Robert South (1634–1716) was one of the great Anglican writers and preachers of his age. A contemporary of Dryden and Locke, he faced the profound political and philosophical changes taking place at the beginning of the Enlightenment in England. With the interdependence of church and state forcing a conjunction of religious and political issues, South's life and work as a preacher show him reacting to changes in civil and ecclesiastical polity over the course of his active public life. Gerard Reedy's book, the first major study of South, makes a strong case for the importance of his sermons, their complexity, beauty and wit, and their place in the history of post-Restoration English literature. Discussing sermons of South which deal with his theory of politics, language, the sacrament and mystery, Reedy reintroduces us to a lively and seminal master of prose, politics, and theology in the late Stuart era.

T0381876

CAMBRIDGE STUDIES IN EIGHTEENTH-CENTURY
ENGLISH LITERATURE AND THOUGHT 12

Robert South (1634–1716)

CAMBRIDGE STUDIES IN EIGHTEENTH-CENTURY
ENGLISH LITERATURE AND THOUGHT

General Editors: Dr HOWARD ERSKINE-HILL, Litt.D., FBA
Pembroke College, Cambridge
and Professor JOHN RICHETTI, *University of Pennsylvania*

Editorial Board: Morris Brownell, *University of Nevada*
Leopold Damrosch, *Harvard University*
J. Paul Hunter, *University of Chicago*
Isobel Grundy, *University of Alberta*
Lawrence Lipking, *Northwestern University*
Harold Love, *Monash University*
Claude Rawson, *Yale University*
Pat Rogers, *University of South Florida*
James Sambrook, *University of Southampton*

This series is designed to accommodate monographs and critical studies on authors, works, genres and other aspects of literary culture from the later part of the seventeenth century to the end of the eighteenth. Since academic engagement with this field has become an increasingly interdisciplinary enterprise, books will be especially encouraged which in some way stress the cultural context of the literature, or examine it in relation to contemporary art, music, philosophy, historiography, religion, politics, social affairs, and so on.

Robert South (1634–1716)

An Introduction to His Life and Sermons

GERARD REEDY, S.J.

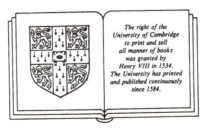

The right of the
University of Cambridge
to print and sell
all manner of books
was granted by
Henry VIII in 1534.
The University has printed
and published continuously
since 1584.

CAMBRIDGE UNIVERSITY PRESS

CAMBRIDGE

NEW YORK   PORT CHESTER

MELBOURNE   SYDNEY

CAMBRIDGE UNIVERSITY PRESS
Cambridge, New York, Melbourne, Madrid, Cape Town, Singapore, São Paulo

Cambridge University Press
The Edinburgh Building, Cambridge CB2 8RU, UK

Published in the United States of America by Cambridge University Press, New York

www.cambridge.org
Information on this title: www.cambridge.org/9780521401647

© Cambridge University Press 1992

First published 1992
This digitally printed version 2007

A catalogue record for this publication is available from the British Library

ISBN 978-0-521-40164-7 hardback
ISBN 978-0-521-04176-8 paperback

For
Paul J. Korshin

The Vein of Preaching which has run so pure since the happy Restoration, that compacted Strength of Reason, that just and natural Method, that Harmony of Words and thoughts, that Devotion without Rapture, that Affection without Violence, that Easiness which is not mean, that Authority which is not Assuming, may contend, in the Praise of sacred Eloquence, with all Rivals of all Countries and Times. Nor will he be charged with Injury to the fathers of the primitive Church, or Flattery to those of our own, who shall affirm that we have seen at one Time more than one Patriarch, who in the Pulpit was not less than a Chrysostome.

Basil Kennet, preface to
The Whole Critical Works of Monsieur Rapin
(London, 1731)

Contents

Illustrations

Acknowledgments

Two fellowships enabled me to do the research for and write the following book: a faculty fellowship from Fordham University for the school year, 1985–86, and a visiting fellowship at the Huntington Library early in 1986. I am also grateful for the help of librarians and for use of books and manuscripts of the following: the British Library; Christ Church Library and Archives, Oxford; the Bodleian Library; the Westminster Abbey Muniments Room; the Lambeth Palace Library; the Huntington Library; The New York Public Library; the Weston School of Theology, Episcopal Divinity School, and Harvard Divinity School Libraries, in Cambridge, Massachusetts; the Library of the Union Theological Seminary, New York; and the Duane Library of Fordham University.

Paul J. Korshin has read the manuscript in full and has corrected many errors. For various sorts of scholarly help, I am also grateful to Vincent Potter, S.J., Herbert Ryan, S.J., Ronald Lau and Albert Loomie, S.J., and to John Kuster and Allen Reddick. The friendships of Harold Ridley, S.J., the late Robert Hayhurst, James Loughran, S.J., and Alvaro Ribeiro, S.J. enlivened and enlightened a year of research in London, Los Angeles, and Cambridge. For help in preparing the manuscript for publication, I thank my office staff, especially Veronica Boland.

Since my days in graduate school at the University of Pennsylvania in the early 1970s, I have been encouraged in my study of late seventeenth-century Anglican theology and English literature by a generous mentor and friend, to whom I dedicate this study of Robert South.

Abbreviations

Ecclesiastes	John Wilkins. *Ecclesiastes, or a Discourse Concerning the Gift of Preaching*. 6th edn. London 1679
FS	Edward Stillingfleet. *Fifty Sermons Preached Upon Several Occasions*. London, 1707
Simon	Irène Simon. *Three Restoration Divines: Barrow, South, Tillotson*. Paris: Société d'Edition "Les Belles Lettres," 2 vols., 1967, 1976
Webster	G. M. Webster. "The Life and Opinions of Robert South, D.D." B.D. thesis, Exeter College, Oxford, 1957

Note on the text

For quotations from the works of Robert South, I have used throughout *Sermons Preached Upon Several Occasions*, in seven volumes (Oxford: Clarendon Press, 1823). Volume and page numbers will be given in parentheses in the text.

Introduction

This study proposes to provide introductions to the reading of at least four sermons of the seventeenth-century Anglican divine, Robert South (1634–1716). A great writer and preacher in an age of great preachers, South spoke about the political upheavals of his time. His talent earned him stalls at Christ Church, Oxford, and Westminster Abbey, as the talents of his contemporaries such as Edward Stillingfleet (1635–99), Bishop of Worcester, and John Tillotson (1630–94), Archbishop of Canterbury, earned them equal and higher rewards. In late seventeenth-century England the powers of church and state were interdependent; the establishment of this interdependence was one of the principal effects of the restoration of Charles II to the English throne in 1660. South strongly supported the mutual claims of church and monarchy. How he reacted to changes in civil and ecclesiastical polity over the course of his active, public life, from 1660 to about 1700, is a principal theme of the following introduction to his life and thought.

South matched his intensity as a public man with an artistic intensity. The depth and complexity of an individual sermon of South are both my premise and conclusion. The more one gives oneself to South's sermons, I have found, the more their complexity as literary and historical documents is revealed. No single sermon of South is as literarily sophisticated as a major poem by John Dryden or play by William Wycherley, texts which vied for public attention during the years of South's great popularity; nevertheless, the best sermons of South easily bear the weight of careful literary and historical analysis.

In my original plans for this work, I had intended to organize chapters around themes: South's politics, religion, relationship with John Locke, and so on. In the process of research, I became convinced that a better approach lay in singling out specific sermons of South for critical discussion. South worked hard to make his sermons lively and internally resonant wholes; paying close attention to those wholes is, I think, the best way to begin to understand him. I have, moreover, chosen sermons in which major issues in any discussion of South must recur: his changing politics, for example; or his complex sympathies with the thought of latitudinarian divines, who assumed the major sees of England as the seventeenth century closed; or his high church bias; or his glosses on the changing linguistic theory of his age; or his approach to the church's sacramental life.

In the late seventeenth century up until the present time, a preacher must give the appearance of being, in Richard A. Lanham's phrase, *homo seriosus*. Preachers were and are expected to deal in real things and problems, to enunciate their meanings, and to speak as integrated selves to a community of serious listeners, whose moral responsibility is assumed. Developments in the theory of prose in the late seventeenth century underlined the seriousness of anyone, including a preacher, who used expository prose: the age encouraged and felt it had created a newly objective and scientifically based relationship between words and things. The age placed great emphasis on the plain style of writing and preaching. Even scriptural revelation was thought to be most divine when it spoke in clear prose; a passion for the plain style was demanded even from God. At least in expository prose, figures of speech were, on the whole, suspect; among the objects of suspicion metaphor ranked high.

Homo rhetoricus, the other model that Lanham extensively develops, is, nevertheless, not foreign to South's work. More than occasionally South's prose involves a sense of play, a self-conscious pride in the repetition of imagery, and a dialectic between rhetorical pose and moral instruction. South's recurrent anger at the regicides of 1649 and their post-1660 followers (as South interpreted the lineage) is one of his more notable and well-known characteristics. Yet often in these angry passages a stylized definition of attitude accompanies moral outrage; like Hamlet, in Lanham's memorable phrase, South may be observed "dining off his own fury, relishing his sublime passion."[1] One can also observe the rhetorical impulse in South's preoccupation with setting up categories at the start of his sermons, fulfilling them, and then, on occasion, reminding his audience that he has done so. The guidelines for these categories are not South's own; they originate in manuals designed to facilitate moral and theological teaching. Though devised with didactic intent, these serious, elaborate categories may seem now to be the rules of a rhetorical game whose point is also to publicize the wit of the speaker.

My starting-point is, then, that at least some of South's sermons richly repay contemplation of their inner workings; they exist as play and reflexive structure as well as social and moral commentary. In the following I devote equal attention to outer and inner; I try to establish historical contexts for the sermons I have chosen for analysis, as well as to discuss their individual artistry and, at times, their internal inconsistencies.

[1] Richard A. Lanham, *The Motives of Eloquence: Literary Rhetoric in the Renaissance* (New Haven and London: Yale University Press, 1976), p. 135. See pp. 1–35 for Lanham's discussion of *homo rhetoricus* and *homo seriosus*.

The knowledge one gains from any exercise in intellectual history depends on where the historian places his camera, and in the following study of Robert South, I have placed the camera fairly close to the subject. I write about his life, his background at Christ Church, Oxford, his training as a preacher, and his editorial methods. For purposes of comparison and contrast, I frequently discuss what South's contemporaries were writing about the subjects on which he preaches. Most of all, I outline and discuss the contents of South's sermons. The camera is rarely placed at a great distance, so that the reader will rarely learn, from this source, how the grand currents of English and European philosophy flow through South's work, or are abetted or twisted by it. To place the camera at such a distance from his work is, almost inevitably, to begin to ignore it; South was not a thinker of the first rank and may deserve only a footnote in the grander scheme of things. At this moment in the history of the post-Restoration Anglican sermon, a need still exists to understand the principal subjects in their fullness; to understand their role in building post-Restoration England, one must treat them as if they were great even if, by some fair measures, they were not. This is especially true for South, whose conservative view of things tends to be ignored by histories that aim to chronicle budding enlightenment. A sympathetic treatment of South may, moreover, give those histories pause.

Like many writers of an *œuvre* of magnitude, South assumes, as he writes, a number of *personae*, or partial, created selves, some consciously created and some, perhaps, not so. South rarely assumes the *persona* of self-revelation: there are no extant diaries or records of spiritual struggle. It is probable that South regarded communication with God as at best vulgar and at worst seditious if it occurred outside the liturgy of the Church of England. Almost no personal letters remain.[2] As I have said, preachers usually adopt the semblance of an integrated self that shares the sure meanings it has found, and South excels at creating and maintaining this kind of self. For example, even though his political opinions, especially in the late 1680s, radically changed, he enunciates this change not in the narration of what must have been painful struggles of allegiance; he successively and successfully creates the same firm persona that emphasizes, nevertheless, different ways of conceiving loyalism. South tries to exclude his personal problems from his public presentations.

Even after the intervention of many years between delivery and publication, many of South's sermons remain angry, vitriolic, satirical. One reason why I include an analysis of South's sermons on "the fatal imposture and force of words" is to give an example of how, at times, South's anger overrules his thought, and how the serious man estranges himself

---

[2] See Webster, pp. 64–67, 78–79, 82–84, 100–01, 145–46, 148–51, 301–3, 306–07, 330–31, for texts and summaries of South's letters, almost all of them about public issues.

from the rhetorical. South was a careful artist and, when bursts of anger break his artistic stride, one may catch sight of an angry self, within an angry pose, that perhaps he did not fully admit to. South's epitaphist notes his emotional outbursts and tries to enclose them in an observable cause-and-effect sequence: the vice, vileness, and counterfeit nature of contemporary life caused him to react, *liberrima indignatione* (I, xcix). The reader of South may not find such closure altogether convincing. One is tempted to embark on a psychological explanation, although the absence of autobiographical material renders such a quest difficult indeed.

There are few substantial secondary materials on Robert South. Those which exist bring up some myths to be corrected and some problems that continue to invite solution. Frederick H. Forshall wrongly writes that South was married, and F. P. Wilson that he was a bishop.[3] South's sharp tongue and ability thereby to make enemies principally account for his failure as an episcopal candidate. Commentators usually portray South as an opponent of the Royal Society and what it stood for, though there is evidence of a more complex attitude.[4] Among churchmen of his time, South was not alone in being ambitious, an aspect of his life which I will discuss in detail in chapter 1. Anthony Wood, the seventeenth-century Oxford antiquarian and reporter of gossip, disliked South for personal reasons and depicted him as a man embittered by frustrated ambition. The picture of South that emerges from other historical records and also from the generosity of his art does not wholly support Wood's caricature. Lastly, South is usually understood as a spokesman for a high church view, and I will spend some time, in the following chapters, defining what this might mean.

South shares the latitudinarian preference for the plain style in prose writing, for a theology built on the literal sense of Scripture, and for the linear, compartmentalized development of homilies set out in the latitudinarian classic of John Wilkins, *Ecclesiastes, or A Discourse Concerning the Gift of Preaching, As it Falls Under the Rules of Art* (1646, and at least five more seventeenth-century editions). Wilkins (1614–72) was one of those figures whose career successfully bridged the Restoration. Although the brother-in-law of Oliver Cromwell, Wilkins was made a bishop of the reestablished church after 1660. He had close ties with the Royal Society

[3] Forshall, *Westminster School: Past and Present* (London: Wyman and Sons, 1884), pp. 175–76; and Wilson, *Seventeenth Century Prose: Five Lectures* (Berkeley and Los Angeles: University of California Press, 1960), p. 105.
[4] See I, 390, where in 1664 South refers to that "great philosopher the Lord Verulam," a figure esteemed by the Royal Society; and *Animadversions upon Dr. Sherlock's Book Entituled A Vindication of the Holy and Ever Blessed Trinity* (London, 1693), p. 13, where he praises Robert Boyle and other authors of scientific works.

of London, and especially approved of its efforts to reform the language; his own work includes an essay on language reform, which I shall advert to later, and *Ecclesiastes*, a very popular work. In his use of the kind of preaching Wilkins represents, South showed himself a theological modern. He also shared with the latitudinarians a predilection for mixed or alternating proofs for any given thesis, from Scripture, necessary reason, common sense and probability, experience, and historical (usually Greek and Latin) example. Such proofs were standard in theological discourse since at least the middle ages and achieve new life in seventeenth-century England.

My research compels me to stress, moreover, that, in the late seventeenth century, one only understands the uniqueness of an individual theological enterprise by closely examining theological proofs. The difference between, for example, a high church and a latitudinarian frame of mind can be understood only by carefully assessing the tension between and interplay of especially Scripture and reason in individual theological proofs. High, broad, low, rationalist, deist – these labels easily obscure understanding of what an individual's theology is about.

South likes to unite disparate aspects of his experience by means of analogies. He is probably one of the last great Anglican preachers with a lively sense of a hierarchic universe full of correspondences, and in this he is not a modern. He writes in 1676:

Order is the great rule or art by which God made the world, and by which he still governs it: nay, the world itself is nothing else; and all this glorious system of things is but the chaos put into order.   (I, 423)

And in an undated sermon on covetousness, he writes:

All parts of the universe, as they borrow off one another, so they still pay what they borrow, and that by so just and well-balanced an equality, that their payments always keep pace with their receipts.   (III, 298)

Kingship, which South understood as God's regency on earth, plays an important part in his analogous view of things. Political changes in the late 1680s forced him to revise his views, although his search for a sublunary entity analogous to divine rule continued.

In the following analyses, I accept as the canon of South only the seventy-two sermons that he edited and that were published between the 1660s and 1717; I have almost completely ignored the further sermons published from manuscript between 1737 and 1744. In accepting only the first seventy-two as a basis for discussion, I follow the bibliographical work of Irène Simon, which is definitive.[5] Besides her work, the only other major contribution to the modern study of South is G. M. Webster's

---

[5] Simon, II, i, 17–28.

unpublished dissertation "The Life and Opinions of Robert South, D.D."
(Oxford, 1957), which I have cited as needed. Although I would, at times,
disagree with Webster's interpretation of data, his amassing of texts and
secondary sources has helped me greatly in what follows.

Westminster and Christ Church

The will

When Robert South died in 1716, at the age of 82, he was a famous man. He had fixed his place in his generation and in the history of Anglican homiletics and controversy by overseeing the publication, from 1692 on, of six volumes of sermons which he had been writing, delivering, and rewriting since the late 1650s. In the decade of his death, another publishing event helped perpetuate his memory in the minds of book-buyers and readers. Edmund Curll, a bookseller just coming into his own at the time, had decided that there was a profit to be made in publishing the wills of the prominent recently deceased, especially of deceased divines. Curll's advertisements in this period announce the publication and sale of the last wills and testaments of Gilbert Burnet, Bishop of Salisbury (*d.* 1715), George Hickes, Dean of Worcester (*d.* 1715), Anthony Radcliffe, Canon of Christ Church (*d.* 1703), Thomas Sprat, Bishop of Rochester and Dean of Westminster (*d.* 1713), Thomas Tenison, Arch-bishop of Canterbury (*d.* 1715), Daniel Williams, a learned, nonconform-ing divine (*d.* 1716), and Robert South, Canon of Westminster Abbey and Christ Church, and Rector of Islip in Oxfordshire.

Curll's motives seem to have been commercial and not political. For the divines whose wills he chose to publish were, politically, a mixed lot of high churchmen, latitudinarians, and dissenters. The collected wills testify to different political loyalties which lasted to death; each of the wills speaks, as it were, from the grave, about the strength and even bitterness of ecclesiastical politics at the close of the seventeenth and beginning of the eighteenth centuries.

Both generic and idiosyncratic, generous and egotistical, the collected wills reveal the divided selves that ecclesiastical existence promoted in this era. A will is, of its nature, a worldly document, and the divines' wills are no exception to the rule. Their careers had often brought them worldly riches, and these are carefully meted out to wives, children, and servants. For these followers of Jesus Christ, the hundredfold had occurred in this life. Yet a thoughtful charity also informs many bequests. South, for example, who was not married, left almost £1,000 to various needy individuals, many connected with Westminster Abbey or Christ Church. He also specified how the income from various other properties should be spent *in perpetuum* for clergy working in the livings of Christ Church. Holders of these livings benefit to this day from his generosity.

High or broad church, these divines were a distinguished, hard-working group. This is shown especially in the voluminous writings they left to posterity, and their wills fussily worry over a proper handling of manuscripts and future reprintings of books, tracts, and sermons. Bishop Burnet directs his oldest son to publish his *History of His Own Time*, but to wait for six years after his death (8–10). Dean Hickes worries about future integration of his writings with those written in accord with principles antithetical to his own; his works are to be "sold by themselves, pure and unmixed with any other books whatsoever" (18).[1] This injunction is promptly ignored by Curll's collection. A codicil of South's will discusses the copyrights of the first three volumes of sermons that he has recently purchased for £107.10s (i, cxi–cxii). On the one hand, these directions from the grave seem to be the vanity of vanities, especially from those who were committed to teaching that we have not here a lasting city. On the other, in complex ways, these divines worked hard to create a religion for rational believers in the world. Their theology spoke not to eremites but to active Christian men and women, and their writings, quite understandably, were important to them, not only for their own reputations but for their lasting effect on believers.

The religious history of England from 1650 to 1714 was turbulent, and the wills reflect the controversies in which their authors took part, and the options and compromises they made. From the 1640s onward, holders of office, especially religious office, had to prove their allegiances in public, swear oaths, and live with the consequences (see appendix 3). South's life, for example, was punctuated by external demands for conflicting oaths of allegiance. He was fortunate to have avoided the rigors of the parliamentary visitation of Oxford in 1647 and 1648, for he was still a youth at Westminster School. Anthony Wood writes of this time:

The generality of the heads of houses, professors and lecturers, doctors and batchelors of divinity, masters and batchelors of arts, undergraduates, beadles, college-servants, and sometimes bedmakers, and scrapers of trenchers, to the number of several hundreds, were thrown out of their respective places, and soon after banished the university by the visitors, for not submitting to their power from parliament and acknowledging their *covenant*.[2]

---

[1] *The Lives and Last Wills and Testaments of the Following Eminent Persons* (London, 1728). Often without title pages, the wills are separately paginated; reference to individual wills, in the text, is made by giving the name of the author and page numbers.

[2] Wood, *Athenae Oxonienses, An Exact History of All the Writers and Bishops Who Have Had Their Education in the University of Oxford*, ed. Philip Bliss, 4 vols. (London, 1820), IV, 118.

Though escaping the full rigor of the Presbyterian crusade, South must have presented some testimony of allegiance to it or to the Engagement oath of the Independents in 1650 when he accepted his Christ Church Studentship in 1651. As South was slowly climbing the ladder of Oxford honors in the 1660s, Wood and others attacked him for his less than wholehearted allegiance to the principle of academic martyrdom.

In 1660 and after, office-holders had to present alternate credentials to another group of visitors, sent by Charles II to purge Oxford of opposition. In 1662 there was the Act of Uniformity; various acts of Parliament in Charles's reign restrained Roman Catholics and dissenters from office, and edicts of James II, in 1687 and 1688, attempted to remove those restraints. The oaths of allegiance to William III in 1689 reversed much that had gone before, and there was, subsequently, parliamentary legislation that some, like South, felt was destroying the integrity of the Church of England. A highly principled churchman had to draw the line somewhere, to refuse allegiance, and to face deprivation of office. The majority of churchmen, for complex reasons, were not so highly principled. One reason was simply to hold on, at whatever the cost to one's integrity, to one's office. Another was obdurate refusal to allow the church to fall into the hands of one's ideological enemies. If the late seventeenth century offers examples of ecclesiastical ambition, it also shows the pain of realistic compromise.

The times encouraged cynicism about the taking of oaths. In response to some demands, it was the easiest course simply to avoid the commissioners. Thus Richard Busby, South's headmaster at Westminster School and a lifelong friend, stayed home sick the day he was required to take the National Covenant in 1645; following his example in 1689, South suggested to a colleague, William Sherlock, that they retreat to the countryside, where the commissioners would leave them alone. This suggestion partly explains why South and Sherlock became enemies and engaged in a bitter theological controversy in the mid-1690s.[3]

The writers of Curll's wills try to enunciate once and for all the principles that a lifetime of compromises may have obscured. Burnet preached at the coronation of William and Mary, and his *History* shows dislike of and puzzlement at nonjurors, those clergy and laity who could not foreswear allegiance to even a Catholic king. In his will he assures us that he dies "a *Protestant* according to the *Church of England*, full of Affection and Brotherly Love to all who have received the *Reformed Religion*, tho' in some points *Different* from our Constitution"; popery, he writes, is more to be dreaded than all other parties (4–5). Hickes, con-

[3] Lawrence Tanner, *Westminster School: A History* (London: Country Life, 1934), p. 13; see Webster, pp. 168–91. For a full description of what nonjuring meant, see John H. Overton, *The Nonjurors: Their Lives, Principles, and Writings* (London: Smith, Elder, 1902), pp. 1–22.

cerned about the purity of his writing in regard to those "some Points
Different," and a nonjuror, was ordained bishop in 1694 by a nonjuring
bishop; this was a momentous step because it threatened to widen a local
dispute about the oath to William into the basis for church schism. In his
will Hickes prays for nonjuring clergymen ejected from their livings and
asks God "to inspire our Superiours with an effectual and speedy Resolution, to make a National Attonement for the Sacrilege of which the
Nation hath long been guilty, by a Pious Restitution to the Church of all
the Lands, Tythes, and Offerings which belong to her Priests" (12).

Neither a political latitudinarian like Burnet or as high a churchman as
Hickes, South also used his will to show his final sympathies. After Busby
died in 1695, South became a trustee of his estate and thus was familiar
with the terms of his will; Busby had provided safeguards that the money
he left for lectures in "practical divinity" would be so spent.[4] In leaving
property which would eventually go to Christ Church, South followed
Busby's example by setting down conditions concerning those who would
profit from his property's income. This might go only to clergymen in
Christ Church livings who led moral lives and who avoided actions
"against the Act of Uniformity or rule of the Church of England, for
religious worship" (I, cvi). South had always preached against toleration
for nonconformists, whom he, unlike Burnet, considered more dangerous
than Roman Catholics. The idiosyncrasy of this clause, written late in
South's life, lies in its invocation of the Act of Uniformity of 1662. That
Act required of established clergy a strict use of the Prayer Book, a
declaration against taking arms against the king, and episcopal ordi-
nation. Charles II and James II had attempted to whittle away at the
Act in various ways. The oath to William III in 1689 explicitly cancelled
some of the Act's provisions. A political document in the extreme, South's
will pretends that these mitigations and cancellations never occurred and
demands more ecclesiastical purity than did the government itself.

South was not a nonjuror; he had taken the oaths to William on 31
July 1689, the last day when it was possible to do so. Burnet tells us that
South "had taken the oaths, but with the reserve of an equivocal sense,
which he put on them."[5] It is difficult to understand what Burnet means,
other than that South felt the oaths to be a problem, and that he resolved
it by saying one thing and meaning another as he took them. The
ambiguity of his action helps to explain a clause in his will leaving £200
to be shared by twenty nonjurors who had been ejected from their livings
because of their principles. Clearly South's conscience dwelt on their suf-

[4] G. F. Russell Barker, *Memoir of Richard Busby, D. D. (1606–1695) With Some Account of Westminster School in the Seventeenth Century* (London, 1895), pp. 138–39.
[5] Gilbert Burnet, *Bishop Burnet's History of His Own Time*, ed. M. J. Routh, 2nd edn., 6 vols.
(Oxford, 1833), IV, 390.

ferings, and his imagination sympathized with a fate that could have been his own.

Ambition

South's decision to sail with the wind in 1689 invites us to make a fundamental inquiry about his character. How ambitious was he? Was his desire for office so great as to prompt him to surrender principles that he regarded as worthy in others? Or was the oath-taking itself a principled act, the sort of gesture one could expect from South, whose sermons generally demand idealistic conduct, and attack politic, "silent candidates for future preferment" (III, 445)? These fundamentally different views of his character form, as a matter of fact, the bases for the two earliest biographical sketches of South – by Anthony Wood in the second and posthumous edition of his *Athenae Oxonienses* (1721), and by the anonymous author of *Memoirs of the Life and Writings of Dr. Robert South*, published by Curll in South's *Posthumous Works* (1717).

These two writers take opposite views of South's ambition. Wood interprets South's life as a continual pursuit of office and money. Much of Wood's account concerns two failures of South, because of nervousness, in the pulpit; for Wood and his sources these failures justly punish South's use of preaching as a means of personal gain. Although Wood does not discuss the oaths of 1689, his sketch ends with a picture of South in 1694 "upon his temporal estate at Caversham (left him by his father) near Reading, in a discontented and clamorous condition for want of more preferment."[6] In this view, the ambition that led South to take the oaths had, paradoxically, permanently embittered his life.

The anonymous biographer, on the other hand, presents South as hesitating and conscience-stricken in 1688 and 1689. The writer makes sense of South's decision by means of several considerations: South had refused to sign the letter of invitation sent to William of Orange in June 1688, above the signatures of prominent politicians and clergy; South believed that the protection given by a monarch and obedience to him were reciprocal, and, James having fled, the obligation to obey had disappeared; and South stood out for some time, for over six months, gained nothing financially or in his career from the oaths, and refused to take the see, in 1691, of an ejected, nonjuring bishop (I, lxxvii–lxxviii).

Both Wood and the 1717 biographer are prone to exaggeration, although Wood, who had a longtime dislike for South, presents by far the greater distortion.[7] The 1717 biography is a genre piece, the worshipful

---

[6] *Athenae Oxonienses*, IV, 637.

[7] Wood's dislike of South is discussed in *The Life and Times of Anthony Wood, Antiquary, of Oxford*. ed. Andrew Clark, 5 vols. (Oxford, 1891–1900), III, 497, n. 2; see also Simon, I, 233. *DNB*

biography of a post-Restoration cleric; other instances of the genre include
Izaak Walton's lives of John Donne and George Herbert, especially as
Walton revised the lives to make them address late seventeenth-century
issues, and Bishop John Fell's lives of Henry Hammond (1661) and
Richard Allestree (1685).[8] Generic, worshipful treatment of these figures
stresses their lives of prayer and their avoidance of politics. One distinguishing characteristic is their portrayed concern for the restoration of
church and church-school buildings. The depiction of such restorations
has a complex purpose: to give biographical fact, to show the recuperative
strength of the post-Restoration church, to denigrate, once again, Crom-
wellian iconoclasts, and to encourage the laity to join the pious work of
rebuilding.

In the light of this generic piety, South is pictured as rebuilding his
living at Islip, including a new vicarage and school (I, lxxi–lxxii) and, in
the years of James II's short reign, avoiding London; in the country and at
Oxford he was "busied in preparing most of those excellent sermons for the
press, which have since seen the light, and exercised himself in devotions to
deprecate the judgements that seemed to hang over the national church"
(I, lxxv–lxxvi). This pretty construction, however, is contradicted by two
extant letters of South from the period. On 27 July 1686, South wrote to
William Sancroft, Archbishop of Canterbury, almost openly begging for
office, "I wish I could bring my ability of Parts to serve the Church equal
to the sincerity of my Resolutions to endeavor it. But I hope your Grace
will pardon all defects in the former; and I will take care, that there shall
be nothing to be pardoned in the latter." The ratio of words and phrases to
thought is extremely high in this letter; its style contrasts with the South's
usually vigorous prose. A month later, something has happened. The king
has given the place to another, apparently because an alleged insult of
South has been reported to him. On 26 August, South wrote a long
anxious letter to Sancroft, asking him not to "retract your good opinion
of me."[9]

To understand that South once or occasionally fawned over his super-
iors in an attempt to become a bishop is not to prove that he was, as Wood
says, consumed and frustrated by his ambitions. There exists clear evidence that South refused, for reasons of age, the see of Rochester and
deanery of Westminster late in his life; it is probable that he was also

(XVIII, 685) summarizes what is known: "Wood's harsh judgment is said to have been
inspired by a jest with which South received Wood's mention of a bodily ailment from which he
suffered."
[8] See David Novarr, *The Making of Walton's Lives* (Ithaca: Cornell University Press, 1958),
pp. 113, 118–26, 242–43, 261–62, 309–17.
[9] Bodl. Ms. Tanner, XXX, 91, 109. Wood reports that the prize South lost because of "a bitter
and satyrical letter" was the see of Oxford (*Life and Times*, III, 195).

offered an Irish bishopric early in James's reign, and refused that also.[10] Further to judge the truth of Wood's charge of consuming ambition, it is necessary to look closely at his accusations and examine them one by one.

(1) *Before 1660, South tailored his preaching and other speaking to the dominant religious party.* Wood charges that, during the 1650s, South catered to his Independent governors, then, late in the decade, sought favor with Presbyterians, and finally joined the royalists as the restoration of Charles II became a possibility. Unlike many other Westminster and Christ Church men, South never suffered for his beliefs; Wood also makes this charge of avoidance of suffering against others as new degrees were awarded and new appointments made in the 1660s.

Most of these charges are found only in Wood. He ignores or does not know about South's participation, as a boy at Westminster School, in the prayers for Charles I a few hours before his execution, and South's friendship with the royalist, Richard Busby.[11] Wood also ignores what the 1717 biographer tells us about South's attendance at illegal services, according to the rite of the Church of England, conducted by Richard Allestree, John Fell, and John Dolben – three ejected members of Christ Church – in secluded rooms in Merton Street, close to Christ Church, in the 1650s. The biographer's account of South's argument about this worship with John Owen, the Independent Dean of Christ Church at the time, sounds fictitious; yet some basis in fact may be assumed (I, v). South preached at Dolben's consecration as Bishop of Rochester at Lambeth Palace on 25 November 1666. The sermon was separately printed in 1666, with a dedication to Dolben, reminding him of their days together at Christ Church (I, 120–21); the affair signifies a long-standing relationship between South and Dolben, who had been ejected in the 1650s, and who saw no contradiction in having the younger Christ Church Student, who had not been, preach. The argument from South's friendships after 1660 to his royalism before that date has been forcefully made by Irène Simon.[12] Besides Wood's bald assertions, the evidence points to South's consistent loyalty to the monarchy and established church from his schooldays until 1660, when he was 26 years old.

(2) *From the early 1660s, South was ambitious to be named a canon of Christ Church, complained in public about his denied right to a stall, and was opposed by the Dean, after 1661, John Fell.*

In the summer of 1660, South preached an anti-Presbyterian sermon for

[10] See Simon, I, 231–32; and, on the Irish bishopric, the 1717 biographer (see South, I, lxxxiv). Alexander Gordon notes that the see of Cashel was vacant from 1685 to 1691 (*DNB*, XVIII, 684).

[11] See the anonymous 1717 biographer of South, who claims that South read the prayer himself (see South, I, iii), and South's own narration of the event (III, 412). Barker thinks it unlikely that South, at age 15, would have been chosen for the office (*Memoir*, p. 16n.).

[12] Simon, I, 235–38.

the king's commissioners at Oxford; as a reward for his views and ability,
he was named Public Orator at the order of Edward Hyde, Earl of
Clarendon, and Chancellor of the University. The appointment required
him to give an oration, usually in Latin, on occasions such as the visits of
English or foreign monarchs to Oxford; the oratorship, perhaps a burden
for an older man, was less so for the twenty-six year-old South, who
thereby achieved high visibility. He kept the position until he resigned it
in 1677. South felt, in Wood's accounts, that from the beginning this office
should have carried with it a canonship of Christ Church, and set out to
remind whomever he could about this. At a 1661 Convocation, with
Clarendon present, South announced, writes Wood, that he was
"deprived of his right of canonship at Christ Church which was annexed
to his place"; he "tugged hard, such was the high conceit of his worth, to
be canon of Christ Church as belonging to that office; but was kept back
by the endeavors of the dean."[13]

The "right" to which Wood has South refer, the dual canonship and
oratorship, is not difficult to verify. The Laudian and Caroline Code for
the reformation of Oxford in the 1630s makes the University Orator a
canon of Christ Church, and the three orators who preceded South,
William Strode (1629–45), Henry Hammond (1645–48), and Ralph
Bulton (1648–60), were all canons of Christ Church. Yet although
Hammond and Bulton received both gifts at the same time, Strode waited
nine years for a stall after his appointment as Orator. The automatic
coupling of oratorship and canonical stall seemed on the wane in the
seventeenth century, for South's two successors as Orator, Thomas Craddock (1677–79) and William Wyatt (1679–1712), were never made
canons of Christ Church. It is perhaps reasonable to understand the delay
in South's stall for reasons of age. South was thirty-six in 1670 when he
received the stall; the ages of the five canons appointed after him were
near enough to his and suggest that there was no bias against him.
Ecclesiastical appointments in the 1660s, because after a time of want,
were not always symptomatic of usual practice; the pattern after 1670
becomes more regular.

What was South's relationship with John Fell, Dean of Christ Church
(1660–86) and Bishop of Oxford (1676–86)? There seems to be no record
of estrangement between the Dean and South, a member of his chapter,
other than that at which Wood hints; the 1717 biographer calls Fell
South's "very good friend" (I, xiii). Wood himself tells us that in November 1666, Arthur Brett, a visiting West Country vicar, returned to Christ
Church, his own college, and preached a sermon that praised the rebirth
of oratory at Oxford and, by implication, Allestree, Fell, and South. Wood

---

[13] *Life and Times*, I, 414; *Athenae Oxonienses*, IV, 634.

notes that this caused "heart burnings among the scholars, strife, envy, and ambition."[14] Here Wood groups South together with his alleged enemy Fell, and Allestree, to show that singling out individuals for praise caused public discontent. The unpleasant fact seems to be that Wood simply disliked South, and did not care whether he drove a wedge between South and Fell, or joined them, so long as it helped a negative portrayal.

Fell's writings indicate one area in which the younger man may have displeased. Fell had a strong aversion to the rhetoric of ridicule and mockery, which he bewailed as symptomatic of the age. In an Oxford sermon before the king in 1675, he attacked the prevalent substitution of wit for understanding, especially in the pulpit, "those Schole divinity Drolls of this our Age, who defend the Faith by destroying Charity. Tis certainly a great pity a good cause should be asserted by such arguments as libel and reproach it." Fourteen years earlier, in his life of Hammond, Fell had praised Hammond's "detestation of all verbal follies ... so that the scurrilous jest could sooner obtain his tears in penance for it, then the approbation of a smile," and the quality that underlay this sensitivity, his "meekness to those that slighted him and disparaged his abilities."[15] Some of South's pulpit behavior would have affronted Fell's values. South enjoyed bringing his congregation to laughter; he loved to ridicule, especially nonconformist preachers, by means of exaggerated description; and he was never meek when arguing. "Piety," South wrote, "engages no man to be dull" (III, 14). His belligerence and verbal violence shocked even later readers; it is a standard feature of Victorian comment on South to note his indecorous language in the pulpit.[16] Fell was against this in principle, and perhaps critical of South in particular. Wood's charge of estrangement between the two is plausible in this context.

(3) *Having sought and received office, South accepted the attached stipends but ignored the pastoral and administrative duties involved.*

In late seventeenth-century England, many churchmen accepted multiple ecclesiastical appointments without the intention of personally fulfilling the duties of each one of them. Pluralism of this sort had long been attacked, in England and elsewhere; it thrived especially in the years after 1660 because, with the return of the king and the Act of Uniformity of

---

[14] *Life and Times*, II, 93.

[15] *The Character of the Last Daies, A Sermon Preached Before the King* (Oxford, 1675), p. 20; *The Life of the Most Learned, Reverend, and Pious Dr. H. Hammond* (London, 1661), pp. 101, 185. For a classic, post-Restoration treatment of jesting and raillery, see Isaac Barrow, *Works*, ed. John Tillotson, I (1683), 193–208.

[16] Charles J. Abbey and John H. Overton, *The English Church in the Eighteenth Century*, 2 vols. (London: Longmans, Green, 1878), I, 487; John H. Overton, *Life in the English Church (1660–1714)* (London: Longmans, Green, 1885), p. 239; and W. C. Lake, "South the Rhetorician," in *The Classic Preachers of the English Church*, ed. John Edward Kempe, 2 vols. (London: John Murray, 1877–78), I, 54, 57.

1662, hundreds of church livings had become vacant, to be filled by churchmen loyal to the king and conforming to the new legislation. South shared in this windfall as canon of Westminster (1663), vicar of a parish in Wales (1667), canon of Christ Church (1670), and rector of Islip (1678). He had to receive a special dispensation to hold the livings of the two parishes, "notwithstanding they are above thirty miles distant," and thus impossible personally to be served by one priest.[17] It was not impossible to serve as canon of more than one cathedral chapter. Canons were, in the main, administrators responsible for the upkeep of the cathedral, for the hiring of chaplains, and for the regulation of cathedral properties. At Christ Church, the canons also governed the college and, as in other sees, elected the local bishop after instruction from the king. Because Westminster and Oxford were not so very distantly situated, it would have been possible for South to have regularly attended meetings of both chapters.

Care of parishes, however, presented more sensitive problems; it was easy to see how pluralism could hurt the care of souls. South left no record at all of any concern for his living in Wales, and the 1717 biographer barely mentions it. South was deeply involved in Islip. He received £200 a year for it from the Westminster chapter, in whose gift Islip is; he gave £100 of this to a curate permanently in residence, and the other £100 to educate and provide apprenticeships for children of the parish. He also built, at his own expense, a new school and vicarage, and repaired the church (I, lxxi-lxxii). It appears that South's inheritance from his father was sufficient for his own needs; it is recorded that he used his income from both Islip and Christ Church, at least, for charitable purposes.[18]

In 1677 South accompanied Laurence Hyde, an ambassador of the king, to Poland to present gifts to Charles II's god-daughter, the daughter of John Sobieski, King of Poland. South sent a long letter about his stay in Poland to Edward Pocock, an eminent orientalist who was South's fellow canon at Christ Church. South's descriptions frequently (but not always) detail church matters. He was an active observer, and although he writes mainly about Roman Catholic practices, he is rarely judgmental. Not without a dig at English stinginess, he relates that even minor clergy in Cracow receive £100 a year. He also notes that some clergy have rights to a canonship and to two or more parsonages, and that "there are none that take any care to perform the duties of their functions" (I, xx, xlvii). It seems inconsistent that South, the holder of two stalls and a parish in 1677, and away from the three of them for a long visit to Poland, should censure Polish canons for non-performance of duty. The point of his remark seems not to be the evil of pluralism, or even of absenteeism, but the lack of

[17] Bodl. Ms. Tanner, XXXIX, 81.
[18] Thomas Hearne, *Remarks and Collections*, ed. C. E. Doble, 11 vols. (Oxford: Oxford Historical Society, 1885–1921), I (1885), 104.

"care." Though the usual sources hold no record of the Welsh parish's transactions, if South was consistent with his practice at Islip and comments about Polish practice, he appointed and paid a curate generously, as he did for Islip, to take his place.

South's performance of his duties as a canon was not wholehearted. Abundant evidence exists to show his active participation in capitular business at Westminster. He served as treasurer of the chapter in 1680, 1681, and 1684, and left a full account, in his own hand, of disbursements, as well as a record of accounts from other years, apparently made for comparative analysis. At the end of the century – South was then in his sixties – he remained active in overseeing much-needed repairs at Westminster Abbey.[19] In addition, dated sermons with the site of their delivery noted in the collected edition show him intermittently preaching at Westminster after 1663.

From 1670 on, South preached somewhat more frequently at Christ Church, but participated hardly at all in cathedral and college business. He almost never was recorded as present at capitular meetings and rarely signed in person for his stipends, paid twice a quarter. The disbursement books from this period are signed, at South's place, by Robert Sheldon, the college account keeper, or Thomas Rookes, a cathedral verger, whom South had appointed to manage his Oxford business. No other canons during these years had a record of absences approaching South's. After 1690, the canons began to appoint and record proxies to vote for them in chapter when they were absent. South's proxies are duly recorded in the secretary's hand. All the other canons during South's tenure were appointed someone's proxy at some time or other; South alone from 1690 to 1716, for whatever reason, never served as proxy for one of his colleagues.[20]

It is not easy to explain South's continued absence from Christ Church during these years. Perhaps there was indeed a long-standing antipathy to Fell and the chapter. Yet South's writings clearly support the Christ Church royalism that Fell consciously constructed, and South and Pocock, another canon, had "a most intimate friendship" (I, xiv). One might follow Wood's view that South had a psychological need for titles and stipends; never satisfied, the more he got, the more he wanted. South's sermons depict rapacious personalities like this, and condemn them. Any psychological portrait of South runs into the same problem: almost all the evidence is public data. No private revelations exist that reveal the heart and soul, as it were, unmediated by a public occasion.

[19] See "Dr. South's Notebook," Muniments Room, Westminster Abbey, and also W.A. 33715, 33716, 33719, 35488, and 35493. South's attendance at Westminster chapter, though better than at Christ Church, was not always regular.

[20] See Christ Church Disbursement Books, 1681–85, and 1696–1700, and Chapter Books, 1648–88, 1688–1712, especially, in the latter, fol. 18r to the end of the volume.

Lastly, South had not hidden his views on administrative work. In an early sermon, he had discussed the ministerial "scribe" and his need for genius, learning, and leisure to write, preach, and ponder moral theology successfully. The church, South announced, must support the work of such men, because the church could not cogently address the world without them (III, 18–20). In practice, support meant recognized, funded positions with no strings attached; a parish in Wales and a stall in Oxford gave South the financial and psychological base he needed for his preaching and study of theology. None of South's sermons was written in a day; years of reading and weeks of construction had gone into them. Because of these efforts, Christ Church lacked South's daily presence as an administrator, yet gained in reputation as the college of a great preacher. In the light of this gain it is not surprising that there seems to be no record of complaint extant, except Wood's, about South's absenteeism.

An Oxford tradition alternate to Wood's had arisen by the time of South's death. This is enunciated by a nonjuror, Thomas Hearne, and like Wood, a great collector of facts. On Thursday, 12 July 1716, in the week of South's death, Hearne wrote:

On Tuesday night last Christ Church bell rang for the Death of Dr. South, one of their canons, a very old man. He was celebrated for his Learning and Charity, and was looked upon as pretty honest, though he was a Complyer. He hath many publick Works existent. He hath founded a school at Islip, and endowed it forever. He was Rector of that Place, as Prebendary of Westminster and ever since he was Rector he spent the whole Income of that Rectory (as I have been well informed) in charity.[21]

The encomium acknowledges South's submission in 1689 and puts it in a larger context of charity, something that neither excuses or explains his political conduct, which Hearne disliked, but exists side by side with it.

South's ambition, such as it was, can only be understood in context. In context, none of his major political decisions is intelligible on the grounds of personal ambition alone. His royalism in 1660 accorded with what most of the evidence suggests was his previous – and impolitic – behavior. If eager for office in 1686, he was selective in what he would accept. Having taken the oath to William III in 1689, he did oppose the government on the issues of toleration and comprehension; he thus further alienated bishops like Burnet and John Tillotson, for whom the flight of James II signalled changes in church discipline and worship. Throughout these times of crisis, South kept up his works of charity and honed his talents into those of a greater preacher. South's integrity was not unambiguous.

---

[21] Hearne, *Remarks and Collections*, V (1901), 264.

South was not a purist, but certainly not a trimmer. He knew when to comply, and how far. He was, as Hearne wrote, "pretty honest."

Education

In Robert South's lifetime, Westminster School and Christ Church were institutions of great national reputation. Busby's long tenure as Headmaster at Westminster (1638–95) had made its methods of teaching and preparation for life, especially clerical life, legendary. Like many schoolmasters, Busby had his favorites, and among them had been, as Lawrence Tanner writes, the "greatest living philosopher, John Locke, the greatest living architect, Christopher Wren, and the greatest living poet, John Dryden." In the first rank of great preachers, South had also received Busby's special attention; though little evidence survives of particulars, South's presence among Busby's executors testifies to a strong relationship. During Busby's lifetime about fifteen of his students became bishops. Thomas Sprat, not an old Westminster boy, but nevertheless Dean of the Abbey and Bishop of Rochester, is reported to have remarked that he thanked God he had received a see even though he was not an ex-pupil of Westminster.[22]

The steady growth of Christ Church in the mid-seventeenth century, unlike Westminster School's, had been checked by parliamentary interference. After a difficult period in the 1650s, when some outstanding canons were replaced by lesser lights, the college quickly regained its prominence under Dean Fell; directing the construction of the new buildings, including Tom Tower, and repairing old, Fell led the college to a commanding place in the intellectual and political life of the university and national church. No college better represented post-Restoration loyalism. "Fell himself," writes G. V. Bennett, "did not doubt that he was creating the future leadership of a ruling class which would be firmly attached to the church and which would see its own security in the defence of the Anglican cause."[23] This was South's world.

The special relationship of Westminster School with Christ Church and Trinity College, Cambridge, is not unknown. Each year, Headmaster, Dean, and Master met to elect outstanding Westminster boys to scholarships on the basis of competitive exams and of Busby's recommendation. In 1650 Dryden was elected to Trinity, and in the next two years South and Locke to Christ Church. There they joined other Westminster boys among the one hundred Students supported by the foundation of Henry

[22] Tanner, *Westminster School*, pp. 20–23.
[23] Bennett, "Loyalist Oxford and the Revolution," in *The History of the University of Oxford*, V: *The Eighteenth Century*, ed. L. S. Sutherland and L. G. Mitchell (Oxford: Clarendon Press, 1985), pp. 11–12.

VIII. These Studentships, pleasant and long standing, entailed few obli-
gations nor even residence after a degree was taken. South gave his
Studentship up in 1670, when he received a stall; Locke lost his late in
1684 at the order of Charles II, who considered him seditious. The
opposition of the king, not Locke's absence in Holland, caused the chapter
to oust him.

There is a not inconsiderable amount of writing about the curriculum
and teaching at Westminster School and Christ Church in the second half
of the seventeenth century, yet we do not get from it, or from South's own
work, a very real sense of what he did from day to day from the 1640s on.[24]
The Latin and Greek exercises at Westminster were very rigorous. South
began his literary studies there and continued them at Christ Church,
where his serious philosophical and patristic studies began. Scripture must
have been a principal topic of study throughout these years. South knew
some Hebrew – an interest of Busby's[25] – but diffidently; in the course of a
sermon, he notes that he has consulted Pocock about the meaning of a
disputed passage in Isaiah (II, 473). South knew Latin and Greek
extremely well. The Westminster training, requiring translation from the
classical languages into English, and back again, and original composition, prepared him well for the Public Oratorship; even Wood praised
the elegance of his Latin orations.[26]

---

[24] See John Sergeaunt, *Annals of Westminster School* (London: Methuen, 1898), pp. 115–24;
Barker, *Memoir*, pp. 77–82; L. S. Sutherland, "The Curriculum," and P. Quarrie, "The
Christ Church Collections Books," in *The History of the University of Oxford*, V, 469–91, 493–511;
Charles Ward, *The Life of John Dryden* (Chapel Hill: University of North Carolina Press, 1961),
pp. 9–13; David Wykes, *A Preface to Dryden* (London: Longman 1977), pp. 11–27.

[25] Sergeaunt, *Annals of Westminster School*, pp. 115–24, and Barker, *Memoir*, pp. 77–82. Many
references to Busby in nineteenth- and twentieth-century books routinely refer to his penchant
for flogging Westminsters into civilized conduct or solid learning. In a sermon written for a
1685 reunion of old Westminsters, and, because of the death of Charles II never delivered,
South allows "austerity" for the training of recalcitrant youths, but argues that "Stripes and
blows are the last and basest remedy." Since Busby was alive and still headmaster in 1685, and
would presumably have been present in the choir or congregation at Westminster Abbey,
where the sermon was to be delivered, one might agree with Barker, who finds South's attack
on flogging "somewhat curious" (*Memoir*, p. 15n.). Did South disagree so strongly with the
pedagogy of his lifelong friend that he felt obliged to a public airing of his disagreement (see
note 32 below)? Lawrence Tanner initiates a discussion that has never been concluded, and
that attempts to resolve the discrepancy between Busby's alleged practice and South's
remarks. First-hand impressions of Busby, he writes, are rare. "It would be interesting to know
if Busby's reputation as the great flogging Head Master is really justified ... tradition in these
matters is apt to become magnified ... " (*Westminster School*, pp. 15, 17). See also John H.
Overton on Busby: "The traditions of his excessive severity are of rather a vague character"
(*DNB*, VII, 30).

[26] *Life and Times*, II, 62, 157. South's exact knowledge of Greek is evident in the many Greek
terms which appear in his sermons, though not in excess, and in his *Animadversions Upon Dr.
Sherlock's Book Entituled a Vindication of the Holy and Ever Blessed Trinity* (London, 1693), where, in
chapter ten, he castigates Sherlock for scores of errors in Greek (as well as English and Latin)
usage. Hearne tells us that South enlisted a young man named Michael Mattaire, another

Two biographies of Christ Church figures in South's time are revealing. From a life of Philip Henry (1631–96), we learn that the four or five former Westminster pupils elected each year received the same tutor; this no doubt permitted the boys, whose preparation for university was excellent, to continue to work at an advanced level. Henry's life also tells of what a week's work looked like and of the peculiar differences between students of opposing political persuasions. From a manuscript life of George Hooper (1640–1727), also a Westminster and Christ Church man, we learn that almost no old Westminsters could converse with Busby at ease; that Pocock taught him "the oriental languages," would take only five pupils at a time, and refused to accept renumeration for his services; and that, by way of implication, few tutors were as devoted to teaching as Pocock was – to whom South refers as his "most honoured instructor" (I, xiv).[27]

South's training in Latin and Greek helped him in other ways. He learned from classical theory and practice to structure carefully his orations and sermons; the rhetorical values of his own time, which held methodical presentation in high esteem, also influenced the architecture of his sermons. From his readings in Aristotle and later manuals of logic, he learned how to separate, analyze, and combine ideas in argument. In a 1677 sermon Edward Stillingfleet, later Bishop of Worcester, discussed the kinds of figures of thought and speech appropriate for a Christian preacher; he finds blameless "the methodizing our Conceptions of things, by bringing them under their due Ranks and Heads ... [and] understanding the Difference of Causes, the Truth and Falsehood of Propositions, and the way of discerning true and false Reasonings from each other."[28] For South, as for Stillingfleet, the categories of classical logic were companions at hand as he prepared his writing; his works show careful reading and retention of Aristotelian logic, learned, presumably, as an undergraduate at Christ Church.

South's studies at Westminster and Christ Church gave him a wealth of classical reference, precedent, and anecdote. In his sermons up to only 1665, eight years after he took his M.A., South mentions or quotes over thirty different classical, medieval, and Renaissance authors, almost all of them written in Latin or Greek. Some of these references, such as his list of moral philosophers permitting regicide (III, 538–48), need not depend on extensive reading, since *catenae* of apt commonplaces were perhaps available to him. Other references do not seem commonplace, and drive points freshly home. An interesting aspect of South's reading, evident in the early

Busby favorite, to hunt down Sherlock's errors, and that both South and Mattaire later regretted their pendantry (*Remarks and Collections*, IX (1921), 258).

[27] See Matthew Henry, *An Account of the Life and Death of Mr. Philip Henry*, 3rd edn. (London, 1712) pp. 13–17; and Abigail Prowse, "Life of Bishop George Hooper," Lambeth Palace Ms. 3016, sig. 1 r–v.

[28] *FS*, p. 710.

1660s, is his familiarity with the Latin works of Socinus and his followers; such knowledge prepared South for the major Anglican–Socinian confrontations of the 1690s.

For all the time South was in school and university, and for most of his preaching years, the best-known book on preaching was John Wilkins's *Ecclesiastes, or A Discourse Concerning the Gift of Preaching, As It Falls Under the Rules of Art* (1646); this work went through six editions between 1646 and 1679, and will be discussed again in chapter 2. If South read Wilkins, brother-in-law of Cromwell, father-in-law of Archbishop Tillotson, and Bishop of Chester in 1668, he would have been warned that preaching required the study of many authors, "a business of vast industry and much time, scarce consistent with the frequent returns of public service required of a constant Preacher, unless he be beforehand qualified for this by education and leisure at the University."[29] From the evidence of quotation in the sermons, it is impossible to attempt to divide South's reading between the pre- and post-degree years. Experience tells us that what we vividly remember from books has little to do with whether we read them recently or long ago. In the years at Christ Church from 1651 on, under the direction of Pocock or Fell, whose clandestine services he attended in the 1650s, as student and emulator of both, South heeded Wilkins's warning to use wisely his university years, and later encouraged others to do so (III, 42–43).

Lastly, South's education, especially at Westminster, influenced his later choice to take the oaths in 1689. Between 1649 and 1660, Busby had learned to survive in office, and the lesson was not lost on his students. Yet the rewards given him immediately after the Restoration show that his compromises were not regarded as seriously disloyal. Busby had not taken the National Covenant in 1645 and perhaps took the Engagement oath in 1650. John Sergeaunt excuses the latter as less aggravating to a royalist conscience; yet Edward Reynolds, Presbyterian Dean of Christ Church, had preferred ejection rather than compliance on the same issue, a personal crisis that Busby, so prominent a member of the Westminster–Christ Church circle, certainly knew about. Busby taught himself, and his students, the tactics of survival in the face of hostile odds. In the late 1680s, writes Sergeaunt, "Westminster sent no man of mark to swell the ranks of the Nonjurors."[30]

Perhaps compromise and conformity, however, are concepts too crude to use to rationalize Busby's influence. For if most old Westminster boys

---

[29] *Ecclesiastes*, p. 44; see also p. 5 for similar remarks. Both passages are in *Ecclesiastes* from the first edition.

[30] *Annals of Westminster School*, pp. 89, 91. For adverse remarks on Busby's compliance, see Walter Pope, *The Life of the Right Reverend Father in God, Seth, Lord Bishop of Salisbury* (London, 1697), p. 38.

took the 1689 oaths, even like South, with reservations, others did not find nonjuring the only alternative. Dryden, one of Busby's favorites, had become a Roman Catholic by 1688, and presumably had some sympathy for the king over the water; Locke, another former Westminster pupil, arrived back in England in the rear of the invading army of November 1688 that prompted James's flight. Still another, Philip Henry, whose recollections of Busby are detailed and moving, attributed his own non-conformity, beginning in 1662, partly to his headmaster's influence.[31] These different choices and fates suggest that, among Busby's favorite students, there was no simple political pattern – that his influence told on them not in clone-like behavior but in independence of thought and action. It is easiest to praise this legacy of independence when it went against the crowd. But independence does not only appear in non-conformist dress. Indeed independence of thought and action seems most heroic – and was this South's situation? – when risking purist scorn, it judges to be right not the lonely but the common cause, and follows it.

Locke and South

There are great similarities between the education and interests of John Locke (1632–1704) and Robert South. They attended Westminster School together and went in the same 1651 election to Christ Church. They corresponded in later years. The same issues prompted them to write: toleration, scriptural interpretation, the nature of polity, and education. Although they differ strongly about these issues, they share a deeper similarity: their works consistently argue that human knowledge, especially certainty, was a rare and hard-won prize.

If the intellectual historian places his camera at a distance from his subject, to repeat a metaphor I used before, similarities between Locke and South, about how difficult it is to know, for example, grow strong. An examination in more immediate contexts, however, despite the similarities of education and the long-term friendship, discourages easy comparison; on most important issues of their time, Locke and South disagree, as a contrast of their views on polity and education suggests.

South suspected that toleration of other forms of worship than that of the Church of England would subvert political order; Locke strongly opposed such a view. South considered a divinely ordered hierarchy of classes, starting with the king, essential to order; Locke considered government a thing to be made and changed by human hands. When South discussed polity he argued from Scripture, reason, and experience, includ-ing the experience of history. When Locke sets out, in his *Second Treatise of*

---

[31] *An Account*, p. 11.

Government, to discuss what polity should be, he very rarely uses Scripture as a source of ideas or of authority. This qualitative difference in methods of proof, I think, matters far more than the difference in conclusions resulting from such proofs. The text of Scripture says various things about kingship to various kinds of seventeenth-century interpreters; to ignore scriptural authority entirely is a radical step at the time. On the subject of polity, there is no meeting-ground between Locke and South.

Separate works of Locke and South discuss the education of youth and were written about the same time: Locke's *Some Thoughts Concerning Education*, written between 1684 and 1691 and published in 1693, and South's sermon on Proverbs 22:6, written to be delivered at a convocation of old Westminster boys in the late winter of 1685 which was cancelled because of the death of Charles II; the sermon was published in 1717. The works are similar in that both have optimistic hopes for moral education. Both assume original sin in some form, South more so than Locke. Both attack education by means of corporal punishment; their articulations of this matter suggest that they are conscious of departing from usual practice.[32]

But fundamental differences in approach exist, especially in the literary structure of the works. *Some Thoughts* has a real but somewhat casual order wherein three topics are discussed in descending order of importance: moral education; the content of education, especially languages; and other suitable areas for a gentleman's study. Moral education takes up about two-thirds of the discussion. The scheme sometimes doubles back on itself; the final version is based on letters which may not have been consistently edited. Inside the threefold scheme there seems to be no inevitable order wherein one paragraph must precede or follow another. Although the work deals at length with the methods of moral training, one can only infer how Locke feels about training young people to be believers in Christianity or good citizens of England.[33] The structure mirrors the philosophy of the piece: successful education occurs in situations that may vary, but close parental contact and supervision are very important. Successful methods vary in individual cases; form is usually more important than matter.

---

[32] Locke, *Some Thoughts Concerning Education*, ed. John W. and Jean Yolton (Oxford: Clarendon Press, 1989), pp. 112–13, 117–18; South, III, 398–400. It is unlikely that South's criticism of corporal punishment implied a criticism of the methods of Dr. Busby, who would have sat in the congregation had this sermon been delivered. South's last remarks on the topic ask that, should such punishment be given, let it appear that "the person is loved while his fault is punished; nay that one is punished only out of love to the other" (400). If Busby indeed gave such punishment, South's final remarks legitimate his practice.

[33] Yolton (Locke, *Some Thoughts Concerning Education*, pp. 1–2) is more hopeful than I am that Locke's theory of education is integrated with this political theory. For an excellent summary of Locke's theology, see John Locke, *A Paraphrase and Notes on the Epistles of St. Paul to the Galatians, 1 and 2 Corinthians, Romans, and Ephesians*, ed. Arthur W. Wainright (Oxford: Clarendon Press, 1987), I, 28–59.

In his sermon on the education of youth South follows, as he does again and again, John Wilkins's tripartite structure for sermons: exegesis, division and confirmation, and application. In this sermon South precedes exegesis with an account of how English society has disintegrated following and because of the regicide of 1649; the scriptural text, "Train up a child in the way he should go, and when he is old he will not depart from it" (Prov. 22:6), shows that reformation of society must begin with the education of the youth of England. South gives six propositions which connect the natural "propensity to vice" to "the ruin and subversion of government" and leads us to the education of youth (III, 386–89). He then develops the theme of education from the point of view of parents, schoolmasters, and clergy. All must educate youth to "a hatred of rebellion" (395) and a love for "obedience and subjection to government" (405). In regard to the content of education South is really only interested in teaching the reasons for and observance of civic and religious obedience. South digresses to allied topics such as nurturing in Israel (391); the revolution in the class system evident in the regicide (393); the relationship between teacher and pupil as an instance of proper, universal relationships (396); discipline in Sparta and corporal punishment (398–400); love and discipline (400); confirmation and the sacrament of the Lord's Supper (402–04); preaching about obedience and the danger of "tender consciences" (405–07); and the falsity of attacks against the rites and ceremonies of the Church of England (408–09). The sermon concludes by urging the congregation to suppress "conventicling schools and academics" and to support "free grammar schools," such as Westminster School (409–12).

The unity of Locke's "thoughts" on education is tonal as well as thematic; the same voice, at times experimental, at times prescriptive, is heard throughout. Besides both theme and tone, careful structuring and one repeated image unify South's sermon. South conceives all units of the educational process to be analogous: king and nation, bishops and faithful, parents and children, schoolmasters and pupils. All these relationships involve loving obedience, which is the law not only of the schoolhouse and family but also of the nation and the universe. South's synthesis is both extreme and beautiful in its symmetry.

The image of the regicide is, at the same time, brought before us again and again, in every division of the sermon. South makes the rhetorical purpose of this clear only at the end, when he reveals that he was present when the king "was publicly prayed for in this school, but an hour or two (at most) before his sacred head was struck off" (412). The rhetorical structure completes, on the level of the speaking self, what it advocates on the public level: that private concerns be integrated with public and even universal order. The history of 1649 is not completely dismal: when the world collapsed, Westminster School stood firm, and South was there.

Given Locke's own background as an old Westminster pupil it is extraordinary that *Some Thoughts Concerning Education* advocates that boys should be tutored at home rather than sent to school. Locke feels that schools encourage roughness and ill-breeding.[34] Historians of Westminster School habitually list Locke as one of Busby's successes, and perhaps he was; but he also rejected the entire concept of education which the school represented. Children, Locke insists, should stay close to their parents. Even tutors should be watched carefully. Education should be private, and tailored to the individual, not public. South's advocacy of Westminster has, of course, personal motivation; his esteem for Busby was lifelong. But the kind of personal education advocated by Locke also presented philosophical and even political problems for South. Almost anything private was threatening to his integralist view of church and state; the education of youth ranked high on his list of activities that had to be engendered by and participate in the life of church and state.

This brief contrast between Locke and South lastly deals with the correspondence. Five letters of South to Locke are extent, from the period 1699 to 1704. Locke mentions "little Robin" once in a letter of 1657; "little Robin" is mentioned again in a letter to Locke in 1658, as is "Mr. South" in a letter, from another correspondent, in 1660. The early references suggest friendship or acquaintance within a larger Westminster and Christ Church group; the later letters from South himself are, at the same time, both more personal and more professional.

In these later letters, South makes repeated requests to have Locke's *Essay Concerning Human Understanding* translated into Latin; praises Locke's intellectual superiority to Stillingfleet and Sherlock, thus involving Locke in his own personal battles; thanks Locke for the gift of four presentation copies; and refers often to their friendship, ending a letter of 6 December 1699, "Your old, affectionate, faithful friend."[35] South refers to his own sickness at the time of writing; there is, at times, a hint of a hunger for Locke's attention. But South's letters also come to grips with the intellectual issues of the controversies in which he and Locke were engaged; strength of mind remains.

How does one reconcile the wide differences between Locke and South on political and educational issues and the unanimity expressed in South's letters? The discrepancy between public disagreement and private like or dislike is a theme of more than one of these letters; in spite of his position here expressed, that public and personal be kept apart, South was not

[34] *Some Thoughts Concerning Education*, pp. 127–33.
[35] *The Correspondence of John Locke*, ed. E. S. De Beer (Oxford: Clarendon Press, 1976–89), VI, 754; for other correspondence, see also, I, 54, 56, 153; VI, 62–63, 196–97, 643–45; and VIII, 356–58.

usually successful at distinguishing the thought of someone he disliked from the person himself.

It is possible that South did not know that Locke wrote *Two Treatises of Government*, *Some Thoughts on Education*, and other works with which South's own writings disagree. This is unlikely if one grants that Locke's author-ship of even the controversial *Two Treatises* was suspected.[36] In the correspondence South stresses his agreement with Locke on issues that are especially technical: the illegitimacy of the concept "common nature"; the credit of divine testimony and the ancients' belief in the materiality of spirit; and the philosophical identification of God and the universe. Even South, who makes most things political, is not compelled to see these issues thus. But why does South give Locke the benefit of the doubt? Why does he allow that Locke be taken in discrete parts, not as an objectionable whole?

The answer is, I think, twofold. South appreciated the simple truth that Locke's works were more wide-ranging and at times more penetrating than his own, particularly Locke's theological works. South's occasional sycophancy in the Locke letters is perhaps not that, but honest admiration of what he knew was a far greater mind. Lastly, the Westminster and Christ Church roots perdured. These roots imply the royalism that Locke rejected, the principle opponent of which, in the eyes of history, he became. South thus hated the politics Locke stood for, yet he struggles to keep the level of discussion cordial and on topics of agreement. South is rarely this agreeable. His letters to Locke testify to the flexible strength of the simple fact of a shared past.

Dryden and South

In 1966 Paul K. Alkon published a seminal article on South, William Law, and Johnson, exploring, in part, how South's understanding of Aristotle's notion of habits may have influenced Johnson; in 1975, Irène Simon broke new ground in comparing South to the "Augustans."[37] Both articles pay high and necessary praise to South's thought by taking it seriously; both show how writers after him might have sympathized with his thought. Simon writes, for example that his "conception of man and of his role in society was one with which the Augustans were in complete agreement," especially in regard to "commonplaces of Christian ethics" of freedom, good and evil, and reason and enthusiasm.[38] Assuming the

---

[36] See John Locke, *Two Treatises of Government*, ed. Peter Laslett (Cambridge: Cambridge University Press, 1988), p. 4.

[37] Alkon, "Robert South, William Law, and Samuel Johnson," *SEL* 6 (1966), 499–528; and Simon, "Robert South and the Augustans," *Essays and Studies*, n.s., 28 (1975), 15–28.

[38] "Robert South and the Augustans," p. 27.

reader's knowledge of Swift, Pope, Edmund Burke, and Johnson, Simon devotes most of her analysis to South, whose philosophical anthropology she fully explores.

It is curious that the obvious relationship between South and John Dryden (1631–1700) has gained little attention. The biographical data suggest how fruitful such attention might be to understanding both South and Dryden. Dryden was born in 1631, three years before South. In the late 1640s they studied together (with Locke) at Westminster School under Dr. Busby, among whose favorite pupils both were reputed to be. The classical learning of each advanced in this period. Dryden went up to Trinity College, Cambridge, in the 1650 election, South to Christ Church a year later. In the tight, loyal, emulous Westminster community, South may have held Dryden up as someone he wanted to be like. After 1660 both became vocal supporters of Charles II and his brother, James Duke of York. In 1667, the same year Dryden's *Annus Mirabilis* praised Charles and James, South became one of the Duke of York's chaplains. Both South and Dryden can be counted among the most energetic expositors of the Stuart myth, according the highest prerogatives to the monarchy. At the same time, both had enough wit to temper the myth with irony, South in a 1675 sermon on kingship (see chapter 3), and Dryden in *Absalom and Achitophel* in 1681. Lastly, both former pupils of Busby watched their careers, for conscience's sake, wither after 1688; both came to feel that the changed nature of English politics could not provide a worthy object for the high emotional hopes they had once felt.

To compare Dryden and South, as I propose briefly to do, assists the reader in two ways. The reader probably knows more about the poet and dramatist Dryden than about the clergyman South; illation to the better-known body of work will make South's clearer. The reader may know something about late seventeenth-century Anglican thought, for there are available a few good studies; the reader will know very little about the relationship between literature and theology in the period, mainly because the relationships have been so little studied. Much prized in today's academy, interdisciplinary study has rarely approached this area. Yet the biographical data of Dryden and South, and other figures of the period, suggest fruitful results for the interdisciplinary researcher. The following, in which I discuss literary, political, and philosophical similarities and differences, begins to address the need, though the effort is meant to be suggestive rather than exhaustive of the richness of the area.

One subject to which South returned again and again in his preaching was the education of the clergy. To trace these returns in his sermons reveals the organicity of his vision, for one cannot discuss clerical training therein without exploring also university education, the need for a peaceful and structured society, and, finally, a strong monarchy. A noneducated clergy would, like several other dark forces in South's vision, ruin the state.

Dryden also found time, late in his life and writing career, to discuss clerical education. He does so in a more indirect way than South does, but the theme recurs. In his late translation from Chaucer, "The Character of a Good Parson (1700)," Dryden communicates what he takes to be an ideal of the clerical life and of the balance between intellect and piety in it. Dryden heightens the pious poverty of the parson of Chaucer's account; he also deemphasizes the learning of the parson. He omits, for example, Chaucer's description of the parson as "a lerned man, a clerk."[39]

For Dryden, the parson's learning is from nature, not art:

> With Eloquence innate his Tongue was arm'd
> Though harsh the precept yet the Preacher charm'd.[40]

The emphasis on innateness is Dryden's own: his parson needs not the spectacles of books to preach nature. Dryden's poem of 1682, *Religio Laici*, seems to require a clergy that is above all learned in the interpretation of Scripture; Dryden's conversion to Roman Catholicism some time after 1685 led him to change his mind. As Dryden turned away more and more, after 1688 and the flight of his Catholic patron, James II, from the English establishment, he began to praise, in the clergy, not the qualities of learning and breeding that are redolent of establishment, but the disarming and impolitic qualities of piety and poverty.

In 1693 Dryden praises the Roman satirist Persius, whose moralism he considers superior to "all the nice speculations of divinity and controversies concerning the faith, which are more for the profit of the shepherd than for the edification of the flock."[41] This might be taken as an expression common to latitudinarians, of annoyance with mistaking the non-essentials for the essentials in theology and religion. Dryden also might be striking out at those, unlike himself, who have succeeded inside the English establishment. As G. Douglas Atkins reminds us, Dryden was contemplating a treatise on the clergy in the years before he died.[42] He would almost certainly have stressed in it the need for clerical piety, humility, poverty, and disestablishment over the opposite qualities. By the 1690s, Dryden was finding in his own poverty and resignation, projected onto the clergy, a paradise within.

---

[39] *The Riverside Chaucer*, 3rd edn., ed. Larry D. Benson (Boston: Houghton Mifflin, 1987), p. 480. The parson's learning may be a rebuttal of the charge of Lollardry made by the Host (p. 104); the parson, unlike the Lollard stereotype, was educated.

[40] Dryden, *Poems and Fables*, ed. James Kinsley (London: Oxford University Press, 1962), p. 811.

[41] Dryden, *Of Dramatic Poesy and other Critical Essays*, ed. George Watson (London: Dent, 1962), II, 123.

[42] *The Faith of John Dryden: Change and Continuity* (Lexington, KY: The University Press of Kentucky, 1980), p. 152.

South's thoughts on clerical education, opposite to Dryden's, are, in any age, extreme. South felt that a clergy reliant for its effectiveness on personal virtue would inevitably present a political problem. Personal virtue and uprightness were wild cards in the political game, which only learning bred by the state could control. In the right order of things, clerical learning, controlled by supervised universities and schools, necessarily preceded clerical holiness. Right thought was more important than right living. South reiterates this eccentric position as late as in a Pentecost sermon of 1692: "The Spirit always guides and instructs before he saves; and that, as he brings to happiness only by the ways of holiness, so he never leads to true holiness, but by the paths of knowledge" (II, 546).

Political changes help to explain Dryden's view of clerical education. Dryden was thoroughly out of the establishment by the 1690s. His king was over the water, and Dryden had to hide his comments on current events in ambiguous *obiter dicta* in his translations from Latin and Greek. He was a Roman Catholic in a country that was not only Protestant but, after 1688, becoming more thoroughly so. His heightened awareness of the innateness of clerical goodness is not inconsistent with his own loss of external position and honors.

South's situation is more complicated. South doubly reiterates his connection of clerical education and state control after 1688: by continuing to preach in this vein and by republishing earlier explorations of the same, such as "The Scribe Instructed" (1660), published in 1715, South seems to want to stress his consistency in this area. Yet political consistency was difficult. After 1688 South increasingly belonged to a losing side in the Church of England; high church political gains in the reign of Queen Anne (1702–14) would also falter. South opposed, for example, along with many others, the position of what often seemed to be the majority on the toleration of dissenters. It greatly troubled South that the alliance of church and state, which he had stridently supported, might advocate a policy that he detested.

South never changed his own argument that a strong state maintaining strong universities led to a strong clergy. Perhaps South felt that the Williamite reform would be shortlived; perhaps he felt that the universities, at least colleges such as Christ Church, would hold onto the old ways. It appears that, because of his own difficulty in maintaining his belief in an integrated state while hating its recent developments, South lived in anger.

Recent commentators on the late works of Dryden stress their peace, the advice they give to come to terms with change. We like to see such final reconciliation in our great poets, and Dryden does not fail us. There is no such peace in South. The nasty remark of Anthony Wood, that South lived his final years "in a discontented and clamorous condition" seems, as we shall see throughout the following chapters, near to the truth, though this truth does not really involve Wood's reductionist interpretation of South's frustrated ambition. It is more likely that South's anger stems from a cause hinted at in his continued defense of clerical learning. He was caught defending that which turned out to oppose him; right thinking about the church and right thinking about the state, which South always insisted were one, had come apart.

Dryden wrote poems, essays, and plays; South wrote mostly sermons. Aside from these obvious differences in choices of form, similarities in literary preferences exist. Both Dryden and South comment on two issues that the late seventeenth century considered important literary questions: legitimacy of metaphor and purity of form.

Both Dryden and South participate in what is commonly called the reform of prose style in late seventeenth-century England. Both authors write in the plain style: neither Ciceronian nor Senecan, the plain style attempts, in the parlance of the Royal Society of London, to be faithful not to a preconceived rhetorical structure but to the object or quality described (see chapter 2). Both Dryden and South temper the potential severity of the plain style with an abundant reliance on metaphor.

As I will later explain, the use of metaphor in expository prose was highly suspect at this time. Both Dryden and South, sufficiently self-possessed to depart from standard practice, allowed metaphor to carry major meanings in their prose. Dryden's brilliant use of imagery, as he moved from verse to prose, and back again, changed in one important respect: in verse he often relied on patterns of images to carry meaning, even, to the ingenious observer, perhaps to carry a meaning counter to the point of the whole. Dryden never did this in his essays. Their imagery is always local: it reinforces, sometimes making a meaning startlingly fresh, but it never repeats itself throughout an essay, and never grows complex enough to take on a potentially disrupting influence of its own.

South also used imagery in an inventive manner. He is not as great in this regard, I think, as Dryden is; Dryden's invention and expansion of a simile can at times take the breath away; South is merely very good. But South does surpass Dryden in one respect: South often creates image patterns in his sermons. There is in fact no greater sign of South's artistic self-consciousness than his pattern-making. My primary reason for picking the sermons analyzed in this study has been that of content, but I also chose sermons in which this patterning would be evident. Only South, among the greatest of late seventeenth-century divines, composes in this way: image patterns are his signature.

As I have mentioned, South likes to punctuate his sermons with humor; the mixing of serious and light confused contemporary and later commentators. This confusion seems irrelevant today: why shouldn't South mix

humor and seriousness in one literary construct? We ask this question
because we have for the most part rejected seventeenth-century anxiety
over mixing literary genres. To mix the light with the serious, the low with
the high, and the comic with the tragic was taken by some not only to be
indecorous but also unnatural. The classical genres of tragedy, comedy,
epic, satire, and so on represented not merely convention but a connection
with nature that was set down in its pure form by classical authors. Just as
one cannot understand South's ideal of clerical education without reference to politics, so the theory of literary genres invokes not only history,
but also philosophy and perhaps theology as well. Interconnectedness is a
seventeenth-century presence, even omnipresence.

Dryden, like South, agreed and disagreed with the theory of genres.
Though not revolutionary, they were independent. In a series of essays
from 1668 to 1700 which change their minds about many things, Dryden
consistently defends the English mixing of genres in drama called tragicomedy. In this defense Dryden argues less philosophically than prag-
matically: what pleases the audience is good dramatic practice. "I dare to
prophesy," Dryden writes in 1681, "that few tragedies except those in
verse shall succeed in this age, if they are not lightened with a course of
mirth."[43] In some cases, Dryden argues, success rather than fidelity to
tradition is necessary.

Although criticized by Fell and by other divines, South understood that
a mixture of seriousness and levity in a sermon would do no great damage
to pulpit decorum. South wrote no extended defense of humor in the
pulpit. When he starts to do so, he tends to turn off to criticism of the
ponderousness of others, as he does in 1660: "piety engages no man to be
dull; though lately, I confess, it passed with some for a mark of regeneration" (III, 14). In theory, South understood rhetorical invention as a gift
from God; all preachers should use all the gifts they have to communicate
the gospel. In practice, South, like Dryden, looked to the audience as well
as to the rules of decorum. For both, within certain bounds, popular
appreciation of a mixed genre supplemented critical narrowness masking
as regeneration as an index of literary value. Dramatists had more
common sense in this regard than homilists: Dryden was certainly in the
seventeenth-century mainstream of approving mixed genres, while South,
in homiletics, was not.

The argument over purity of genre forms one small chapter of a larger
discussion that occurred throughout Europe in the late seventeenth
century. This discussion concerned not only what truths an intelligent
person might hold in theology, natural philosophy, ethics, and history but,
more importantly, on what basis the truths were to be accepted. How did

[43] *Critical Essays*, I, 279.

one prove the truthfulness of a thesis? We usually understand this discussion of sources of verification in terms of opposites: reason against tradition, science against theology, experience against authority, moderns against ancients, education against innate ideas, and so on.

These oppositions point out the special, conflictual nature of late seventeenth-century European thought. An interpreter of a figure such as Robert South must insist that his age not be interpreted as one in which the newer categories and bases for truth steadily overcome the old. This is the Whig interpretation of intellectual history, and one which could understand South only as an irrelevance. Both old and new methods of proof vie with one another in South's time, modifying and gaining strength from one another.

The last similarity I wish to draw between Dryden and South concerns their methods of proving things. Both take somewhat the same attitude towards the newer probational resources; both make a self-conscious effort to diversify. Both again and again rely on mixed proofs; that is, they tend to prove the truth of any statement by complementary arguments from authority, necessary reason, and experience.

When Dryden set out to prove that this or that play or technique or prejudice was right or wrong, he frequently sought to align his argument with that of Aristotle's *Poetics*. Although he at times disagreed with Aristotle, reference to the *Poetics*, he knew, carried great weight. Closely allied to an argument from the authority of Aristotle were arguments from reason: a scene or a judgment was true because it fulfilled the laws of justice, or of probability, or fit the end of a genre. These are arguments from necessary reason: once an axiom stands, certain conclusions must flow from it. Such proofs resemble that from the authority of Aristotle because Aristotle's greatness consisted in part in such keen observance of nature and the extant models that he could set down not only subjective judgments but universal laws.

Dryden most reveres Horace's *Ars Poetica* as a literary authority; this is no doubt partly owing to the casual nature of the verse essay, whose meaning can be twisted to advantage. When Dryden argues from experience, he sometimes opposes it to arguments from authority and reason: we have seen how he praises tragicomedy for its audience appeal, even though no classical precedent stood and though a mixed genre, it could be argued, was inconsistent with a rational norm. Dryden also defended works because they were, in a word, English; he was at times nationalistic. Because he judged not only structure but also individual passages, he helped to establish textual explication as part of the English critical tradition.

In South's or any other time, a theologian works under rules of evidence different from those of a literary critic. A thesis could be admitted by all to be in Aristotle, yet Dryden could still reject it as applicable, without losing his status as a critic. If a truth is clearly found in the Old or New Testaments, the theologian, at least in South's day, had to accept it. To prove that a truth was scriptural was the goal of much theological discourse; a truth not in Scripture was suspect. Nor could an orthodox theologian find a discrepancy in sources and allege that Scripture led one way and reason another. Throughout the seventeenth century Anglican theologians argued that God would never let his coordinate gifts, revelation and reason, contradict one another. Only radical thinkers such as Hobbes, Spinoza, and the deists explored the possibility that the obvious conflicts between Scripture and reason are insurmountable. South argued, as many did, that all available probative resources led to the same truths.

Especially for Protestant theologians Scripture was and had to be the principal norm by which religious truth was proved to be true. One also discussed not whether but how Scripture supported an argument; Wilkins gives an elaborate scheme (see appendix 2) for using Scripture properly. South's other probative resources are, of course, reason, sometimes in the deduction of truth from what were held to be necessary principles; observation and common sense, ways of proof that gave full vent to South's ability to satirize; and confirmation by historical example. Because of his excellent classical education South excelled at the latter; one senses that confirmation by parallel anecdote from Plutarch or Livy had a nearly scriptural efficacy for him and his more educated hearers.

One can analyze a given proof of Dryden or South and note that one or other probative resource is stressed. But the general picture leads one to believe that both greatly prized diversity: they both loved to show as much as they knew, to be evidentiary virtuosi. Both believed that different sorts of argument were equally useful; South had the added motive of showing that all sources of truth agreed on the central Christian truths. As men of their time, with a keen eye on old and new, Dryden saw merit in the authorities, sometimes conflicting, of both Aristotle and Shakespeare; and South, when he felt a doctrine was clearly in Scripture, would set about to prove it instead by reason.

As their careers progress and as they mature, is there evidence that South and Dryden came to favor one type of proof over another? Dryden's most famous prose work, *An Essay of Dramatic Poesy* (1668), seems incapable of integrating arguments from different sources into one critical voice; it creates different characters arguing different theses based on different types of evidence. As attractive as *An Essay* has been felt to be, it does not offer a brave solution to the problems of conflicting evidence. Many readers have felt that Dryden reaches a peak of resolution of variety in his "Heads of An Answer to Rymer" (1678); there he mediates between conflicting sources of neo-Aristotelianism, honoring but correcting

Aristotle, and balances arguments from reason and experience to argue the greatness of English tragedy. But Dryden's development is never simply linear, and subsequent essays lean one way or the other along the evidentiary continuum.

In the 1690s, his last decade of writing, South makes a significant change in procedure. The context is the Socinian debates (see chapter 6), wherein the central Christian mysteries were held to be (a) rationally absurd, and (b) not in Scripture. South and others wrote against Socinian argument, but South seems unique in at least two ways. He refused to use analogies between the mysteries of nature and the mysteries of Scripture; he regarded the latter as absolutely unique. He also preached that the Christian mysteries served as a useful chastisement to reason and humbled the searcher for truth in a salutary way. The latitudinarians, truly on the same side here as South, did not argue this way. South's voice here hardly confirms the universal validity of proofs that, in theory and practice, he had before asserted. There is no easy way to explain away his methodological inconsistency. Even after the 1690s debates, of course, he edited and published many sermons written in his earlier and usual mode.

One final question remains: did the literary critics read the proofs of the theologians, and vice versa? Did South influence Dryden, or Dryden South, in the matter of mixed proofs? The question is impossible to answer in a fully verified way. But it is historically useful to remember that in the 1670s and 1680s the sermons of South were at least as popular and commented upon as the essays of Dryden, and it is perhaps more probable, if any influence at all occurred, that Dryden learned from South and, marvelling at the mixed proofs of the divines, introduced them into his own writing.

2

South's *Sermons* in context

Collecting

In the late 1680s, South set about the task of collecting and editing his
sermons – even as he continued writing new ones, as he would do until
1699. In 1692, he published the first collected volume of twelve sermons
(six of these had been published before), and volumes of twelve each
followed in 1694, 1698, and 1715. In 1717, the year after his death, the
fifth and sixth volumes, again with twelve sermons each, were published.
These last two volumes have dedications written by South; he had
planned the volumes himself. In the years from 1692 on, it began to be
clear to South that his rise in the church had stopped; the excellence of the
seventy-two sermons would have to compensate, in the eyes of history, for
their author's lack of episcopal office.

South was aware of different ways of organizing one's collected sermons,
for, in the twenty-five years it took him to edit his own, a number of other
divines (or their editors) were occupied in similar tasks. Most prominent
among these were Edward Stillingfleet (*d.* 1699), Bishop of Worcester, and
John Tillotson (*d.* 1694), Archbishop of Canterbury. Both had published
several volumes of sermons during their lifetimes and, following previous
practice and instructions, after their deaths their chaplains compiled fuller
editions. The principles of organization of Stillingfleet's *Fifty Sermons*
(1707), volume 1 of the *Works* in folio, and of Tillotson's fourteen volumes
in octavo (1695–1704) differ greatly and indicate the choices South
himself faced as he set about deciding, from 1692 on, which of his sermons
to publish and how.

Stillingfleet's and Tillotson's collections give evidence of alternate exercises in specificity and generality. Tillotson and his editor usually sup-
pressed the date when, and place where, individual sermons were given, as
well as any internal signs in the sermons that might indicate these.[1]
Though some references to Whitehall, where Tillotson frequently
preached, remain, the vast majority of the two hundred sermons in the

---

[1] See Simon, II, ii, 358, 360.

1695–1704 edition are cut off from time and place, Of the twenty or so sermons where circumstances of delivery are alluded to, the annotation often reads simply "Ash Wednesday," "All Saints' Day," or "Christmas" – datings that increase the generic nature of the sermons, placing them not in a linear and secular, but rather in a cyclical and liturgical calendar. Even the apparently specific dating on one sermon, "Ash Wednesday, 1689" (volume VIII, sermon four) – only a few months after William III's arrival and devoid of political reference – seems in retrospect to undercut the significance of that historical moment; kingdoms may rise and fall, but the liturgical year endures.

The true principle of organization of Tillotson's collection is thematic. Seven of the fourteen volumes have thematic titles, such as *Several Discourses on the Attributes of God* (volume VI) and *Several Discourses on Death and Judgment, and a Future State* (volume IX). These volumes and almost all the others, even those without thematic titles, list, on their title pages, the themes covered in the particular volume. By suppressing dates and places, and by arranging his sermons according to themes, Tillotson and his editor suggest that these works belong not to historical theology, but to systematics; the principle of organization stresses the use of these sermons as a perennial resource, rather than as a means of insight into the English church in the late seventeenth century. In this case history vindicated editorial decision; Tillotson's sermons became standard reading for eighteenth- and nineteenth-century students of divinity.

Where Tillotson is generic, Stillingfleet is specific. *Fifty Sermons* surprises, first of all, by its exclusivity. Tillotson provided his editor with two hundred sermons, Stillingfleet with only fifty.[2] The principles of organization seem to be to create a sampler, repeating no theme or occasion and, vying with this, to include sermons preached before distinguished audiences. Stillingfleet firmly places thirty-seven of the sermons in space and time, and is very specific about audience: before the king at Whitehall (sermon XVII), before the king and queen at Whitehall (XXVII, XXXI, XXXII), before the king and queen at Hampton Court (XXXIV), before the Princess of Denmark at Whitehall (XXXIII), and so on. Until sermon XXXIII, the arrangement is chronological, so that the reader can observe the increasing fame and art of the author.

Stillingfleet also cultivates the relationship of several sermons to their contexts of controversy, mentioning doctrinal opponents in prefatory

---

[2] See Gerard Reedy, S.J., "Stillingfleet's *Fifty Sermons*," *Papers of the Bibliographical Society of America*, 73 (1979), 254–57; since this note was published, four manuscript sermons, none of which is in *FS*, have been called to my attention in Ms. 0.81 (St. John's College, Cambridge); Lambeth Palace Library has recently acquired a manuscript, some of it in shorthand, of Stillingfleet sermons. Some of these sermons seem to be already in *FS*, and the manuscript waits for an interested decipherer. If the shorthand pages are pulpit notes, then the manuscript may tell us more than we now know about Stillingfleet's revisions.

material, marginal notes, or the text itself, as in sermon XVIII, part of a
discussion on church definition and nonconformism, sermon XXIV, part
of an argument of Scripture and tradition with Roman Catholics, and
sermon XXVIII, on the theological mystery, part of the Socinian controversy of the 1690s. Lastly, unlike Tillotson, Stillingfleet never repeats a
category: he includes one Christmas and one Pentecost sermon, for
example, one for 30 January, the anniversary of the regicide, one for 5
November the anniversary of the discovery of the Gunpowder Plot, and so
on. In a passing gesture to Tillotsonian thematics, he includes six sermons
on one text (John 6:68) and one topic, the relation between happiness and
immortality; this kind of multiple exploration of a single text was a
common *tour de force* among contemporary preachers.

It is clear that Stillingfleet presents his sermons not as a generic manual
of topics for future readers, but as symbols of a successful, prominent life,
full of hard work, homiletic art, and high recognition. He invokes history
– the prominence of where and when, of audience – as components of our
enjoyment as we read. He compliments us by placing us in such distinguished company. He invites comparison and contrast with sermons of
others given on the same days of similar occasions in other years. He has
achieved his goal of variety, as Tillotson has succeeded in giving each one
of his volumes uniformity and sameness, even as his themes change. Stillingfleet challenges the reader to guess how the preacher's art will function
on this occasion; his transition from explication of the biblical text to a
statement of what the sermon will demonstrate is usually surprising and
unpredictable. But a successful career exhibited in the self-congratulatory
folio publication of a life's sermons is its own reward; unlike Tillotson's
sermons, which were reprinted again and again, *Fifty Sermons* was never
reprinted after the first edition.

The principles on which each of the six volumes of South's *Sermons* are
organized are more complex than those of either Stillingfleet or Tillotson.
Only volume III, dedicated to Oxford University ("having by the favour
of your patience had the honour of your audience" [I, 345]), and with five
out of seven placed sermons given at Christ Church, begins to make its
principle of organization obvious. That two sermons in the volume were
given in Westminster Abbey and that five are not placed at all testify to
South's aversion to simple patterning. Volume III collects sermons on
Jesus and the Holy Spirit – the dedication speaks of the dangers of
Socinianism – and on the moral life, but other themes are also present.
Four of the sermons in volume V, published after South's death, deal with
the English Anniversaries of 30 January, 29 May, the anniversary of the
king's return in 1660, and 5 November; these contain some of the most
royalist passages, from sermons of 1662 and 1663, that South had written,
and the delay of their publication suggests that South had second thoughts

about the warmth of his early sentiments. South was sick in his last few years; unwilling to destroy the fruits of his early art, yet perhaps ashamed of their naiveté, he may have been hoping that, as happened, the natural course of events would excuse him from witnessing publication.

Like Stillingfleet, South dated and placed a number of sermons, about forty of the seventy-two, of volumes I through VI. Thirteen of these are placed at Westminster Abbey, and sixteen at Christ Church, almost all of the latter, "Before the University." In the same category are five sermons at St. Mary's Oxford, all given before South received his stall at Christ Church, along with the privilege accorded to canons there, of delivering university sermons in the cathedral rather than the university church.[3] Headnotes describe two sermons as given at Whitehall and before the court at Christ Church. It may have been an embarrassment to South that he could collect so few sermons preached, in a forty-year career, before the king and court; this lack of royal attention hints at something prickly and independent in South that never attuned itself to courtly ways. South includes one sermon for 30 January (1662–63), two for 29 May, the anniversary of the King's return (1670, 1672), and three for 5 November (1663, 1675, and 1688). Volume 1 comes close to Stillingfleet's *Fifty Sermons* in at least one respect, for it is organized around prominent places where sermons were preached: Christ Church, Westminster, St. Mary's, St. Paul's, Lincoln's Inn, and Lambeth, the last three apparently one-time appearances for South.

Like Tillotson, South leaves many sermons undated and unplaced, about thirty in all. The possibility arises that South had forgotten where and when he delivered certain sermons by the time he set out to edit them; one sermon on the Trinity is situated, along this line, somewhere "between the years 1665 and 1670" (III, 194). At least in volumes III and V, thematic principles seem to have helped organize the contents. Volume VI begins with three sermons on the same text, Isaiah 5:20, on the theme, a favorite of South's, "the fatal influence of words and names falsely applied"; there follow seven sermons on temptation, using different texts, giving the whole volume a thematic appearance only slightly marred by the addition of two last sermons thematically unrelated to the first ten. Thus South shares to some degree Tillotson's desire to leave for posterity systematic treatments of moral questions.[4] Yet part of his twenty-five year planning and editing seems to have been given over to frustrating the

---

3 See Henry L. Thompson, *Christ Church* (London: F. E. Robinson, 1900), p. 92, for the controversy, around 1670, concerning this privilege of the canons of Christ Church.

4 Other examples of multiple treatments of the same texts and themes by South are: two sermons on Eccles. 5:2, against long *ex tempore* prayers (I, 405–63); two on Rom. 1:32, on taking pleasure in others's sins (II, 1–79); two on 1 John 3:21, studies of conscience (II, 163–224); two on 2 Thess. 2:11, on the power of affections over the judgment (III, 224–86); and two on Luke 12:15, on covetousness (III, 287–347).

attempts of future readers too easily to categorize him as either a trumpeter of his own successes or the self-effacing author of a *summa theologica anglicana*.

South's sermons range between 7,000 and 10,000 words. The obvious question about such lengthiness, quite common in his day, is whether such sermons could possibly have been delivered in the pulpit. Were the pulpit versions shorter than the printed? Did South habitually revise, always with a view to lengthening? The truth is that we have no way of answering this question in regard to South because all we have is his printed text. We have no manuscripts or pulpit copies of even one of his sermons. South never prefaced a printed version, as Stillingfleet once did, with the notice of "Additions which the straits of time would not then permit me to deliver."[5] Does the rarity of such a remark signify that usually sermons were *not* revised, that the printed copy was the same length as the pulpit copy? Here and there in South there is evidence of revision: Simon has caught him, in a sermon of 1663, printed in 1717, anachronistically referring to the Popish Plot.[6] Likewise, in a sermon of 1668 published in 1717, discussing the proud poverty of the English clergy, he writes that the church should not have "naked gospels or naked evangelists" (IV, 138), alluding to Arthur Bury's deistical *Naked Gospel*, published in 1690. There are probably a number of similar anachronisms, but evidence of this sort cannot solve the question of whether or not South greatly augmented his preaching text as he edited it.

Dedications

Like many of his contemporaries, South practiced the art of the fulsome dedication. To a certain extent he followed the prevalent, generic formula of magnifying the virtues of the dedicatee, including condescension in accepting the work, and of deprecating his own abilities. It is difficult to accept such dedications today at their face value, and at times they seem to be exercises to test the gullibility of the figure so laboriously honored; we must remember the great capacity for flattery in South's day. Even in the last volume of sermons, published posthumously in 1717, South follows the formula and laments his inequality to his patron's virtues; he cannot "reach the very lowest parts of them by the best and highest of my expressions" (IV, 201–02). Over eighty when he wrote this, South could not have been hoping for preferment from George Hooper, Bishop of Bath

---

[5] *FS*, p. 275.

[6] Simon, II, i, 20, n2. "None of the autograph versions of South's sermons seems to have survived," Simon writes, "but it is clear that he revised them for publication and that the printed text differs from the sermon as preached" (II, i, 24). No evidence is given to support this clarity; the second part of this statement seems to assume what the first has denied. It is clear that we know very little about how South composed.

and Wells, the dedicatee; in fact, few of South's dedicatees were capable of helping him in any substantial way. There were good reasons for South to praise Hooper, who had been trained by Pocock, and was known as his finest student of Hebrew, Arabic, and Syriac. One may surmise that by praising him South was also praising the Christ Church establishment, of which South himself was known to be a prominent member. On the other hand, perhaps the process of dedicatory hyperbole was such an ingrained habit in South and other writers that he and they thought very little about the reality behind their praises and self-deprecations.

South's publications of single sermons all occurred in the 1660s, early in his career. he wrote a dedication for each single publication; a later sort of dedication, still generic but more revealing of his own politics, appears in volumes II through VI, from 1694 on. In the early group, a dedication to Edward Hyde, Earl of Clarendon (1665), was inevitable; he was South's first patron in the great world, whose influence brought South the Public Oratorship and his D.D. The dedication of two sermons (1660) to Sir Edward Atkins (1587–1669), whose parliamentary sympathies were known to go back to the 1630s, is puzzling. South concentrates his praise on Atkins's resistance to Cromwell in 1654, when the Protector sought to change court rules, and his presence as a presiding judge in the regicide trials of 1660. This is not the only instance of a South dedication that selectively interprets the dedicatee's life to make the political points South wants. Bishop Dolben was the natural dedicatee of the sermon preached at his consecration in 1666, which I have mentioned in the previous chapter.

Lastly, a single sermon delivered at St. Paul's in 1662 gave South a chance to honor the Lord Mayor and Aldermen of the City of London. This is more than a decade before the City became a center of resistance to the Stuarts. South's lyrical praise of the City resembles Dryden's in the dedication to *Annus Mirabilis* (1667), and South's dedication, like Dryden's poem, mentions the profanation of old St. Paul's by parliamentary troops, who had turned it into stables. South's sermon concerns fallen human nature, and the dedication involves him in an uncharacteristically elaborate conceit: "my business is, by describing what man was in his first estate, to upbraid him with what he is in his present: between whom, innocent and fallen (that in a word I may suit the subject to the place of my discourse), there is as great an unlikeness between St. Paul's a cathedral, and St. Paul's a stable" (I, 29–30). South usually avoids such "metaphysical" imagery, and his parenthesis perhaps shows his uneasy feeling at not doing so; his indulgence is part of what in his dedication he calls "the raw endeavours of a young divine" (I, 29).

The dedications of volumes II through VI tell us a great deal about South's political sympathies towards the end of his life, a period when he was living with and making sense out of his taking of the oaths in 1689.

The dated sermons of the 1690s are not political in nature, and only in the dedications did South reveal his hand; having rejected nonjuring, but wary of the accommodating new bishops of William III, South dedicated the volumes to those who were, like himself, carving out a loyalist and non-Jacobite, but high church position. The dedication of volume V (1717) to Robert Freind, Headmaster of Westminster, and past and present masters there, is the least complex of the lot; it offers thanks for "the author's education in that renowned seminary of learning, loyalty, and religion" (III, 373). Even here, however, the abstractions "loyalty" and "religion," present a complex code to those readers who have Busby and the center of Stuart loyalty he had established in mind. The dedication of volume II (1694) to Oxford University attacks the "innovating spirit ... striking at the constitutions of our church," and praises the work done at Oxford and Cambridge "to support and recover her declining state" (I, 345, 347). In the 1690s and after, the idea of the church in decline was a stock item in Christ Church arguments that opposed changes in episcopal jurisdiction, comprehension, and toleration.

In his dedication of volume III (1698) to Narcissus Marsh, Archbishop of Dublin, South sets out to create the myth of a unified Church of Ireland, where church and parliament work together, to contrast the lack of similar unanimity in England. South knew Marsh for only a short period in the late 1680s, when Marsh, having fled Jacobite risings in Ireland, visited Oxford, where he had connections at Magdalen Hall and Exeter College. Sometime after his return to Ireland and elevation to the sees of Cashel (1691) and Dublin (1694), Marsh had abetted the prosecution of the deist John Toland – "a certain Mahometan Christian," South calls him (II, 228) – resulting in his flight from Ireland in 1697. South uses the willingness of the Irish parliament to punish Toland for a heterodox theology as a symbol of ideal cooperation between church and state. In the Marsh dedication, South makes a rare allusion to "high churchmen," but as a term invented to abuse "the ancienter members of her communion, who have all along owned and contended for a strict conformity to her rules and sanctions" (II, 226).

Volume IV (1715) is dedicated, in a brief citation, to William Bromley in "high esteem and sincere affection" (III, 1). The dedication does not allude to the decay of the church caused by theological innovation, but Bromley's political stands, as M.P. for Oxford after 1701 and, from 1710 to 1714, Speaker of the House of Commons, were solidly high church. In particular, he championed a controversial bill against occasional conformity, that is, the practice by nonconformist officials, who may have belonged to disestablished or unestablished congregations, of only occasional attendance at the services of the established church. The issue of occasional conformity was one of the five or six battlegrounds that high church forces chose to contest in the reign of William and Mary and after.

Perhaps the most revealing dedication is the last, of volume VI (1717), to Bishop George Hooper. In Christ Church and in study under Pocock, Hooper and South shared a common history; Hooper was also an old Westminster student. Even with this background, Hooper had taken the oaths early and had encouraged others to do the same. Like South, Hooper had taken the risk of complying, and, unlike him, had gone further. In 1703, he accepted the see of Bath and Wells, from which Bishop Thomas Ken had been evicted for nonjuring; mitigating circumstances included Ken's urging him to do so. Notwithstanding the appearance of submission, Hooper, like Bromley, had gone on to fight another day. Associating himself with anti-latitudinarian causes, he defended the prerogatives of the lower house of Convocation (the upper house of bishops being latitudinarian), opposed the union of England and Scotland without full extension of the Anglican hierarchy, and like Bromley, openly sided with Henry Sacheverell, a strident high church-man, in his trial in 1710 for libel of the government. In Hooper, South saw the reflection of his own compliance, and how it could be turned into vigorous independence.

Through his dedications, South chose his friends and defined himself in the last decades of his life. Like Marsh (or at least like the idealization presented), Bromley, and Hooper, South believed the church to be in a state of crisis. Already in 1666, in the dedication to Dolben, South had commiserated with the new bishop, elevated when "the church is in its wane" (I, 121). The developments of the next fifty years convinced South and many others of his party of the essential correctness of that diagnosis. The term, "high church," means different things in different contexts, but at least refers, in the years around 1700, to the conservative perception that the church as it had been known was in decline. The research of Geoffrey Holmes into Anglican churchgoing and faltering urban growth indicates that South's party's fears had a basis in fact.[7] As the high church–latitudinarian conflict developed and intensified, South moved into his old age; he could do little actively to help. He responded to the crisis by reaffirming the solidarity of the opposition: Christ Church, Westminster, Bromley, Hooper, and South. The dedications lack the drama of parliamentary debate; they are the contribution of a man away from the center of political action. The governments after 1688, mostly sympathetic to latitudinarianism, could easily read a firm opposition in the dedications to South's *Sermons*.

---

[7] Holmes, *The Trial of Dr. Sacheverell* (London: Eyre and Methuen, 1973) ch. 2.

Pulpit reform

Irène Simon's research has articulated the self-conscious reform of pulpit oratory in late seventeenth-century England.[8] South partly inherited and partly advanced the principles of that reform. Even if he was not familiar with the small library of manuals Simon has located and summarized, he was clearly filled with their spirit. From two sermons he gave in the 1660s (29 July 1660, 30 April 1668) on the function and practice of preaching, and from parallel suggestions of representative preachers and theoreticians such as Stillingfleet and Wilkins, one may construct a four-point summary of what South considered reformed homiletics to be.

(1) Every sermon must show planning and method; the preacher must not rely on the inspiration of the Holy Spirit to do his work for him. For John Wilkins, this means a tripartite structure, to which the sermon itself would call attention, of explication of a scriptural text, demonstration of truths drawn from the text, and an application of those truths to Christian life or thinking. Wilkins warns against varying this structure; a desire for variety "May be true of itching curious Hearers, but not of such as regard their own profit and Education."[9] In his printed text, South always sets out, after his explication of Scripture, what he wants to do for the rest of the sermon. It was then necessary to develop these points in order; such a procedure both helped and challenged him, especially if he had memorized the sermon (see below, point 4). It was at this juncture, in a lost sermon on Ecclesiastes 7:10 given before the king on 13 April 1662, that Wood tells us that South was "taken with a qualm, drops of sweat standing in his face as big as pease," and lost his voice.[10] True or not, the anecdote vividly pictures the fears of a young preacher about what might happen when his nerves got the better of him. Especially because the printed sermons were edited sometimes long after their delivery, they give us no evidence about such failures of nerve or loss of memory in the pulpit. South occasionally repeats his outline, five or six thousand words later, when the demonstration is finished, a tactic signifying proud completion of a challenging task, and one of which Wilkins would not disapprove. South's sermons must be grasped as wholes, since the structuring of compelling wholes formed part of his intention and part of the pleasure and profit gained by his audience.

(2) The preacher needs learning. Wilkins lists page after page of commentaries and authorities for preachers who have not had time to do their own research or to augment their own studies. Besides learned content, the sermon-writer should master the rules of classical rhetoric. One senses that South and Stillingfleet, writing on this point, are conscious

---

[8] Simon, I, i, 1–73.   [9] *Ecclesiastes*, p. 6.   [10] *Athenae Oxonienses*, IV, 636.

of opposition from the same quarter – either preachers of the Spirit or, more simply, the slothful – that impugned orderly method. Stillingfleet writes: "if there be one way of speaking better than another, more apt to please, to ravish, to move, to inflame, why should this not be esteemed a Gift of God which tends to the most useful Improvement of Speech?"[11] South and Stillingfleet also detail modes of writing and argument that have no place in Christian homiletics, but the principal message is clear: the greater familiarity with ancient and modern learning, the greater the likelihood of good preaching.

An insistence on method and learning had political as well as rhetorical consequences. For South, the Interregnum, particularly the rise of the Independents, had encouraged *ex tempore* preaching, political sedition, and the decline of the universities. At times South has difficulty proving the encouragement of the last by historical example; the examples he gives seem insignificant in proportion to the amount of time he spends deploring Independency's alleged belittling of university education. Still, it was inevitable that long training, familiarity with authoritative commentaries, and careful method would help weed out the most fanatical preachers and fanatical tendencies in the rest. Moreover, such preparation presupposed leisure, places of study, and beneficed sinecures that followed in the wake of at least royalist stability. Without a political theory that argued against innovation, the reform of pulpit oratory was an unrealistic project.

(3) Granted method and learning, a preacher must still fit his sermon to the congregation. The delivery must be moving and in plain words. Even Stillingfleet, who kept an emotional distance from his material, advocates a spirited delivery: "That is then the best way of Preaching, which hath Light and Heat together; which clears the Scriptures to the People's Capacities and warms the Affections to the Spiritual things." for Wilkins, an emotional delivery is "the evidence and demonstration of the Spirit and the Power" of God accompanying the preacher.[12] Though South may have found fault with Wilkins's exact phrasing, as tending to enthusiasm, he agreed in theory that the emotions of the congregation must be aroused; his own remarks on outward manner reflecting inward appreciation paraphrase Wilkins's (IV, 154).

No one, it was felt, could be moved by diction that was obscure. Only plain speech, suited to the capacity of the congregation, fit the standards of reform. South writes that "it was clearness of the apostles' preaching which rendered it virtuous and irresistible" (IV, 151). "It is very easy to shoot over the Peoples' heads," writes Stillingfleet, "but it requires all our skill to Preach plainly without flatness." Not only a manual writer for

---

[11] *FS*, p. 709.   [12] *FS*, p. 367; *Ecclesiastes*, p. 201.

preachers but also an influential theorist in the vanguard of the Royal
Society's plan to purify speech, Wilkins writes: "The greatest learning is to
be seen in the greatest plainness."[13] The latitudinarian and scientific
circles in which Wilkins lived sponsored a spirited campaign in favor of the
plain style of writing, and writers such as South, whose intellectual and
social connections were somewhat different, also felt that plainness was a
desirable goal in oral and written communication.

(4) A preacher had to choose whether to read his sermons, memorize
them, work from an outline which he filled in as he spoke, or speak *ex
tempore*. W. Fraser Mitchell is certainly wrong to assert that there was a
single, acceptable post-Restoration style in these matters: "the Restoration preachers," he writes, "favoured notes and schemes retained by the
memory"[14] The longest essay we have on preaching styles, Gilbert
Burnet's *Discourse of the Pastoral Care* (1692), distinguishes three types of
delivery: reading, memorization, and *ex tempore*. He greatly favours the
last, though he insists it can only succeed when it rests on many years of
reading and prayer.[15] Burnet's analysis demonstrates that all three styles
are flourishing as he writes. South discusses the need for a preacher to have
a good memory for several reasons, among them the desire to please
congregations which demanded "homilies." Opposed to read sermons,
these presumably are something more casual and fit to the occasion than a
sermon that has been written out and memorized (III, 13–14).

Some writers realized that delivering a sermon from memory might be
as boring as reading it. The mature preacher, Wilkins suggests, should not
write down his entire sermon beforehand, for "the judgment will be much
weakened, and the affections dulled, when the memory is over-much
burdened and vexed." One way to avoid this was to use a method
somewhere between memorizing and *ex tempore* delivery: to prepare a text
but to leave gaps to be filled on the spot, as a sense of the congregation and
the spirit dictated. Philip Henry endorses this method, advising preachers
"to allow themselves a Liberty of Expression, such as a Man's Affections if
they be well rais'd, will be apt to furnish him with." A nonconformist after
1662, Henry preached at Christ Church several times in the late 1650s,
when South could have heard him. But we know little about South's own
method of preaching. While seventeenth-century memory skills were more
highly developed than our own, it is still difficult to imagine South
memorizing the long sermons we have. The existence of his sermons only
in printed, edited form again hampers our understanding of the steps
leading up to the final copy. A careful reading of Wood's account of

---

[13] *FS*, p. 367; *Ecclesiastes*, p. 199.
[14] W. Fraser Mitchell, *English Pulpit Oratory from Andrewes to Tillotson* (London: SPCK, 1932),
    p. 26.
[15] Gilbert Burnet, *A Discourse of the Pastoral Care* (London, 1692), pp. 229–41.

South's failure in the pulpit in no way provides "good evidence," as Mitchell writes, for supposing that South habitually preached *ex tempore*, since a failure of nerves could equally have disrupted acts of reading and memory.[16]

Style and metaphor

A number of studies of late seventeenth-century preaching and prose style mention South's contribution to the reform of prose going on at that time. In one view, South and others after 1660 distanced themselves both from the self-consciously oratorical style of the Ciceronians and from the choppy, Senecan manner of Donne and Launcelot Andrewes; South satirizes the "little affected sentences" and "quibbles and trifles" of what he understood to be writing in the Senecan mode (III, 32–33). In reaction to that mode he advocated a "plain style." The fact of such a style is easier to demonstrate than its manifold kinds. Robert Adolph shows that there were at least two plain styles current in the seventeenth century, and that later commentators sometimes confuse them.[17] Although South occasionally expressed dislike for the virtuosi of the Royal Society, his prose clearly has affinities with theirs, and it would be difficult, on the basis of a selection of short passages from sermons, to distinguish South from, say, Sprat or Wilkins. Their common plain style tried not to express personality, but only the shape of the topic of discussion. A typical strategy was to try to make word choice and sentence and paragraph structure fit the object described, rather than to insist that the object fit into preconceived figures such as balanced periodic sentences, epigram, or paradox.

The entire plain style movement is a phenomenon which seems to grow more indistinct the more one knows about it. The movement is easier to define in reference to what is absent – highly stylized parallelisms and metaphysical conceits, for example – than in reference to its inherent qualities. Brian Vickers has even attempted to deny the phenomenon a philosophical core, asserting that the plain style movement was a matter of politics; he calls attention to "the myth of plainness which the established church created for itself" and in opposition to which the style of puritans or dissenters or revolutionaries was defined.[18] Vickers's thesis is attractive,

---

[16] *Ecclesiastes*, p. 202; Matthew Henry, *An Account of the Life and Death of Mr. Philip Henry*, p. 53, and Mitchell, *English Pulpit Oratory*, p. 24.

[17] Adolph, *The Rise of Modern Prose Style* (Cambridge, MA, and London: MIT Press, 1968), pp. 129–32. For useful summaries of the disputed divisions of seventeenth-century prose style, see Adolph, pp. 10–25; and James Thompson, *Language in Wycherley's Plays: Seventeenth-Century Language Theory and Drama* (University, AL: University of Alabama Press, 1984), pp. 6–23.

[18] Vickers, "The Royal Society and English Prose Style: A Reassessment," in *Rhetoric and the Pursuit of Truth: Language and Change in the Seventeenth and Eighteenth Centuries* (Los Angeles: William Andrews Clark Memorial Library, 1985), pp. 3–45; 45.

although I think that some comments on style, like those of Hobbes and Locke, for example, may be understood as philosophical statements; political motivation accounted for much, but not all of the plain style movement.

South wrote several times, usually in highly figurative language, of the difficulty of arriving at truth. One such passage occurs in his 1694 sermon on mystery, which I will discuss later in detail. An earlier treatment of this theme occurs in an undated sermon, published in 1679, on the rejection of Christ's doctrine:

> Truth is a great strong hold, barred and fortified by God and nature; and diligence is properly the understanding's laying siege to it: so that, as in a kind of warfare, it must be perpetually upon the watch, observing all the avenues and passes to it, and accordingly makes its approaches ... plants this reasoning, and that argument, this consequence, and that distinction, like so many intellectual batteries, till, at length, it forces a way and passage into the obstinate enclosed truth, that so long withstood and defined its assaults. (I, 163; see also III, 31–32)

This passage summarizes South's ethics of learning early and late in his career. It also embodies a mighty and labored conceit. Such theorizing about the difficulties of arriving at truth presupposes a commensurate style. Although aphorism and balance require hard work of the writer, once in place they tend to give the truths expressed the appearance of being easily won. Some of South's early writing may seem excessively balanced; while his sense of truth as difficult of access remained constant, his style only gradually caught up with his philosophy. An unpredictable, unbalanced style seems more attuned to the philosophy behind it, and the later sermons at times show these qualities.

The alleged stylistic reform in which South participated called for brevity and the excision of unnecessary words. South praises brevity in writing in extravagant terms (I, 435–42), as do others. Some years after Tillotson's death, Thomas Birch praised him because he "cut off all superfluities and needless enlargement; he said what was necessary to give clear ideas of things and no more." In a much-quoted passage from the 1660s, Thomas Sprat wrote that the Royal Society aimed in its prose "to return back to the primitive purity, and shortness, when men delivered so many *things*, almost in an equal number of words."[19] In Sprat's analysis brevity becomes not only the current ideal but the key to understanding the primitive past.

One casualty of this campaign for brevity was figurative language, and after 1650 there is much writing against metaphor in prose. The argument for brevity and against metaphor clearly had denominational and political

---

[19] Thomas Birch, *The Life of the Most Reverend John Tillotson* (London, 1752), p. 21; Sprat, *History of the Royal Society of London for the Promotion of Knowledge*, ed. Jackson I. Cope and Harold Whitmore Jones (St. Louis: Washington University Press, 1958), p. 113.

origins. The stereotype of puritan preaching included preaching at great length; lush, wild metaphors were held to account partly for this. Anti-puritan writers such as John Eachard and Samuel Parker, who replaced Fell as Bishop of Oxford, attacked puritan metaphor-making; Parker especially denounced metaphors in sermons as the practice of anti-establishment fanatics.[20] The attack on puritan metaphors was, in a way, simply royalist triumphalism: everything that went before 1660 could be routinely condemned. yet a more subtle argument runs through these harangues: metaphor-making is to language what rebellion is to civil and church polity. Because metaphor hides things under alien terms, it was alleged to confuse a congregation. Although it is difficult to find royalist writers providing exact examples, it was generally held that puritan metaphors disguised and distorted kingship and the English Constitution is such a way as to convince people that rebellion was necessary and encouraged by God. In four sermons I will discuss later, South attacks linguistic distortions of political reality at length, although in that discussion he does not single out metaphor for special indictment.

In a separate but related development, a number of writers attacked metaphor – I am using the term to refer to all figures of comparison – not on political but on epistemological grounds. Metaphors interfered with knowledge. In order to understand this complaint, I make two preliminary observations. These attacks on metaphor did not concern imaginative literature such as poetry and plays. The critics had in mind expository speaking or writing that described or advised about the true nature of physical, political, moral, or supernatural reality. Even Hobbes, whose attack on metaphor in his kind of writing is harsh, allows several "special uses" of language, one of which is "to please and delight ourselves and others, by playing with our words, for pleasure or ornament, innocently."[21] Since seventeenth-century attacks on metaphor seem mirthless in the extreme, it is important to realize that not all writing had to be free of metaphor; sermons, however, were clearly among the genres to be purified.

Second, several expository works which attack metaphors as an obstruction to efficient, true communication also freely use them. It appears that only certain types of metaphors are proscribed, although individual passages attacking metaphor rarely make distinctions. Beginning with its title, Hobbes's *Leviathan* does not lack metaphorical structures, "the subtle imagery," as Michael Oakeshott writes, "that fills its pages." About forty

[20] Eachard, *The Grounds and Occasions of the Contempt of the Clergy and Religion* (London, 1670), pp. 45–64; Parker, *A Discourse of Ecclesiastical Politie* (London, 1670) pp. 75–77. South also attacked metaphorical preaching (IV, 151–53).

[21] Thomas Hobbes, *Leviathan*, ed. Michael Oakeshott (Oxford: Basil Blackwell, 1947), p. 19. For a fuller view, see Charles Cantalupo, "Hobbes's Use of Metaphor," *Restoration*, 12 (1988), 20–31.

years after *Leviathan*, John Locke writes that "all the artificial and figurative application of Words Eloquence hath invented are for nothing else but
to insinuate wrong *Ideas*, move the Passions, and thereby mislead the
Judgement."[22] Yet it is not difficult to find telling use of metaphorical
language in *An Essay Concerning Human Understanding*, in whose pages this
attack occurs.

In Hobbes, Locke, and others, three problems arise which the successful
metaphor-maker had to solve in order to be an effective communicator.

The problem of added meaning: metaphors should illustrate, make clearer,
or drive home something previously explained. They should not add
meanings to the truth already stated, or even try to enrich it, if such
enrichment becomes a distraction. Because of the possibly complex associations of metaphorical vehicles brought in to carry the truth, metaphors
often involve the passions, which as Locke writes, "mislead the Judgement." Thus all metaphor should be long on denotation and short on
connotation.

The problem of analogies between levels of being: in the second half of the
seventeenth century, the modern disciplines of academic study were being
defined, not only in the sciences but also, notably, in political philosophy.
To divide a reality from other realities, to separate its primary and
secondary causes, and to ascertain what sort of certainty its study would
offer were to begin to understand it. By linguistically uniting object and
vehicle, metaphor tended to confuse the borders that the division of
disciplines required. Confusion would especially result if a writer, reader,
or audience still lived in a universe of metaphysical or mystical correspondences. Surely many still lived in such a universe after 1660; the founding
of the Royal Society by no means dried up the many backwaters of belief
in such a universe. The progress of learning was slow and and sporadic;
advanced thinkers, such as the anti-metaphor writers often were, saw
metaphor as a potentially conservative force that would make their
rational endeavors all the more difficult by encouraging old-fashioned
world views.

The problem of the true vehicle: quoting Eachard, Joan Bennett notes that
not only had the point of the metaphor to be true, but also the vehicle
itself: "the resemblance should not only be a true likeness to the thing to
which it is compared, but should also be itself an accurate account of the
facts."[23] The laws of nature or Scripture also apply to the term brought in
from the outside as illustration. Both the vehicle and the whole comparison must offer true knowledge.

A delightfully self-conscious metaphor of Eachard alleges an example of

---

[22] *Leviathan*, p. xviii; *Essay Concerning Human Understanding*, p. 508.
[23] Joan Bennett, "An Aspect of the Evolution of Seventeenth-Century Prose Style," *Review of English Studies*, 17 (1941), 286.

a successful solution to all three problems. He writes that Cicero and Caesar avoided "frightening Metaphors":

> We may read many a Page in their Works, before we meet with any of those Bears; and if you do light upon one or so, it shall not make your hair stand right up, or put you into a fit of Convulsion; but it shall be soft, significant, and familiar, as if 'twere made for the very purpose.[24]

The metaphor persuasively solves problem three: in or out of a metaphor, bears frighten people, convulse them, and perhaps even make their hair stand right up. The comparison of metaphors to bears is also, in regard to problem two, only rhetorical; it in no way alleges a deeper connection than the precise one for which it has been created, to illustrate a truth about metaphor. Likewise, the comparison firmly illustrates that truth and no other; denotative meaning seems carefully circumscribed.

It is doubtful, however, whether even this metaphor, chosen precisely to exemplify correct usage, provides a full solution to the problem of added meaning. Eachard shows here how hard it is to control a good metaphor and how right, after all, critics were to be vigilant. The wit of the metaphor stops, for the moment, the forward progress of the argument. Hence language ceases to be a Hobbesian means of communication and enters into his category of "special uses," of innocent play. The metaphor also begins to involve the "passions" of the reader, at the very least, admiration for the aptness of the comparison and amusement at its contents. If he has been frightened by a bear, moreover, the reader's more complex feelings doubtless interfere with full attention to the argument. Even one who claims to be a specialist in such matters has difficulty restraining the meaning of a good metaphor merely to illustrate a previously stated idea.

Many sermons of Robert South develop such extended metaphors; some sermons incorporate them into broader patterns of imagery that reflect on the meaning of the whole. To survey South's hundreds of metaphors used in this way or singly is to understand that, not always but by and large, he solves the three problems set by contemporary theorists. He accurately restrains the vehicle to the meaning given by the context, does not usually try to unite orders of being by means of his metaphors, and his vehicles tend in themselves to be true. The following analyses of individual sermons will quote many of his metaphors, and his fidelity to these rules will be evident. Perhaps more than any preacher of his time – certainly more than Stillingfleet and Tillotson – South depends on metaphors to develop the arguments of his sermons, and does this in a way sanctioned by the popular linguistic thought of his time.

There are, however, two major exceptions to South's conformity to

[24] Eachard, *Contempt of the Clergy* pp. 45–46.

these rules. First, when he creates an especially involved metaphor, based on several points of comparison, the ingenuity with which he does this becomes in itself the focus of a reader's attention. The problem of added meaning, which even Eachard could not elude, remains unsolved, for an extended metaphor cannot help calling an attention to itself which disrupts the flow of the argument. An even greater distraction occurs when South incorporates the metaphor into an extended pattern of imagery reinforced by other elements such as historical and biblical allusions or quotations. When this occurs, the metaphor and the larger pattern become objects of contemplation in themselves; the sermon begins to lose its argumentative value and may move over into becoming something like art for its own sake. Metaphor-making, as well as the argument, becomes a theme in the reader's consciousness. Indeed in at least one political sermon, which I will discuss in chapter 3, the pattern of imagery, including metaphor, makes a statement counter to the announced intentions of the rhetorical divisions.

Second, South at times held to a belief that individual realities were symbolic of a hierarchical, ordered universe. At least before 1685, his political theory, in which the king shared God's power, was one expression of the continuities he believed to be in the nature of things. When he came to write extensively about mystery in the 1690s, he also discovered that this concept united disparate levels of the history, psychology, and theological doctrine he knew. Insofar as he used metaphor to express the unity of his experience, he encountered and perhaps refused to accept the grounds for the second problem of metaphor I have discussed. South never made a universe of real correspondences a central issue between himself and the puritans, latitudinarians, or Socinians he sometimes argued with; he tended to begin an argument with a clear-cut doctrinal or political disagreement in mind, and only in the course of developing his own position did his presuppositions become clear. Affirming a universe alive with analogy, however, he could not but welcome metaphor, which of its nature unites different levels of reality, into his complex schemes of argument.

3

South and the political sermon

South's interest in politics

Robert South often preached about the imperatives of social morality; for him as for most preachers, then and now, vice and virtue were not private affairs. South also frequently instructed his congregations about what to think and how to act in the world of politics: about how the king should perform his offices, about strategies the nation should take in times of crisis, and especially about the ideal forms of civil and ecclesiastical polity. Although such subjects appear in the sermons of others, South made politics his homiletic theme in an intense and prolonged manner; political sermons were his specialty. These political sermons fall into three categories: (1) sermons given on English anniversaries such as 30 January and 5 November, in which whoever was preaching was expected to defend the English church and state; (2) sermons on church matters that, because the Church of England is an established religion, involved questions of national politics; and (3) sermons on moral issues such as the right use of speech or conscience, or the immorality of lying, that could have been treated as private matters but were in fact treated as contributory to political peace or disruption. South left a total of about twenty sermons in all three categories, or about 25 percent of his published sermons. No contemporary of his has left us a body of sermons that suggests a similar intensity of political interest.

In addition to the sermons devoted mainly to political questions, many others slide, as it were, into politics. South's sense of how actions on different levels, psychological, social, political, were related, was acute; for him, disorder in one sphere brought disorder in another. South thought that he could show by historical proof, for example, that a freedom of conscience which was not restrained by Scripture and human law had revolutionary implications. Thus in a sermon on Satan disguised as an angel of light, he talks mainly about theological error, but towards the end slips into discussing the error that grants "such a kingdom to Christ, as shall oppose and interfere with the kingdoms and governments of this world" (III, 489). He could not rest on the level of academic theology, and launched an attack on those sects, still extant after 1660, that considered human kingship idolatrous.

For South, such thinking was doubly troublesome: it encouraged sedition and abetted regicide and, more importantly, it separated concepts South wished always to keep, perhaps somewhat vaguely, together. For him all kingly dominion, in Christ or in a prince, was analogous; all legitimate dominion, which was, for South, always kingly dominion, was hierarchical, as was the universe itself, when properly understood. This hierarchy, which South's generation was perhaps the last easily to perceive, was both a fact and a value, how things were and how they should be. Likewise, in a sermon dealing mostly with the personal and social effects of lying, South cannot avoid looking at recent political history to comment on the wilful deception of the English people in the 1640s that culminated in the regicide (I, 327). There were many more occasions when, in the middle of a discussion which seems nonpolitical, South veered into the political implications of his topic; for him there was no such thing as a moral issue that did not have a potential effect on the government of church and state.

Each generation sets its political standards of judgment by previous successes and failures: a Munich or a Vietnam inevitably becomes the means of understanding or misunderstanding further sets of events. For South the fundamental norm by which to judge political life after 1660 was the execution of Charles I on 30 January 1649. It is difficult to overstress the importance of this event for him. He was a boy at the time at Westminster School, not far from the Banqueting Hall in Whitehall, outside of which the execution took place; the Westminsters prayed openly for the king on the morning of his execution and, even if Busby did not allow them to attend, they would have known about the beheading minutes after it had taken place. In a sense, all of South's reinforcement and supernaturalizing of kingship attempted to ensure that it would never again be violated as it had been at the start of 1649. South brought all moral issues to the bar of the regicide to be judged: in regard to any vice, he asked whether it was present in those responsible for the king's death – and would indulgence towards the vice lead to a similar event in the future? Any attempt at toleration, any lie or false use of speech, and any disrespect for religion paved the way for a repetition of the regicide. Like many of his contemporaries, year after year, especially on the anniversary, South dwelt in detail on the regicide, contemplated it, and plumbed it for political instruction.

The English anniversaries, including 30 January, gave South ample opportunity to develop his ideas about church and state, which, especially in the 1660s and 1670s, put Charles II firmly in the center of things. For South and others, the nature of the anniversary dictated the nature of the

sermon. The anniversary of the Gunpowder Plot on 5 November suggested a sermon that would attack Roman Catholics; the 30 January
anniversary encouraged a preacher to speak against Protestant denominations other than the established church. Choosing to preach or not to
preach on 30 January – it appears, for example, that John Tillotson never
did – declared one's sympathies of party. Latitudinarian divines such as
Tillotson did not willingly choose situations that prompted attacks on
those they wished to reconcile to the establishment.

Both high church and latitudinarian divines were at home in the 5
November sermons, which commemorated a frustrated Catholic plot:
Rome was always an acceptable target, especially in the late 1670s and
early 1680s, during the Popish Plot. Because of latitudinarian sympathies
with the disestablished and unestablished, and because commemoration of
the regicide tended to involve glorifications of the monarchy sometimes
eschewed by latitudinarians, 30 January became a high church occasion.
Especially as the Popish Plot unfolded, Charles II issued several calls for
days of national penance; these days involved church services for the
Houses of Parliament and in parish churches which gave other opportuni-
ties for divines – though not South – to reflect theologically on the national
crisis.

In the reign of Charles II a preacher either supported the monarchy or
did not talk about it. The dominant ideology was termed "passive obedience," passivity being the attitude of subjects in the face of potential
injustice on the part of the monarch. God, not the people, was responsible
for punishing a sinful king, and whole sermons were devoted to assembling
texts from the literature of the early Christian church, including Scripture,
that showed the passivity of believers in the face of unjust treatment. In a
sermon of 30 January 1668/9 Stillingfleet clearly states the ruling theory:

> Another principle, which tends to the subverting [of] Government under a
> pretence of *Liberty*, is, that in case of *Usurpation* upon the *Rights* of the *People*, they
> may resume the exercise of *Power*, and punish the *Supreme Magistrate* himself, if he
> be guilty of it. Than which there can be no principle imagined more destructive to
> civil *societies*, and repugnant to the very nature of *Government*.[1]

From this royalist position, two roads of argument, a high and a low,
diverged. Most preachers, while using both on occasion, had their preferences. Taking the low road, Stillingfleet goes on to explain, in the sermon
mentioned, why the punishment of the supreme magistrate by the people
is wrong: it destroys reliance on oaths, it justifies any rebellion that
happens to be successful, it makes governing a perilous occupation, it

---

[1] *FS*, p. 97. For another classic statement of the theory, see Isaac Barrow, *Works*, ed. John
Tillotson, I (1683), 135–36. For background to the various anniversary sermons, see David
Cressy, *Bonfires and Bells: National Memory and the Protestant Calendar in Elizabethan and Stuart
England* (Berkeley and Los Angeles: University of California Press, 1989), pp. 171–87.

encourages princes to curry favor rather than do the right, unpopular thing, and so on. Thus he finds the reasons for passive obedience in commonsense observations on probable human behavior – in experience. having proved his point this way, he reverses himself and takes up the higher argument: "But on the other side," he asks, "what mighty danger can there be in supposing the *Persons* of *Princes* to be so *sacred*, that no sons of violence ought to come near to hurt them?"[2] Having established the inviolability of kingship on a rational and experiential basis, Stillingfleet then treats kingship as a value in itself, as something so sacred that it needs no rational justification. Such double proofs occur everywhere in Anglican preaching, and not only in regard to kingship, after 1660; argument from intrinsic rational merit coexists with argument from authority of one sort or other, especially Scripture. The order and syntax of Stillingfleet's argument in this place have significance: the argument from authority not only takes second place, but it is also hidden in a rhetorical question that diminishes the force of its being proposed at all.

From the early 1660s, South took as his special province the defense of kingship on the highest road possible; even in an age of royalist propaganda, his sermons stand out for their exposition of the sacramental nature of kingship, of the value not reason but divine providence bestowed on it. While he did not ignore arguments for kingship based on experience or its intrinsic merits, his primary grasp of the subject concerned its sacramentality. That is, kingship for South, at least in the 1660s, and 1670s, was a sign that revealed and participated in the divine governance of the world. The king was God's "vicegerent"; he ruled in God's place, received extraordinary gifts to do so, and had to be honored accordingly. Although South himself never retracted his many enunciations of the theory of the divine rights of kings, changes of government in England certainly gave him second thought; after 1685 he went through what one may guess was a painful period of watching events undermine his political philosophy.

What reason bestows, reason can take away. In the late seventeenth century, the arguments of many, especially John Locke, made the theory of divine right more and more untenable. The sacramentalism of kingship, on the other hand, could not be reasoned to, and could only be intuited. Its natural linguistic milieu was not philosophical argument and analysis but metaphorical discourse. The act of philosophical analysis in the late seventeenth century was, in fact, inimical to kingship, although this enmity is more easily perceived in retrospect. Having analyzed kingship in terms of its rational benefits, Stillingfleet could have asked – but for many reasons did not – whether another form of government could be

---

[2] *FS*, p. 98.

equally or more beneficial, without waiting for God to step in and punish the supreme magistrate. The argument from utility was a two-edged sword.

Metaphors, however, sidestep analysis. South's rich use of metaphor unites different levels of reality and, though hardly unintellectual, insists on an emotional connection also between the sacred and human realms. South's metaphors portray a complex reality which invites contemplation and withers under rational analysis. In a sermon of 5 Novemter 1675, he writes:

> this is that properly which in kings we call *majesty*, and which no doubt is a kind of shadow or portraiture of the divine authority drawn upon the looks and persons of princes ... There is a majesty in his countenance that puts lightning into his looks and thunder into his words ... Certain it is, that the virtues of a prince are a blessing to more than to himself and his family. There are a public seminary of blessings; they are the palladiums and the strongholds, nay the common stock and the exchequer that can never be shut up.   (II, 562–66)

The emotions that unite the terms of these metaphors are complex: pride in the public stability the Restoration brought, anxiety that the politics of the 1670s might disrupt that stability, personal delight in enclosing political complexity in rhetoric, and a shared sense of security between preacher and audience, who could speak and listen to such hyperbole without irony. It is likely that these political metaphors perfectly exemplify what many in the late seventeenth century objected to about metaphorical discourse; the metaphor seeks to hide the tendentiousness of the point being made, as a more rational, image-less analysis would expose latent fallacies.

South did not lose standing by so greatly praising the reigning power. In this case, however, the character and appearance of Charles II, as we know them, give South's metaphors an air of unreality. Did the audience seriously entertain the possibility that the plain face of Charles II was an emblem of divine majesty? Would not the king, who was not present, have enjoyed any such public support for his prerogatives, but snickered at such an appeal to his vanity? South's metaphors seem part of an ongoing ritual in support of kingship first, and, second, the individual holder of the seat of power.

By so amplifying the power and dignity of kingship, South made his emotions and reputation hostages to political fortune. It was not difficult to call an establishment and its leader divinely founded as long as one agreed with their politics. The theory of passive obedience could rationalize even gross immorality in a monarch; the theory was framed, in a sense, to face this eventuality without flinching. But because of the particular relationship of church and king in England, a terrible flaw lay hidden in

the passive acceptance of a king's wrongs. What if the divinely confirmed
king should begin to tamper with the divinely founded constitutions of the
church? To which of the diverging divine mandates ought believers to give
their obedience? South and his generation faced this situation twice: once
between 1685 and 1688, when God's vicegerent was a Roman Catholic of
aggressive views, and again after 1688, when William III and his ecclesiastical advisers began to revise the traditional centrality of the established
church.

Through sermons such as that of 5 November 1675, South left himself in
the worst possible position to accommodate such change. If he had been a
little milder in his assertion of the king's rights, or if he had, like others,
more fully developed the idea of England, not the king, as the object of
God's election, he would have had more ideological flexibility as kings and
their politics changed. South's response to political change, which is the
plot of this chapter, can be seen in a comparison of his 5 November
sermons of 1675 and 1688; these two sermons demonstrate the heights of
South's royalism and his subsequent descent from them.

In the following pages, I will examine and explain South's political
theology in four stages: (1) summary and discussion of the structure,
content, and imagery of the sermon of 5 November 1675; (2) for the
purpose of comparison and contrast, summary and discussion of the
structure, content, and imagery of five other political sermons given after
the above, on national anniversaries or fast days, by John Fell, William
Jane, Thomas Sprat, Edward Stillingfleet, and John Tillotson; (3) a brief
return to South's sermon of 1675 to estimate its uniqueness; and (4)
assessment of South's later changes in politics by analyzing a sermon given
on 5 November 1688, the day that William of Orange landed in England.

What characteristics mark a late seventeenth-century Anglican sermon
and, in particular, a political sermon, as an outstanding representative of
its genre? First of all, the sermon must be of a certain magnitude: it has to
be long enough that it runs the risk of coming apart and of degenerating
into digression, yet so under the control of authorial intelligence that it
coheres as a sustained development of the ideas it sets out at the start.
There must, in this sense, be a tension between the parts and the whole.
The sermon must be more than an insight or a simple explication of the
biblical text chosen; it must explore various aspects of a chosen subject in
an observable order. Several systems of unity were available to divines of
the time. The length of the sermon allowed some divines to develop
patterns of imagery or wordplay that strengthened the effect of unity.
Emotional attitude and tone also created unity; in political sermons, a
sense of urgency, of a need to develop a theology in the face of national
crisis, often pervades the whole. In addition, the categories of Wilkins's
Ecclesiastes came into play; these suggested to the divines numerous

avenues of development that led away from yet returned to the central themes. In the following pages, I will stress Wilkins's rules for the first part of the sermon, the section devoted to explication of the text (see appendix 2). Preachers after 1660 found that they could not create the tension between variety and unity in fewer than 5,000 words, and that to write just over twice that number was to stretch the genre to its limit.

Second, learning had to be evident. A primary need was a full quoting knowledge of the Old and New Testaments, for the initial text was always accompanied by many other texts supporting subsidiary points made in the sermon. The Fathers of the Church and other sacred and secular authors, ancient and modern, also provided sources for arguments. In addition to references to authoritative sources, the preacher had to display arguments from reason; these included arguments from necessity – from those things that must necessarily follow from an accepted or proven truth – and from experience. Mixed proofs from authority and reason were, in fact, the particular speciality of sermons of this period. Mixed proofs make up a methodology that in itself reinforced a dominant argument of almost every major sermon available: that the truths enunciated did not depend on either Scripture or reason alone, but on a mutual working of both. This thesis was occasionally argued in plain sight; more often the structure of proofs, moving rapidly back and forth from authority to reason, implicitly illustrated that the truths of the Christian religion were not narrowly based.

Political sermons also involved their own kind of learning. They placed a primary obligation on the preacher to address the occasion: the problem Roman Catholicism presented to a national, Protestant church on 5 November, Protestant political dissent on 30 January, and, on fast days proclaimed by the king, whatever particular problem was announced as a threat to the nation. The greatest preachers, in addition, used the particularity of these occasions as a starting-point for a more ambitious project: to construct a general theology of English history that defined how God had worked and would work for England, and what the response of English men and women should be. This practice of historical generalization tended to distance the congregation from the emotional violence of the moment, especially during the Popish Plot. While Stillingfleet, Tillotson, and others were not averse, especially in their conclusions, to strident warnings against enemies of the state, the multiple developments and subdevelopments of their treatments tended to dampen hostility and invite the audience to dispassionate intellectual analysis.

Lastly, the plain style had to be maintained, yet varied in different ways. It could be played off against colloquial diction, as in South's remarks in his 1675 sermon that if we do not acknowledge the divine hand in certain political situations, we "cashier all providence," and that, in the

Gunpowder Plot, Rome "had other designs upon the anvil at that time" (II, 558, 572). Image patterns could also be introduced and reaffirmed; writers as good as South accomplish this technique not only in similes and metaphors, but also by reintroducing the images in strong verbs, anecdotes, and quotations from Scripture. Greater or lesser control in the use of anecdotes is particularly revealing of the artistic abilities of individual authors, for not all could resist the appeal of an interesting story from history that did not quite attune to the point being made.

In political sermons it was customary to enrich the plain style by use of typology. It is rare in South's time to find the fully typological scheme of an extended comparison of Charles II to, for example, Moses or David. But vestiges of this typology remain in the sermons. For in a time of shifting political allegiances, when plain speaking might involve the statement of truths later to be regretted, the vagueness of typology had its attractions. In the myth of the Restoration, Charles/Moses had passed through the English Channel/Red Sea without harm; the later employer of the typology could decide whether, continuing the game, France or Holland was the Egyptian enslaver – although Catholic France seems to have won the title more often than not.

South: 5 November 1675

For 5 November 1675, in a sermon preached in Westminster Abbey, South chose as his text Psalm 144:10: "It is he that giveth salvation unto Kings." His brief exegesis ignores the questions of language, of Davidic context, and of scriptural parallels that Wilkins's paradigm might have suggested. He moves immediately to a single doctrine deduced from the text, that "God in the government of the world exercises a peculiar and extraordinary providence over the persons and lives of princes" (II, 548). The brevity of the exegesis suggests that South first found his topic, then his text; the slim theological content of the text will, in fact, scarcely bear the great weight South places on it as he explores the various ways divine providence aids kings.

According to Wilkins's method, South divides and subdivides his 9,000-word treatment. An outline looks like this:

I *Exposition of the text* (547–48)
II *Division and confirmation*
    (1) How an act of providence might be called extraordinary (547–51)
        (a) when it falls outside of the usual operations of a cause
        (b) when it falls contrary to the design of its expert agent
        (c) when it comes to pass beyond the power of its cause

(2) by what extraordinary means God saves princes (551–66)
   (a) giving them added intelligence
   (b) giving them singular courage in danger
   (c) disposing of accidents to concur with their preservation
   (d) inclining the hearts of men and women to follow them
   (e) rescuing them from unknown mischief
   (f) imprinting on subjects an awe of their persons
   (g) disposing their hearts to virtuous causes
(3) why providence is concerned with the salvation of kings (566–73)
   (a) to support civil society
     (i) monarchy is the most excellent form of government
     (ii) its strength rests on the personal qualities of the monarch
III *Application* (573–75)
  (1) how princes should behave to their subjects
  (2) how subjects should behave to their princes

South never moves from one division to another without calling attention to the transition, that is, his closure and new beginning. In the printed version, the only text extant, South summarizes, after II.2.g, the seven extraordinary means God uses to save princes. Thus readers receive a succession of pauses and recapitulations so that they are never in doubt about where they are in the sermon.

Not all parts of the sermon presuppose other parts, but ample evidence suggests a very firm authorial sense of the whole. Part II.2 needs II.1, for a definition of extraordinary providence is useful before one reads of specific instances. Part II.3 seems to start afresh, showing the greatness of the institution of monarchy, but returns, in II.3.a.ii, to the personal qualities of a monarch, which refer the reader back to II.2.a.b. and g. The painstaking structure makes one set of obvious closures; similar content in different parts of the structure invites another set. In this case, the closing of a development, only to be opened again, seems to produce a meaning that is important for the sermon as a whole. South repeatedly stresses that the list of gifts in II.2.a–g is directly providential; II.3.a.ii does not make this point so clearly, and it need not if one keeps the wholeness of the sermon in mind. Only by referring back to previous, similar content does South's point become clear: that a king must never regard his gifts as attributable only to a human cause. South grants a king innate ethical excellence, but never lets him rest in the idea that this can be understood apart from the continued providential action of God. For example, in II.3.a.ii, South writes that "the activity and bravery of the prince is the soul politic which animates and upholds all" (II. 569). Since he has already written (II.2.b) that courage in a king is a gift of providence, he clearly intends to ascribe to the king – a warning is, in fact, implied – very little of natural endowments.

The seven-fold list of divine gifts, occupying over half the sermon, has a rhythm of its own: South begins in the king's person, moves out to the king's subjects, and ends again in the king's mind and heart. South illustrates five of the seven gifts with scriptural references; anecdotal illustrations from secular authors also occur. The second discussion, of a king's courage and presence of mind in dangerous situations, rests on a fully mixed proof: South first quotes from the Old Testament, then describes King Saul's swift rise to power, then narrates a humorous anecdote from Roman history, then comments on Henry VII's wisdom, valor, and riches, and ends with an analytical discussion of the "enthusiasm" of kings (II, 554–56). Not all proofs are as fully mixed as this, but most seek credibility by using more than one source of reference.

Imagery of copy and coinage reinforces the theme of the tension between the king's will and God as the author of all gifts. Monarchy "is an image of the divine supremacy ... a copy of God's government of the universe in a lesser draught," and the king's face "is a kind of shadow or portraiture of the divine authority" (II, 568, 562). Monarchy and princes take their power and dignity from God; these qualities are lent to them. But more is wanted: a response from the king. Money, military power, and laws fail unless the king knows how to use them: "surely the bare image of a prince upon the coin of any nation can neither improve or employ the treasure of it; nor can the military force of a kingdom do much to strengthen it, should the prince either wear a padlock upon his sword, or draw it in defence of his enemies" (II, 570). The country does not lack resources, but the king must know how to use them, and such knowledge is a divine gift.

These meditations upon kingship seem to provide unpromising and even dangerous grounds for irony, and though irony certainly plays a part in the sermon, South never backs away from his central position, to affirm special providence for kings. Alongside this argument, South clearly makes a counterstatement of warning. In a South sermon, irony takes two forms: verbal irony, where amplification is expressed and diminution intended, a technique he usually reserves for Protestant dissent; and structural irony, where statements or images tend to counter the main argument when at first they seem to support it. The slow progress of division and subdivision in the Wilkins paradigm easily contains this type of counterstatement, and the 1675 sermon capitalizes on the possibility. It is rarely in the interest of homiletic art for a counterstatement to cancel the main argument. The counterstatement rather gives, as here, the unpleasant side of the argument, or the price that has to be paid for the implementation of a policy that seems, on the surface of things, painless.

South begins his sermon with a brief discussion of the monarchy of God, and of how kings will have an account to make of their own use of their share in God's rule. The admonition to kings, and to Charles II, seems at first convention, yet it is later reinforced with other warnings:

He who meets his enemy in the field, knows how to encounter him; but he who meets him at his table, in his chamber, or in his closet, finds his enemy got within him before he is aware of him, killing him with smiles and kisses, and acting the assassinate under the masquerade of a counsellor or a confidant: the surest, but the basest way of destroying a man. (II, 553–54)

God can turn the hearts of a nation suddenly and irresistibly. He has done so more than once or twice, and may do so again. (II, 559)

No prince can tell what the discontents of evil subjects, the emulation of neighboring states and princes have been designing, endeavouring, and projecting against him: all which counsels, by a controlling power from above, have from time to time been made abortive and frustraneous. (II, 561)

Although the sermon as a whole is positive in tone, an anxious counterstatement occasionally clouds it. Kings can frustrate the divine will, particularly as they respond to enemies masked as friends, discontented subjects, and foreign princes.

The ending of the sermon reinforces and specifies the counterstatement. Not unusual in this type of sermon, reference is made to King David: "he tells us that he would neither trust in his sword nor in his bow, nor in the alliance of princes. All auxilliaries but those from above he found weak, fickle, and fallacious" (II, 573). The reference to David suggests a typological frame of mind, but in fact this is not the case; the sermon here reads David's psalms tropologically, as teachers of good advice for others, especially kings like David himself. If, like David, a king has been delivered by God from dangers to his reign – as Charles had been in 1652 and 1660 – "it will concern him, not to court the mischief from which he has been delivered" (II, 573).

What is the "mischief" that Charles courts and from which he has already been delivered? South preached this sermon on 5 November 1675. On 27 August of that year, Charles had concluded a secret agreement with Ruvigny, Louis XIV's representative in London. This stated that if Parliament showed further hostility to France, Charles should suspend it; since he would thereby cut off a source of necessary revenue, Louis would agree to pay him £100,000 a year for the period of suspension. In the fall of 1675, Parliament voted to recall English mercenaries in Louis's army; Charles interpreted this action as the kind of anti-French hostility the secret agreement involved, suspended Parliament, and received his first payment.[3]

[3] See George Clark, *The Later Stuarts 1660–1714*, 2nd edn (Oxford: Clarendon Press, 1955), p. 87.

South's sermon of 5 November, with its warnings against foreign alliances and closet politics, addresses this situation. It is not clear how much South knew about the agreement with Louis; an alliance with Catholic France was always an option for the English government. Perhaps in the vaguest of terms, South knew that some further development had occurred, and he uses his sermon partly to warn his audience about the dangers of an Anglo-French alliance. Of course he does not warn the audience (and the absent king) explicitly. He first constructs his theology of God and kingship, reminds kings of their obligation to trust in the God who supports them, then gives warnings about foreign alliances, and finally interprets foreign alliances, in the words of King David, as failures of trust in God. The warning appears with a semblance of logic, at least when it is abstracted from the text. But the 9,000-word development so spreads out the logic as to make its immediate force softer and more acceptable to the guilty king. South and other divines were not afraid of openly attacking the immorality of the court, but a preacher who suggested a state policy which, for all he knew, was already changed, walked more gingerly.

By means of a carefully constructed pattern of water imagery, South reinforces his counterstatement about the dangers of foreign alliances. The central exposition of this imagery occurs in II.2.d, in a discussion of how God turns subjects' hearts to their princes. In what amounts to a second setting of a text for the sermon, South quotes Proverbs 21:1: "the heart of a king is in God's hand, and that as the rivers of water, he turneth it which way soever he will." The quotation does not exactly serve South's purpose, except that it contains the water imagery he wants, and he expands its point about whose heart is in God's hand:

so are the hearts of the people too; which like a mighty stream or torrent he turns this way or that way, according to the wise counsels of his providence. For if he intends to advance a prince, they shall be a stream to bear him up from sinking; and if to forsake or ruin a prince, they shall overflow, and swell, and rush in upon him with such a furious, ungoverned tide, as no power or arts of state shall be able to divert or withstand.   (II, 558–59)[4]

The supportive or ungoverned water represents the people's will, that God alone, not a king, controls. The benign aspect of this control had been seen in the Restoration, "an universal, invincible current of the people's wills and affections" (II, 559). God holds over a prince's head the threat of reversing the tide of popularity. Water also represents a prince's dis-

---

[4] South uses imagery that is similar to that of Sir John Denham at the end of the 1668 edition of the popular *Cooper's Hill*. The poem ends, as in South's later sermon, with a torrent of politically symbolic water; though more detailed than South's, Denham's imagery leaves out the providential vision. See Brendan O Hehir, *Expans'd Hieroglyphics: A Critical Edition of Sir John Denham's Cooper's Hill* (Berkeley and Los Angeles: University of California Press, 1969), pp. 160–62.

position; his strength "ebbs and flows according to the rising or falling of his spirit" (II, 569). Here the tides signify not the people's fickleness, but the king's, especially failures of nerve resulting in foreign alliances. Complex in meaning, the tides represent the ambiguity at the heart of the sermon: a king can destroy the nation on his own, but the courage needed to save it is God's gift.

To complete, at the sermon's end, the water imagery, South pulls out a stock typology from the 1660–61 period that had acquired classic status: Charles II's miraculously sudden crossing through the sea to England as prefigured by Moses' crossing of the Red Sea to the promised land: "Is this not he, whom God brought back again by a miracle as great as that by which he brought Israel out of Egypt, not dividing, but, as it were, drying up the Red Sea before him?" (II, 574). The dominion of God over the waters – the people's changing wills, the king's failures of nerve – is reasserted and proved in biblical terms, with reference to recent history. South invokes the supercharged atmosphere of the Restoration itself to put steel into the king's resolve. In general, the sermon proposes a theology of kingship that instructs kings to rely on God, who will reward them for this trust in ways that Scripture and secular history show. In specific terms, in the early winter of 1675, the sermon reminds the audience that Egypt/ France, the land of bondage, still lures innocent Englishmen, and that any attempt to return there will risk alienation of the people's affections and encourage God to initiate violent political change at home. South's development of a theology of kingship and specific political advice could not be better or more fully accomplished.

Political sermons of other divines

On 2 December 1680, as the excitement of the Popish Plot was winding down, Charles II issued a proclamation calling for a general fast on 22 December; on that day, in churches across the land, his subjects were to pray for an end to the popish conspiracies "fomenting Divisions among our Loyal Protestant Subjects."[5] As was usual in such proclamations, the king ordered the bishops to compose and circulate a special service for Morning Prayer, Holy Communion, and Evening Prayer on that day. At the celebration of these services in the House of Lords, John Fell, Bishop of Oxford and Dean of Christ Church, was asked to preach. At this time the House of Lords itself was especially afflicted by the divisions of which the proclamation had spoken. Early in December it had tried and convicted one of its number, William Howard Viscount Stafford, for complicity in the Plot, and had sentenced him to death – but by a vote of 55 to 31,

---

[5] *A Proclamation for a General Fast* (London, 1680).

indicating substantial dissent from the verdict.[6] Stafford would be executed nine days after Fell's sermon.

True to the occasion, Fell's sermon of about 6,500 words on Matthew 12:25, "Every kingdom divided against itself is brought to desolation," deplores national disunity. Without calling as much attention to his divisions of the text as suggested by Wilkins, Fell divides the sermon into three parts: an analysis of unity and disunity, strongly dependent on the analogy of how the parts of the state, like the parts of the human body, must work together to survive; a listing of six false methods for healing disunity, with succeeding reflections; and the extended suggestion that, if the audience were to heal their own "lusts," national unity would be easier to achieve. Fell's initial exegesis deals with the text only from the point of view of the applicability of its warning to all nations. He later gives a longer, second text from I Corinthians 12, about disunity in the body, that seems more appropriate to his material, especially in the first and third divisions. He chooses the Matthean text about divided kingdoms to address the divisions deplored in the king's proclamation; the text from Corinthians more adequately indicates what Fell wants to do, that is, to conduct an extended meditation on the analogy of the physical to the political body.

In the second part, Fell echoes South's sermon by making the first, false means of recovering national unity "to strengthen ourselves by Alliances abroad."[7] Unitive in purpose, the sermon does not spell out which alliances are more to be feared than others, either with Catholic France or Protestant Holland, though he warns that Dutch toleration of dissent will not work in England (15). Although Fell refers several times to contemporary issues in recent English history, and takes a stand in some current controversies, such as the question of a standing army, he conceives it his duty, as a parliamentary homilist in the midst of a national crisis, to offer somewhat old-fashioned remedies. These depend not on new legislation but on personal self-discipline.

The third part of the sermon reduces political to personal option: can there be peace, he asks, "when lust engages in wild pursuits, in quarrels and expences, and wages amidst all a perpetual war in the members?" (20). All, but especially those governing the nation, must seek to control the lusts in their own bodies; by lust, Fell means not only sexual desire but also an immoderate desire for "Riches, Plesures and Preferment" and, lastly, "misguided zeal ... which in our world usurps the enclosure of

---

[6] See John Kenyon, *The Popish Plot* (1972; Harmondsworth: Penguin Books, 1974), pp. 230–32. I have relied on Kenyon for the historical background to the sermons of John Fell, William Jane, and Edward Stillingfleet that I discuss here.

[7] Fell, *A Sermon Preached Before the House of Peers on December 22, 1680* (Oxford, 1680), p. 8. Further page references will be given in parentheses in the text.

godliness' (21–22). Fell does not specify whose zeal is usurping, but the code words zeal, usurp, and godliness seem to indicate Protestant rather than Roman Catholic zealots. Private self-discipline in all these matters will cure the national disunity. If everyone works to quiet the war in his own home, the disunity of society will be eased: "Let everyone sweep before his own dore, and then, but not till then, the whole Street will be made clean" (24).

Fell's sermon lacks the extended dividing and subdividing of the Wilkins paradigm; it also refuses to advise its audience on an exact political stand. It compensates for these defections from the genre by a great burst of imagistic energy. Fell especially excels at inventing similes and metaphors that breathe new life into the old, medieval analogy of the physical and political bodies. He dismisses four of the six false methods for healing disunity by showing the absurdity not of their contents but of physical analogies to them. Foreign alliances are bad:

Tis to like purpose as if for an Impostume in the brain, or Ulcer in the bowels, the Patient should put a helmet on his head, or apply a plaster to his breast.   (8–9)

As is a multiplication of laws:

a Physician may as well hope to cure his Patient by writing of long bills, and prescribing several recipes, which will never be taken or regarded.   (9)

As is a standing army:

Empirics indeed, who to cure an Ague think it advisable to throw the patient into a Feavor.   (9)

As is clearing the public debt:

The dying Miser may as well hope for life by applying a bag of money to his heart, as a sick State expect a remedy from pecuniary supplies.   (10)

Although Fell opposed the use of humor in the pulpit, it is difficult to imagine that the listening peers did not smile, as it became clear that Fell was exercising his ingenuity in repeated forays into parallel images. Each successful comparison, dismissing an argument, celebrates a linguistic triumph of the preacher, putting him, not his thesis, on center stage.

To Fell's credit, each analogy hits the mark; none wanders off into irrelevant detail. Fell uses four parallels and anecdotes from classical history with equal strictness: a speech of Menenius Agrippa about bodily rebellion (3), also used by Shakespeare, earlier in the century, in *Coriolanus*; a generalized account of how the vanquished in a war learn from their victors, with a denial that this happens in a civil war (4); a list of individuals who caused national disasters, in an attempt to recall each individual Englishman to his duty (5); and a quotation from the fourth-century Roman historian Ammianus Marcellinus, recounting that Julian the Apostate attempted to extirpate Christianity by encouraging "several sects of heretics in their different ways of worship" (14). The last example probably hints at Christ Church opposition to toleration of non-Anglican protestantism and encourages opposition to a Bill of Toleration before Parliament at that moment. The aftermath of the Plot and the approaching execution of one of its members for complicity in it held Parliament's attention. Fell intends to draw his audience away from concern with the Plot – surely part of the king's intention also, in calling for a fast day – to an inner healing from which, he insists, outward healing will result.

Fell's conception of a political sermon, insofar as the 1680 sermon enunciates this, is both similar and dissimilar to South's. Both attune their remarks to an exact appreciation of the political context. Fell speaks directly to the divisions announced in the king's proclamation and evident in the House of Lords as Stafford awaited execution; South brings in the generic problem of foreign alliances for the king's specific use late in 1675. Both sermons oppose foreign alliances, though South makes this point much more central to his application. On the other hand, the structures of the sermons, in the weight they give to the specific advice on foreign alliances, are dissimilar. Fell deals with specific political proposals in his second division, and his applications concern the personal morality of his hearers; South develops the theme of alliances slowly and drives home, at the end, their danger. South develops both a theology of kingship and a specific political program much more fully. If Fell's body imagery makes a counterstatement, it is that the political crisis will not be resolved on the level of political action. He advises a retreat to the personal sphere; it is possible for the moral and physical bodies to be healed, but not, as a separate entity, the body politic. Fell's discipline in responding to the occasion, in not forwarding a specific policy that would cause more disunity, forces him to abandon half his analogy: he shows how the person may be healed, and insists that such healing will spread to the state. For the health of the body politic by itself, he can only reject false remedies.

Public days of fast and "humiliation," not a common occurrence after the Restoration, increased in frequency during the Popish Plot; Charles II found them useful, perhaps to give the impression of constructive action from the throne, while he tried not to act against the Roman Catholics he habitually protected. During what John Kenyon calls the "high tide" of the Plot, at the end of March 1679, the king proclaimed that 11 April would be such a fast day, its special aim being prayers for reconciliation with God and his renewed blessings on the work of Parliament.[8] The

---

[8] *A Proclamation for A General Fast* (London, 1679) announces the date of the fast day, in London as 11 April; the published prayer service, *A Form of Common Prayer for God's Blessing Upon His*

House of Commons asked William Jane, a canon of Christ Church, to preach; during this time, emotions were high, since the testimony of Oates and others about the reality of the Plot was still widely believed. As fellow canons of Christ Church, Jane and South knew each other well; Jane was later to seek, in William III's reign and equally without success, the see of Oxford which South had sought in vain from James II. Jane's published sermon of 1679, over 11,000 words in length, a little-known but worthy example of the Wilkins mode, ably fulfills and expands the requirements of the genre.

Jane's text is Hosea 7:9, a personification of Israel as an old man: "Strangers have devoured his strength and he knoweth it not, yea, gray hairs are here and there upon him, and he knoweth not." The exegesis, of about 1,000 words, follows Wilkins's model in "unfolding difficulties in the sense," perhaps a requirement when dealing with such a metaphorical text; Jane analyzes, in an historical context, what the strength and weakness signified in "gray hairs" meant for Israel, and what they might mean for any nation. The last meaning he assigns to weakness, "a general senselessness of that people, notwithstanding all the judgments of God,"[9] leads him to the main, pessimistic topic of the sermon: how the judgments of God, because of a nation's sinfulness, sometimes fall on deaf ears. After Jane gives the marks of moral decay in a nation – to which I will return – he notes: "These are the gray hairs of the people in the Text. I leave to you to judge by comparing our condition at present with that of the Ten Tribes before their carrying into Captivity" (10). This appeal for audience interpretation was one of the several techniques divines used to distance themselves from a fully typological equation of Jewish and English history. On the one hand, the problem having being raised, some affirmation of congruence was expected; on the other, by insisting that the audience make its own judgment, Jane backs away from full authorial responsibility for the typology of national sin followed by divine punishment.

Jane divides his confirmation into four points: the nature of God's judgments on a Nation (12–28), the effects contrary to repentance such judgments often have (28–34), some causes of human ignorance in these matters (34–42), and the greatness of the provocation offered to God (42–45); he ends with an application (45–51). Jane argues almost exclusively by means of examples and anecdotes from Scripture and secular history, all carefully linked to the context; though his proofs are mixed in that they rest on both Scripture and other sources, he generally avoids the

---

Majesty and his Dominions (London, 1679), gives the wrong date, 10 April. Outside London the fast day was observed on 24 April.

[9] Jane, *A Sermon Preached on the Day of the Public Fast, April the 11th, 1679* (London, 1679), p. 10. Further page references will be given in parentheses in the text.

rational arguments from necessity, probability, or experience that would have made his sermon a more eloquent manifestation of the genre.

One of his historical sources is of special interest. He twice quotes Salvian (24, 49), a fifth-century Latin historian of, among other things, the barbarian invasions of the late Roman Empire. Salvian's principal work, *De Gubernatione Dei*, purports to be a study of divine providence, but, especially in its second half, turns into a jeremiad about the folly of sin in the face of successive barbarian invasions.[10] Jane's use of Salvian indicates that like South he felt the nation had entered into a period of decay. Divines of this persuasion became interested in the historical signs of other dying civilizations that such accounts as the dreary pages of Salvian could supply. By their readings in Salvian and others, divines hoped to assemble a set of parallels that would lead to a theology of history, that is, a casebook of the causes which led God to punish a nation. Here is a list Jane gives:

general dissolution of manners, an impudent boldness in the practice of iniquity, a neglect and contempt of all the duties of Religion, the loosing the joints of Government by Treasons and Conspiracies, divided interests and Dissensions among the people, Confusions and Divisions in the Church are as infallible symptoms of a dying State, of the dissolution of a Commonwealth and the funeral of a Kingdom, as if a flaming Sword had hung over it, or voice from Heaven had revealed its doom.   (10)

In his employment of this traditional imagery, including the comparison of the body politic and physical body, Jane is doubly pessimistic. He interprets national reverses as signs of God's anger, and he pretends to hope for little change in the national conscience.

Jane's sermon is specifically political in several ways: he depicts a return to Roman Catholicism as the divine punishment threatened if England does not mend its ways (47–48); he attacks those of "stiff Zeal," clearly intending Protestant zealots (40–41); and he has no qualms about encouraging further extirpation of the Plot. Like Fell, Jane prescribes the generic solution of private penance for public sins; individual reform will remove the threat of popery (49–50). His final application does nothing to allay violent reaction to "a Hellish Plot for the Assassinating of our King, and the Subversion of our government and Religion" (50). He thus removes some of the distance between text and Plot that his divisions and subdivisions had created.

---

[10] *De Gubernatione Dei* was translated into English, after many years of English interest in it, in 1700; see *A Treatise of God's Government and of the Justice of His Present Dispensations in This World*, trans. R. T., intro. Thomas Wagstaffe (London, 1700). Although John Fell does not mention Salvian in his December 1680 sermon, the historian's presence is felt when Fell develops the idea of one man's capability of bringing down an empire (*A Sermon*, pp. 4–5). This was a theme favored by Salvian (*A Treatise*, pp. 157–60, 232).

When either House of Parliament asked a divine to speak, it invariably followed the delivery of the sermon with a vote of thanks and an order that the sermon be published. This procedure did not always embellish the preacher's reputation, since he sometimes did not have enough time adequately to revise his sermon before it was printed. Simon tells us of the difficulties John Tillotson ran into because he lacked sufficient time adequately to prepare or edit before publication.[11] Thus also Thomas Sprat, Canon of Westminster and future Bishop of Rochester, may have had similar difficulties in the preparation, preaching, and publication of his 30 January 1677/8 sermon before the House of Commons. This sermon lacks control and carefulness of thought, faults which appear doubly curious in Sprat. Not only was he capable of a good sermon, for his other sermons show his competence at constructing a sustained treatment in the Wilkins mode, Sprat was also, as we have seen, an advocate of the spare prose fostered by the Royal Society; the faults of his 30 January 1677/8 sermon seem to conflict with this advocacy.

After introductory praise for the martyr-king and a lament for his execution, Sprat announces that his theme will be Charles I's magnanimity in suffering. The theme accords with the chosen text, Matthew 5:10, "Blessed are they which are persecuted for Righteousness' sake: for theirs is the Kingdom of Heaven." The introduction is about 800 words out of a total sermon length of about 8,700 words, and Sprat then divides his work in good Wilkins fashion: (1) that persecution as a blessing is a peculiarly Christian paradox; (2) that it must be for righteousness' sake; and (3) what its reward is. Having announced this division, Sprat reverses himself: "I cannot now stay to insist directly on these Particulars, or to handle the Argument in my Text, as a Common place of Divinity. It will neither agree with the present temper of your Minds, or my own, to treat of it in such cold, and general terms."[12] In other words, the emotion of the day, the pain still felt almost thirty years after the regicide, makes following an outline indecorous. Since many divines experienced no dichotomy between following an outline and writing with emotion about the regicide, Sprat's remarks are not self-explanatory. His retreat from the outline he

<hr>

[11] Simon, II, ii, 357–58.

[12] Sprat, *A Sermon Preached Before the Honourable House of Commons, January 30th, 1678* (London, 1678), p. 7. Page references will be given in parentheses in the text. John Evelyn, the diarist, casts an interesting light on Sprat's preaching and, by implication, the deficiencies I find in this sermon. On 26 November 1679, Evelyn writes: "Dr. *Sprats* talent was, a great memorie, never making use of notes, a readinesse of Expression, in a most pure and plaine style, for words & full of matter, easily delivered" (*Diary*, ed. E. S. De Beer [Oxford: Clarendon Press, 1955], IV, 188). The stops and starts of the 1678 sermon may be owing to a lapse of Sprat's "great memorie" on one occasion. Still, one would like to know more about the printing history of the sermon; Sprat's decision to give an outline, then abandon it, is still unexplained. If one postulates both a failure of Sprat's preaching method and a hurried printing, the disorder in the present text may begin to be explained.

has set does in fact allow his sermon to ramble. Beginning in its announced theme, magnanimity in suffering, the sermon makes longer and wilder leaps away from it, until the theme is scarcely in focus at all.

Sprat's use of classical anecdote also lacks control. For example, when he wants to tell us how Charles I wrote his *Eikon Basilike* in prison, he compares the king to Julius Caesar:

They tell us that when *Caesar* swam for His Life amidst His Enemies, He had such Presence of Mind, as to swim with one hand, and in the other to hold up His own Book, and save it from perishing. But, when the King was incompassed with far greater, inevitable dangers, He not only preserv'd but wrote that Book. (37–38)

So striking are the dissonances between image and reality, one wonders why Caesar is brought in at all; the comparison muddles rather than clarifies Charles's achievement. Caesar swimming is not Charles writing; the tenor and vehicle never quite get together. Sprat has similar difficulties with the particulars of comparisons between Jesus and Augustus and Charles I and Pompey (9, 26). The trouble with using anecdotes is that they are never, strictly speaking, necessary; they must convince us, by their aptness, that they have earned a right to be present. The ineptitude of Sprat's use of anecdote starkly contrasts with the particularly rigorous theory of disciplined prose that he elsewhere forwarded. His sermon shows that even accomplished preachers, in straining to appear learned, could fall flat; South consistently avoided this fault.

Sprat also wanders off into what becomes, in his creation, a minefield of recent history. Some aspects of Charles's fall were embarrassing to his eulogizers, particularly his connivance at the execution of his adviser, Thomas Wentworth, Earl of Strafford, in May 1641. Sprat introduces the Strafford affair, although he did not have to, and fails to come up with a convincing exculpation of the king. He quotes Charles himself, that the abandonment of Strafford was a "Weakness"; not leaving the king to explain his own faults, Sprat continues, "he could never at last have been drawn to it, had He been half perswaded, that 'twas better for one Man to die, than for the whole People to perish" (23–24). The typology, comparing Charles's rationalization to that of the Pharisees and Sadduccees about Jesus' death (John 11:50), does not flatter the king, although Sprat does not seem to know this. Indeed Charles's *Eikon Basilike*, the source of Sprat's quotation, calls the opposition between "one Man" and "the whole People" a "fallacy."[13]

Towards the end of the sermon, when Sprat speaks of the king's pitiable farewell to his children and, in Whitehall, the scenes "of His former Splendour," the text indicates that his emotion breaks the order of his

[13] *Eikon Basilike: The Portraiture of His Sacred Majesty in His Solitudes and Sufferings*, ed. Philip A. Knachel (Ithaca: Cornell University Press, 1966), p. 8.

thought and syntax: "Or when – I can go no farther," Sprat writes, "For this can scarce be spoken without Tears: and Tears will not become a Death so Triumphant" (41). Sprat has not sufficiently thought his matter through, and, unable to decide whether triumph or tears will dictate his tone, writes and publishes not a finished sermon but the notes towards such a composition. The trouble is not emotion, but a failure to come to grips with it, an inability to choose a structure. The emotion leads nowhere, for the sermon lacks a political resolution. The application to the present is weak: audience and preacher should be watchful "that the same Schismatical Designs, and Antimonarchical Principles ... may not once more revive"; pardon must be sought for sin (47–48). The sermon's wandering structure, outburst of emotion, and lack of political resolution are interrelated. The form and the occasion suggest that, by means of a discussion of Charles's death, the sermon will address immediate problems. Perhaps desiring not to offend, Sprat retreats into a display of private emotion and lets this rupture his announced plans; he loses control of his material.

Ten months after this performance, the nation plunged itself into the Popish Plot. In mid-October 1678, Sir Edmund Berry Godfrey, the justice who first took Oates's testimony, was murdered in mysterious circumstances that have never been explained; Godfrey's funeral, on the last day of October, was a major public event. A few days before this, the king issued a proclamation calling for the first of his fast days during the national frenzy over the Plot. For the fast day service on 13 November, the House of Commons asked Edward Stillingfleet, Dean of St. Paul's and future Bishop of Worcester, to preach. His sermon classically illustrates the genre.

The greatness of Stillingfleet's sermon is that it exists fully on two different levels: it is a political sermon, given at this place and time to counsel a group caught up in a crisis which it had to control, and it also attempts to make theological statements that pertain to any such crisis. In particular, Stillingfleet addresses an issue that always hovers near the surface of late seventeenth-century divinity that deals with politics: how is England a chosen nation? How firm are the parallels with Israel? Is typology a correct means of understanding England's chosen-ness? Stillingfleet refuses to answer these questions simply, yet conducts his inquiry with a vigor and clarity missing from the work of many other preachers. For example, it occurs to him to inquire about the difference between the divine punishments of nations and individuals. Since nations do not have an afterlife, and thus no possibility of eternal punishment or reward, their punishment must occur in history, and therefore be available to observation.[14] This insight is not astounding; its merit lies in Stillingfleet's stopping

---

[14] *FS*, pp. 237–38. Further page references will be given in parentheses in the text.

to face the problem, and in his examining his methodology at the start to discover its unexplained premises. Making it clear that God punishes nations in space and time, and establishing the possibility of empirically locating such punishments, allow Stillingfleet to proceed to generalize about how God acts in history.

About 11,000 words long, the sermon begins with a text from the Davidic cycle dealing with Samuel and Saul: "Only fear the Lord, and serve him in truth with all your heart: for consider how great the things he hath done for you. But if ye shall still do wickedly, ye shall be consumed, both ye and your King" (1 Sam. 12:24–25). In this case, at least, the aural effect alone of reading the text, with its epigrammatic whip, "both ye and your King," must have been telling. After a brief reflection on the gifts of divine providence to England – to which gifts he will return in his application – Stillingfleet examines, according to the first half of Wilkins's model for exegesis, the speaker, occasion, and matter of the quotation from 1 Samuel. Anglican divines of the late seventeenth century prided themselves on their reconstruction of the historical meaning of a text; such reconstruction enabled them both to exhibit their scholarship and to provide an alternative model to a spiritual exegesis that depended on the subjective dispositions of the exegete. At this point in the sermon Stillingfleet tries to stay in the context of the past, yet obliquely involves English history and even current events. Samuel has called a fast at Mizpeh, and the reference to Charles's proclaimed fast, not overtly stated, cannot be avoided by the hearer or reader. "And to let mankind see," Stillingfleet writes, "what influence a general and serious Fasting and Humiliation hath upon the Welfare of a Nation, we find from the day of this *Fast* at *Mizpeh* the Affairs of *Israel* began to turn for the better" (234). Thus the affairs of England may also turn because of this fast day, 13 November, wisely called by England's Samuel, Charles II.

But Stillingfleet makes his typology difficult to follow; Charles is and is not the Samuel of the text. In his gifts of leadership, his confrontation of disgruntled citizens, and his call for an "*established Religion*" (236), Samuel prefigures Charles; but he does not prefigure Charles in that he is, quite simply, not a king and, in one tradition, an anti-monarchist. There is no fully satisfactory explanation as to why Stillingfleet and his peers squinted at typology in such ways as this. Perhaps typology recalled excesses of spiritual interpretation associated with the Cromwell years; perhaps involvement in the typological sense threw a wild card into the exegetical game that the orderly post-Restoration theologians found distasteful on something like aesthetic grounds. Whatever the case, it is rare to find a straightforward typological positioning of type and antitype, of Charles II, for example, and Samuel, in political or nonpolitical sermons;

Stillingfleet's coyness in affirming the Samuel/Charles parallel shows the practical results of the theoretical bias against typology.

During his further exegesis of the text, Stillingfleet gets slightly distracted into a discussion of why Samuel opposed a king for the Jews (235). This opposition, fraught with interpretational tangles for a royalist divine, occurs in texts which had been used many times by anti-monarchist preachers. In Stillingfleet's time, only advanced thinking on Scripture, especially that of Richard Simon, the French Oratorian, was beginning to separate different sources of composition in the Old Testament. Without a knowledge of the different traditions that were responsible for writing the Davidic literature, Stillingfleet simply notes that Israel was, elsewhere, promised a king, and passes on.

Stillingfleet's main division of the text, after the exegesis, is clear and elegant: to show that God exercises a particular providence with respect to the state of kingdoms (237–42), that the state of a kingdom corresponds to the people's actions, good or bad (242–46), and that certain kinds of sin hasten a nation's ruin (246–48); there follows an application that is, for Stillingfleet, somewhat lengthy (248–52). He carefully subdivides each of his main points. Mixed proofs abound here and give the linear progression of argument a needed variety. From his first division, Stillingfleet shows his skill at arguing both from Scripture and history and from necessity and probability: "since mankinds entring into *Society* is both necessary and advantageous to them; and God doth not barely permit and approve, but dispose and incline men to it; and hath given them *Laws* to govern themselves by, with respect to *society*; it is but reasonable to suppose that *God* should call men to an account in that capacity ..." (237). By 1678 Stillingfleet had been arguing in prose for well over a decade, had learned to make his syntax serve his argument, and had mastered his sources of argument and his rhetorical aims. Here his approach is intellectual; he wants to expand the thinking of his audience about its common experience, and not, at this point, to encourage them to action.

He also excels at arguments from scriptural texts and extra-scriptural historical examples. In a subdivision of his first major point, that God exercises particular providence, he suggests two different kinds of negative divine action towards a state: God pulls a state down by causing internal disunity and by raising up enemies external to it. Stillingfleet demonstrates this second point by historical example, for the very nature of the matter demands historical rather than necessary reasoning. "Look over all the mighty Revolutions which have hapned in the *Kingdoms* and *Empires* of the *World*," he bids the reader, to note the strange risings of external opposition to evil nations. Similarly to South, Stillingfleet tends to define suddenness and strangeness in historical events as divinely providential

Beginning in Scripture, he quotes Jeremiah, Judges, Ezekiel, Nahum,

Zephaniah, and Isaiah to illustrate providence's use of foreign enemies to punish an evil nation. He refers to Alexander the Great and Salvian, the latter to show how the conquerors of Rome were in many ways inferior to the Romans; then to Machiavelli, on the impossibility of finding consistency in Rome's reaction to victory and defeat; and then to Hyacinth Jordanus, a medical writer of the seventeenth century, who discusses the possibility that some diseases that will not respond to human remedies may be divinely caused. Thus Stillingfleet brings the classic analogy of the body politic into the sermon, noting and bringing the argument home to the occasion, concluding that some diseases of the body politic require, for their cure, prayer and fasting (239–41). Such units of richly mixed argumentation occur everywhere in the sermon, yet it never gets distracted from the central points it purports to make.

The sermon is neither rich in nor devoid of imagery and anecdote. Besides the use of Salvian, Stillingfleet quotes a remark of Asinius Pollio to Augustus that he would be on the winner's side, whichever that was; sincerity in religion, Stillingfleet notes, abhors such hypocrisy (243). Extended comparisons occasionally occur and, as in his treatment of classical history, he holds all imagery tightly to the argument. There are differences in the ways of sinning, he writes:

> sometimes the stream of wickedness hides its head, and runs underground, and makes little noise, although it holds on the same course; at other times it seems to break forth like a mighty torrent as though it would bear down all before it, as though the fountains of the deep were broken up, and Hell let loose.   (247)

Another extended metaphor concerns the members of the Society of Jesus, who even early in the Plot were called its principal perpetrators:

> The Vipers seemed to have changed their natures, and to have lost their teeth, and to be a very soft and innocent kind of Creatures. Insomuch, that they were hardly brought to believe there could be a plot among them, especially of so horrid a nature as this appears more and more to have been, where such a viperous brood were suffered not only to lie quiet in the Shade, but to sport themselves in the Sun, and to enjoy the freedom of their own retreats. But God doth bring to light the hidden things of darkness.   (251–52)

As the similitude unfolds, its very extension creates, on a rhetorical level, what Stillingfleet desires for the nation at large. Carefully following post-Restoration rules for similitudes, his rhetoric captures and controls the enemy, rendering him easily and wittily surmountable. The rhetoric removes the teeth that the unwary nation and tolerant monarch had forgotten existed. Extended comparisons such as this are not common in Stillingfleet's sermons; they are usually local effects, used to help make individual points and not, as in South, to subtly change the nature of an entire sermon.

Stillingfleet seems firmly to believe in the reality of the Plot, and also that the murder of Godfrey is connected with it. "There was a reason for all this," he writes; "he had taken the Examination; he knew too much to be suffered to live, and they hoped by his death to stifle his evidence, and to affright others from searching too far" (249).[15] Raising the emotions of the audience, he nevertheless distinguishes between the "seduced party" of Catholics and "the busie *Active Faction*" (250). The latter he compares to Canaanites and Jebusites, "*scourges in our sides*," in the book of Joshua (23:13). This is the third time the sermon uses this imagery: first from Salvian, who wrote that a barbarian general called himself "*Flagellum Dei, The Scourge in God's hand*" (240); and again, quoting the Old Testament, and making a general comment also. "Thus for a time, a Nation may seem to flourish exceedingly; and be victorious over others while they are as *Scourges in God's hand* for the punishment of others" (245); and, thirdly, to characterize some Roman Catholics in England. The image unites biblical, late Roman, and contemporary history, and contains in itself the theme of the entire sermon: that throughout history God is concerned with the behavior of nations and operates through an observable type of secondary causes.

How and to what extent does this sermon advocate political measures? The proclamation for the fast day stressed prayers for the king's person, as that for the April 1679 fast day, on which Jane would preach, would stress prayers for Parliament. Stillingfleet does not dwell on the person of the king, as South, had he been given the opportunity, would surely have done. Stillingfleet prefers to work out the relation of providence to England as a corporate state, among the many such states in history. Again and again he comes close to asserting the mutual chosen-ness of Israel and England; he gives the evidence for making such as assertion – as in his two essays on God's particular gifts to the English (232–33, 248) – but never explicitly draws the typological conclusion.

At the end, in his application, Stillingfleet encourages moral change in his audience. As in Fell's sermon, a gap appears here between the problems of national infidelity and personal renewal. On the other hand, Stillingfleet carefully shows how the lack of the virtues he inculcates has caused the present crisis. He tries to offer real solutions towards handling the Plot, and his solutions involve attitudes rather than specific, legislative acts. In his references to national blessing at the beginning and end of the sermon, and to "fear of the Lord" in the same places, he creates a chiasmic

---

15 The first part of Stillingfleet's reasoning is not serious, since Oates could simply have gone to another Justice and repeated his evidence; besides, the king and his closest advisers already knew of Oates's accusations. The second part – the murder as a warning – is interesting and not discussed by Kenyon in his excellent study of the reasons for Godfrey's murder (see *The Popish Plot*, pp. 302–09).

structure that rhetorically suggests an enclosure of personal and political. The advocacy of such an enclosure diverts attention from the absence of more pragmatic solutions.

Because of John Tillotson's peculiar editorial annotations, we know that he delivered a 5 November sermon in 1682, but we do not know where. The excitement of the Popish Plot was only a memory by this date, but Tillotson's sermon keeps alive the spectre that Roman Catholics were continuing to undermine the government. The Roman Catholic vice chosen for particular condemnation is an excessive "zeal," and Tillotson's text is: "I bear them record, that they have the zeal of God; but not according to knowledge" (Rom. 10:2). For Anglicans, the word "zeal" had long been associated with Protestants to the left of the established church. Jane used it in that context in his 1679 fast day sermon. Sprat had preached a few months before that, on 22 December 1678 before the king at Whitehall, and had widened the zealous opposition by picturing the church attacked on both sides by them: "the sad influence of a Fiery, Fierce Religion, on all sides of us: Here from an Enthusiasticall, Private Spirit; there from a pretentious Catholic Spirit, but Private too."[16] In 1682 Tillotson moves to the opposite extreme from Jane: although anyone could at times be guilty of the zeal indicted in his sermon, in the main the vice characterizes Roman Catholics.

In his exegesis Tillotson distinguishes between the good and bad senses of zeal, by giving a number of scriptural examples from the New Testament. He develops the notion of a zeal "concerned about lesser things, to the prejudice of the greater,"[17] and of zeal "not according to knowledge." The sermon is, in effect, an extended definition of false, knowledgeless zeal. Tillotson nods in passing at those parts of Wilkins's paradigm for exegesis that concern context. He devotes only a paragraph to St. Paul's relationship with the Jews of his day, about whose zeal the text speaks (357–58); a longer contextual analysis would not have served his preoccupation with Catholic zeal. After the exegesis Tillotson divides his matter into the three topics of zeal with knowledge (359–64), zeal without knowledge (364–69), and the possibility, fully dismissed, that doing evil because of zeal might mitigate the evil involved (370–73); an application, somewhat lengthy in relation to the 5,000-word whole, follows (374–81).

The brevity of his sermon does not prevent Tillotson from subdividing his tripartite structure. The effect of the whole is somewhat sketetal; Tillotson's bias against unnecessary ornament is evident here. At one point he moves quickly through a list of Catholic offenses, from equivocation to general councils prescribing persecution for heresy (364). In such a discussion, South and Stillingfleet tend to enumerate and quote instances and

---

[16] Sprat, *Sermons Preached on Several Occasions* (London, 1697), pp. 175–76.
[17] Tillotson, *Sermons*, II 3rd edn. (London, 1704), p. 354.

authorities; Tillotson assumes the audience's knowledge of these and moves on. The argumentation of the sermon combines demonstrations of how various aspects of zeal follow one from another and case histories of false zeal; the latter methodology characterizes those parts of the sermon attacking Roman Catholics.

The sermon is not totally free of imagistic argument. "Zeal is an Edg-tool," Tillotson writes, "which Children in understanding should not meddle withal" (374). With more sustained artistry, there is an extended comparison of zeal to fire:

There is nothing oftner misleads Men, than a misguided Zeal; it is an *ignis fatuus*, a *false fire*, which often leads Men into Boggs and Precipices; it appears in the Night, in dark and ignorant and weak minds, and offers itself as a guide to those who have lost their way; it is one of the most ungovernable Passions of Human nature, and therefore requires great knowledge and judgment to manage it and keep it in bounds. It is like fire, a good Servant but a bad Master; if it once get head, it consumes and devours all before it, and the great danger and mischief of it is, that it is most commonly found where it should not be, and possesses those most, who are least fit to govern it.   (378–79)

In spite of the nervous return ("it is like fire") midway, lest we have lost our bearings, Tillotson handles the similitude very well; the nervous repetition symbolizes the voice of the times, of an overly rigorous sense of the plain style, reasserting itself in the midst of a perfectly pleasant and already clear simile. Beneath the image lies a parody of Exodus, an anti-pillar of fire, aberrant behavior masked as providence. The image suggests that true knowledge is hard to come by. The bogs, precipices, and night of confusion and error – compelling in their psychological truth – are a refreshing antidote to the seemingly easy purchase of truth made by the skeletal structure of the sermon and by Wilkins's rules in general.

The sermon contains a useful enunciation of the theological latitudinarianism that Tillotson often expounded. "A zealous strictness about external Rites and Matters of difference," he writes, "where there is a visible neglect of substantial Duties of Religion, and the great Virtues of a good life, is either a gross ignorance of the true Nature of Religion, or a fulsome Hypocrisie" (362–63). Like Gilbert Burnet's will, the sermon suggests that Protestants join together on essential concerns, especially moral concerns, and tolerate "Matters of difference." Much has been written about the latitudinarian aspect of Tillotson's thought: often in historical surveys, it is the only aspect of his thought discussed. It is too often omitted that latitudinarianism did not give its adherents a license to jettison essential Christian beliefs in the interests of smooth sailing on the sea of Christian fellowship and toleration. Tillotson himself wrote extensively in defense of the doctrines of the Trinity and the Incarnation, as did Stillingfleet. These divines clearly thought that core Christian doctrines were not simply "Matters of difference"; they were not deists who rejected a doctrine only because it caused disunity. In the context of this sermon of 1682, two examples of false matters of difference precede this retelling of the latitudinarian creed: the long controversy over the dating of Easter and the controversy between Jews, during Jesus' time, over inner and outer cleanliness (361–62). The triviality, in contemporary terms, of Tillotson's examples lends no support to the view that latitudinarians were careless about doctrinal purity in the interests of an interdenominational moral crusade.

Tillotson's suppression, in the edited text, of the place where this sermon was delivered makes interpreting its political significant difficult. The penultimate paragraph, preceded by a discussion of conscience, suggests that the sermon addresses a particular congregation in a particular crisis.

God hath given us Understandings, to try and examine things, and in the light of this Word to direct us in this Tryal; and if we will judge rashly, and suffer ourselves to be hurried by Prejudice or Passion, the *Errours of our Judgment* become *Faults of our Lives*: For God expects from us that we would weigh and consider what we do; and when he hath afforded us light enough to discern between *Good* and *Evil*, that we would carefully follow the direction of it; that we should be suspicious of ourselves, when our Zeal carries us to do things that are furious and cruel, false and treacherous, and have a horrid appearance even to the light of Nature; we should question *that zeal* which is so contrary to Christian Goodness and Meekness, to Peace and Charity, and which tends to *Confusion and every Evil Work*.   (380)

What is "this Tryal"? What political options are against "the light of Nature" and tend to "*Confusion and every Evil Work*"?

The sermon could not have been written for a parliamentary audience, since the king had suspended Parliament in 1681 and would rule until his death in 1685 without one. The sermon may address this suspension – perhaps it was delivered in a church in the City of London, where real opposition to Charles had existed for some time – and, if so, moderation in opposition to rule by royal decree is urged. A plea for discernment, consideration, and suspicion and questioning of self seems to dampen whatever revolutionary movements were extant rather than to encourage them. The sermon does not defend Charles, but shows the darker side of what zealous opposition means: such opposition would make Englishmen indistinguishable from Roman Catholic zealots. Tillotson had preached on this theme at least once before.[18] But any attempt at constructing a context is only conjecture. Without editorial information about the place

18 See *A Sermon Preached November 5, 1678* (London, 1678), pp. 28–30.

where a political sermon was given, it is impossible to establish a correct context – and without this, the full meaning of a sermon.

South's uniqueness

From the preceding discussion, the uniqueness of South's political sermon of 5 November 1675, and perhaps, of his sermons in general, is clear. The sermon is not unique in terms of any one of the qualities that I have discussed: not in its royalism, structure, use of imagery as a unifying device, or interest in both the theory and practice of government. All of these qualities are present in the sermons of others. One cannot even say that South's practice excels that of others in exemplifying some of these qualities in some ultimate way. For Tillotson's sermon, partly because it is relatively short, seems to exemplify the Wilkins structure in an ideal way, and Stillingfleet's inquiry into the chosen-ness of England is more sustained and profound than South's. South is unique only in that he handles so many of the qualities of the genre so well in the same homiletic moment. His strength lies in his awareness and conquest of all the genre can afford. To this one, overwhelming uniqueness, one may add, with qualification, another. Many authors around South's time learned to use images in the post-Restoration, rationalist mode, but South uses image patterns in a more sophisticated way than does any other preacher at whom I have looked. His ability to elaborate an image pattern in various modes – historical analogy, similes, scriptural quotations, and so on – is especially interesting. In this one possibility offered by a lengthy sermon, it would be difficult to find a rival to South.

During the 1660s and 1670s a number of different political circles, with different loyalties and theories of the monarchy, existed in England. Terms like "Royalist" and "Parliamentarian" allude to only the most basic facts of political loyalty and theory. Among the secular and ecclesiastical figures most loyal to the king, South, if we can judge from his theology of kingship, supported the idea that the king should rule as independently as possible, without interference from elected legislative bodies. South was not alone in believing that God favored England in a special way, but, in his theology, the only avenue by which this favor is extended runs through the monarch. At various times during South's life, his patrons were Edward Hyde, Earl of Clarendon, and the king's brother, James, Duke of York. It is likely that in the circles surrounding Clarendon and James were loyalists who not only supported the king but also conceived of God's special help for England almost solely as a function of the relationship between God and king. South was a prominent spokesman for these loyalists.

South may also have represented these hyper-royalist circles in his "high" theology of kingship. That is, as I have noted, kingship has its primary value for South in that it is the human analogue to God's rule and, only secondarily, in that it may turn out, in empirical observation, to be a good form of government. South writes in the 1675 sermon:

monarchy, in the kind of government, is the first, and consequently the most perfect of all other sorts. It is an image of the divine supremacy, man's imitation of Providence, a copy of God's government of the universe in a lesser draught. For the world has one sovereign ruler, as well as but one maker; and every prince is both his lieutenant and his resemblance too.   (II, 567–68)

After 1660, many wanted the king to be a strong ruler; many also believed that his rule was a divine gift to England. South was among those who carried these ideas out rigorously and to their extreme, giving a monarchy that was analogous to divinity a central place in his political theology.

Simon sets up the frame of reference of seventeenth-century political philosophy spanning the years from Richard Hooker to John Locke, from the idea that human laws are descended from and reflect divine laws to the idea that human reason may conflict with and remake human law. She writes that South is on Hooker's side, as Tillotson is on Locke's.[19] Clearly conservative in his politics, South writes, in one sense, at a vast distance from the innovative republicanism of late seventeenth-century England. Yet South's excited advocacy of an extreme theory of divine right may have its eye on the newer political theories being promulgated; the sway of the latter affects at least South's tone. South speaks his royalist views with a shrillness and emphasis that would not be necessary if those views were not being challenged.

One way of reading the sermons of South and other post-Restoration preachers has been to try to understand them as sermon-essays. In her study of the late seventeenth-century sermon, Caroline Richardson writes:

essentially it was a secular work intended to appeal to the thoughtful, philosophical, well educated person who recognized foibles and weaknesses in himself as quickly as in his fellows ... Take a dozen or more of Robert South's sermons, behead them of their texts, cut off their extremities of perfunctory reminder that souls should be saved, and what remains is a group of essays well worth reading.[20]

To confirm her strange thesis, Richardson offers the titles of eight sermons of South that resemble essay titles. All of the titles she gives, however, are those of later editors; none were composed by South himself.

South's political sermon of 5 November 1675 offers at least three

---

[19] Simon, I, 154–62.
[20] Caroline Richardson, *English Preachers and Preaching, 1640–1670. A Secular Study* (London: SPCK, 1928), p. 86.

arguments that deny Richardson's thesis. First, his extremist theology of kingship is not for "the thoughtful, philosophical person"; in its own day and in ours, the calculated effort to confuse the borders between God and king was suspect and perhaps offensive. It is no honor to South to consider it in any other way; to palliate his extremism is to misunderstand him. Some of his political sermons are not essays but violent manifestos, calculated to arouse intense loyalty as well as opposition and hatred. Second, South often but not always writes about human "foibles and weaknesses." The sermons that do this are, in my opinion, his dullest, although with the proper hermeneutic anything can, I suppose, come alive. South's political sermons sharply focus on contemporary problems; many of his sermons outside the area of politics address specific and contemporary issues and writers. He writes about human nature, for we can still, sharing that nature, understand him, but it is human nature at a specific time and place.

Third, Richardson's curious tactic of lopping off beginnings and ends sends one back to South to discover how integrated the various parts of his sermons are. At his best South positions these parts against one another; beginning and middle are enriched by the ending, and this leads firmly from them. In the 1675 sermon, for example, the references to the Red Sea and King David add important meaning, at the end, to what has gone before; the admonition to kings at the sermon's beginning seems at first conventional, but then it is picked up and developed into a carefully structured counterstatement. South's sermons are not fictional narratives wherein the loss of one part may ruin the whole, but certain aspects of his sermons suggest that the idea of an organic or architectural whole is not the worst model by which to understand them.

Thirteen years to the day after South's sermon on the ways God helps kings, William of Orange landed at Torbay in the West Country and began his slow march to London. South preached that day, 5 November 1688, in Westminster Abbey, at either Morning or Evening Prayer, and later published his sermon. As a preface to any discussion of this sermon, one has to ask whether South knew about the invasion. Is this the context of the sermon as it was given? It is unlikely that London was informed of the invasion, given slowness of communication, at any time on 5 November. William had not been silent about his intentions, however; James II expected an invasion at any time. It is probable that talk of William's imminent landing was current in London and Oxford, and such public awareness provides, I think, at least one context for understanding South's sermon. It clearly provides a context for any editing South did between 1688 and the date of publication.

Simon understands the sermon as it comments on the reign of James II; she avoids the possibility that it might address the threat of William or his

possible landing, "of which South could not have known."[21] It is my view
that the sermon addresses both the fact of James and the possibility of
William, that it shows the end of South's dream of a divinely elected
monarchy, and that it equally condemns the Houses of both Stuart and
Orange. The sermon is a jeremiad upon England, inspired by an Isaian
text, "What could have been done more to my vineyard, that I have not
done in it?" (Isa. 5:4). Except for the briefest of exhortations, at the end, to
national repentance, the text of about 6,500 words leaves no hope for a
change. Though the sermon has multiple divisions, it is one of the few of
South that does not follow the form of exegesis, confirmation, and application. The whole sermon lingers in the first division, explication of the text.

   I *Introduction*
      (1) Many Protestants have been as disloyal as the Roman Catholics
           who were in the Gunpowder Plot (IV, 79–80)
      (2) Roman Catholics at least have the virtue of consistency (80)
      (3) Complaints of God against the Jews have a "parallel instance"
           in England (80–81)
  II *The form and manner of the divine complaint in Isaiah 5:4*
      (1) Its strangeness (81–82)
      (2) The unusual indignity of ingratitude (82–83)
 III *The contents of the complaint (85–97)*
      (1) The person complaining: God himself (83–84)
      (2) The persons complained of: the Jews, the "select people of God"
           (84–85)
      (3) The grounds for complaint (85–97)
         (a) Previous grants of sacred words, oracles, and other gifts
         (b) Continual mercies
         (c) Judgments and lack of response evident in
            (i) injustice and oppression
            (ii) covetousness
            (iii) luxury and sensuality
      (4) The result of the complaint: the destruction of a nation's
           defenses (97–101)
         (a) its laws
         (b) its military power resulting in
            (i) "sects and factions"
            (ii) destruction of the vineyard

More about England's infidelity than Israel's, only in its earliest parts
does the sermon not refer explicitly to England, and implicit reference is a
possibility everywhere. South almost never speaks only about Israel, and

---

[21] Simon, I, 163.

very often only about England. In a major change from his political
theology of the 1670s, South here discusses the chosen-ness not of the
monarch, but of England: the nation rather than the individual has
become for him the subject of divine election. James II had led the nation
astray and was tampering with the church establishment; from what
South knew of the supporters of William of Orange, the government
escaping the Catholic frying-pan would jump into a Whig fire. The
available personal subjects of divine election had eliminated themselves
from South's consideration. By the 1688, he had retreated to what was in
essence the latitudinarian position: that the nation not the individual
monarch was the heir to the promises made to Israel. South repeats and
perhaps darkens the latitudinarian emphasis: England again and again
refuses to repay the gifts of an ever-generous God. In this corporate
relationship, one party repeatedly fails to fulfil the contract.

Southean mannerisms appear throughout. The imagery of the sermon
corroborates that of the text: England is God's vineyard on almost every
page. South's wit occasionally transforms this imagery: he refers once to
"the gentle manurings of his mercy" (90) and warns that "we have lived
under a long sunshine, and God knows that it has ripened our sins apace"
(100). The sermon drops the coded opposition to France of 1675 and
openly attacks "the French fashion and French vices that have invaded,
and conquered, and spoiled our land" (96). The traditional imagery of
illness in the body politic and the falsity of most suggested cures occurs
here. South also alludes at the beginning of the sermon to the practice of
putting good names on evil realities, a practice that he had already
castigated in four sermons that I will discuss later (chapter 4).

South is ominously dire about his main theme, England's repeated
refusal of divine help. To be elected by God, in 1688, means sure punishment. Except for a brief call for national repentance, the conclusion
concerns God's final actions in response to betrayal. After the vineyard is
opened, it is "trodden down":

It was first to be choked up by a growing evil from within, and next to be laid
waste by a force from abroad. The non-execution of laws caused the first, and a
failure of power occasioned the next.   (IV, 100)

The conspicuous feature of this scheme of thought and language, which
almost abandons the allegory and becomes openly seditious, is its inability
to locate salvific power in either of the two obvious political options. God
only acts in 1688 to destroy, or to allow the English to destroy themselves.
James II is guilty of non-execution of law and failure of power; William of
Orange is the new Sennacherib who will destroy the land. No available
political force can allay the disillusion of the English prophet, once a
strident supporter of the established monarchy.

An interesting feature of this sermon is the general comments it twice makes about the nature of English society. South praises "the mutual interchange of good offices" as the only thing that stands between civilized behavior and the animal nature of man (82–85); he attacks newly rich magnates who try to concentrate the nation's wealth in their own hands and "transmit the fruits of their sins and rapine to their posterity" (94). The first aside sounds a bit like Hobbes, and the second, proleptically, like Swift, although it is not necessary to resort to either to understand South, who here follows traditional biblical morality. Once South lowered his sights to envision England, not the king alone, as God's elected, he became more interested in the secondary causes that made English society habitable. In these brief remarks, South again echoes latitudinarian thought, which, though supportive of late seventeenth-century capitalism, condemned its grosser manifestations.[22]

Conclusion

Nothing better illustrates South's changing ideas about kingship than a parallel change in his thought about the function of human conscience. Near the end of the 1688 sermon, he notes that the English still wrongly accept "pretences of conscience" from those who had consistently fomented rebellion since the 1640s. South here enunciates his usual view of conscience as a force in the political subject that encourages dissent and rebellion. In the 1660s and 1670s South occasionally praised conscience, yet could never free it from its associations with rebellion. In a sermon on the subject in 1672, he writes:

whereas heretofore the magistrate passed for God's vicegerent here on earth, the weak conscience is now resolved to keep that office for itself ... for the magistrate must make only such laws as such consciences will have made, and such laws only must be obeyed, as these consciences shall judge fit to be obeyed.   (II, 373)

Even though the sermon praises a "strong conscience," which is, in South's definition, obedient, the idea of a free conscience in a free society frightened South, who felt he had ample historical foundation for his fear.

After 1688, when his own conscience found it impossible fully to assent to the ruling magistracy, South reassessed his position. In November 1691 and October 1692, in two sermons given at Christ Church on conscience, South apprehends conscience as a positive force in that it fights political fashion. Conscience

is no less than God's vicegerent or deputy, doing all things by immediate commission from him. It commands and dictates everything in God's name, and stamps every word with an almighty authority. So that it is, as it were, a kind of copy or

[22] See Margaret Jacob, *The Newtonians and the English Revolution* (Ithaca: Cornell University Press, 1976), p. 53.

transcript of the divine sentence, and an interpreter of the sense of heaven . . . [it] has one prerogative above all God's other vicegerents; to wit, that it can never be deposed.   (II, 197)

South had habitually reserved the imagery of vicegerency and of divine copy for the person of the king. The deposition of James II, as South's wit makes clear to his Christ Church audience, caused him to transfer the imagery to a once-suspect entity, human conscience.

One wonders at the pain and fear of inconsistency latent in such a transference; the Christ Church audience must have been aware that South was abandoning what he had strongly espoused. Only utter disillusion with the Houses of both Stuart and Orange allowed South so to go back on himself. South hides the personal anxiety; the same, firm persona governs both the 1672 and 1692 sermons. South never abandons what he conceived pulpit decorum to be. Each text is internally consistent, and we can sense, in them, none of the ambiguity about rulers that, for example, the poetic structures of Marvell's "Horatian Ode" or Dryden's *Absalom and Achitophel* encourage. Only by comparing texts twenty years apart do we understand South's radical change, as he was forced to work out his disillusion with individual monarchs on the level of the psychology of the subject Englishman.

To observe these changes is to call attention to what is perhaps the best and worst of South as a political writer. He rarely chooses to be subtle; he may bully his hearers toward his thesis, even when he has, in the past, bullied them in an opposing direction. He can be fairly perceived as, in a word, insincere. Yet, sincerity, or fidelity to interior dispositions, surely was not South's principal aim in delivering any sermon. In each of his political sermons, South wanted to present both a plan for correct behavior and an image of the strength that followed from adopting that behavior. He was a public man who did not regard the pulpit as a place to show inner conflict; he lived fully in a rhetorical world. The worst thing that a prominent divine of the Church of England could do was not to change his opinions, but to flounder, and thus to bring the charge of weakness or instability on the church itself.

4

South and the misuse of language

Contexts

The late seventeenth century in England was a time of great ferment in the theory of language. The gradual decline in the "tyranny" of Aristotle over natural philosophy and the rise of experimental science set many wondering whether similar scientific reforms could be made in the use of language. The triumph of the vernacular in many areas encouraged new study of how concepts in English were formed. Nationalism and the breakdown of major religious denominations into sects also played a part in the new interest in language: too many wars had been fought, it was felt, that were abetted by ill-digested slogans and theological terms. Reformation of the national languages might have a real effect on bringing peace and toleration to Europe. Both in England and on the continent, the problem of the relationship between words, particularly abstract words, and things and ideas moved to the forefront of theological, philosophical and political discussion.

The best-known discussion occurs in book 3 of John Locke's *Essay Concerning Human Understanding* (1690), where Locke grapples with how abstract ideas are formed and what it means to say that things have "essences," on which abstract words are based. Between 1660 and 1700, as James Knowlson tells us, at least nineteen separate attempts were made to write a "universal" language, which, through the use of specially constructed signs, might make minimal the linguistic possibilities for ambiguity and misrepresentation of things and ideas.[1] Theologians such as South and Stillingfleet moved the discussion to the metaphysical plane; they felt that it was impossible to discuss the misnaming of good and evil without establishing anew that good and evil existed in an objective manner, independent of opinion. In the background of their treatments, and also those of more secular thinkers, lay the ideal of an Adamic language: Adam had once given things their natural, correct names. Centuries of abuse had displaced those names, but the ideal of a purely objective naming lingered

[1] Knowlson, *Universal Language Schemes in England and France, 1600–1800* (Toronto and Buffalo: University of Toronto Press, 1975), pp. 226–28.

1   The Christ Church portrait of Robert South, the most severe in appearance of the extant
portraits. The artist is unknown.

2   The Oriel portrait of Robert South. The words "Dochtr. South by W. Dobson. 1640" are printed in the lower right; the date and artist are inaccurate, since South was six years old in 1640 and Dobson, a fashionable portrait painter, died in 1646. Whoever painted this portrait, like South's other portraitists, did not try to make him handsome. The Oriel South still seems preferable to the sterner portrait at Christ Church.

3   George Vertue (1684–1756) engraved this portrait of Robert South. It does not resemble
the other outstanding portraits and may be an original of the elderly South. Vertue set up shop
in 1711, four years before South's death. Vertue includes South's coat of arms (bottom center):
three rectangular figures (Delfts or Billets) with a golden crown (Chaplet or).

4 Richard Busby and a pupil. Although attributions have been attempted, the identities of the painter and of the pupil are unknown. Busby has the schoolmaster's eye here, as he points to a passage that has been misquoted or mistranslated; the pupil dreamily stares at a living monument.

5 John Fell, John Dolben, and Richard Allestree. Painted by Sir Peter Lely (1618–80), this study commemorates the celebration of the offices of the Church of England in the 1650s, in rooms in Merton Street, when that celebration was proscribed at Oxford. After the Restoration the rewards of such fidelity were great: Fell became Bishop of Oxford and Dean of Christ Church; Dolben Bishop of Rochester; and Allestree Canon of Christ Church and Provost of Eton. South probably attended the clandestine services.

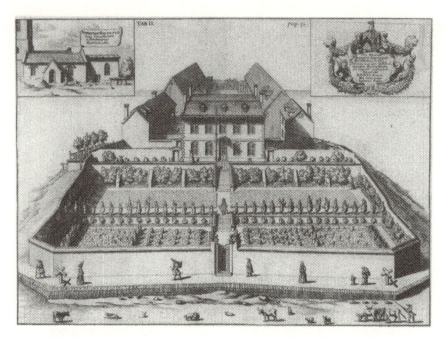

6   The Rectory at Islip. South funded the building of this imposing structure in 1689; it
remains standing and occupied today, though not by the Vicar of Islip. South also rebuilt the
chancel of the parish church, shown in the upper left inset, in 1680. The engraving, by
M. Brughers, was commissioned by White Kennet (1660–1728), Bishop of Peterborough and
antiquary, for his *Parochial Antiquities* (1695), where it appears after page 50.

to motivate systematic reforming of the connections between words and things. The relative idealism or skepticism about such reform itself provides an interesting index for sorting out differences among a number of late seventeenth-century writers.

From 1649 to 1688 radical changes in English government provided ample opportunity for winners and losers to establish their own meanings for abstract political terms. In the eyes of many, language had become the plaything of party. Thus John Dryden's *Absalom and Achitophel* (1681) satirizes political misnaming by the opponents of Charles II in the twin crises of the Popish Plot and the campaign to exclude James, Duke of York, from succession to the throne. In Achitophel's two great speeches tempting Absalom to treason, he cynically proposes to manipulate language in the interests of revolution:

> All Sorts of Men by my successful Arts,
> Abhorring Kings, estrange their alter'd Hearts
> From *David's* Rule: and 'tis the general Cry,
> Religion, Common-wealth, and Liberty.
> The publick Good, that Universal Call,
> To which even Heav'n Submitted, answers all.

The narrator of the poem later reflects on Achitophel's successful duplicity:

> Yet all was colour'd with a smooth pretence
> Of specious love, and duty to their Prince.
> Religion, and Redress of Grievances,
> Two names, that always cheat and always please,
> Are often urg'd; and good King *David's* life
> Indangered by a Brother and Wife.
> Thus, in a Pageant Show, a Plot is made;
> And Peace it self is War in Masquerade.[2]

Religion, commonwealth, liberty, public good, civic love and duty, religion, redress of grievances, and peace itself: like many thinkers of his time, Dryden knew that the danger of these words lay in that they were "general" and "Universal." In frequent use, their referential values dependent on self-serving demagogues, such words became, as South says, "fatal." In the wrong hands, their meanings undermined the reality they were supposed to represent. This eventuality was virtually certain when the citizenry did not use its reason to determine its own political good. As in Dryden and South, attacks on abuses in political language often went hand in hand with a low estimate of the reasonableness of the masses.

Readers have long felt that Dryden's satiric diagnosis of this and other

---

[2] Dryden, *Works*, II, ed. H. T. Swedenberg and Vinton A. Dearing (Berkeley and Los Angeles: University of California Press, 1972), 14, 18, 27–28.

political problems is more convincing than the cure that *Absalom and Achitophel* applies. Poems, unlike life, must enclose and end problems. In a speech from the throne at the end of the poem, the king dismisses his enemies partly by correctly defining the political abstractions of established power and the rule of law. The stagey setting in which Dryden places this redefinition suggests its ambiguity: in reality, no single act of speech could heal the long-term damage political language has suffered. Because the king rules by divine right, he can perform the Adamic act of connecting words with the things to which they naturally refer; Dryden's conclusion is theologically decorous. Other speakers in other contexts could not rely on supernatural causes and had resort only to the weak voice of reason to set things right.

To understand Dryden's satire and the four sermons of South that I will discuss in this chapter, it is necessary to gauge three related contexts – political, moral, and philosophical, or linguistic – in which these works live and to which they in turn give life. Each context suggests related but different causes for what many felt were epochal disjunctions between words and things that had occurred by the late seventeenth century.

Political: Adam correctly and by divine inspiration named things. His sin caused a breakup between himself and nature, including the nature of things which he and his descendants continued, often erroneously, to name. The episode of the Tower of Babel (Gen. 11:1–9) offers, in late seventeenth-century exegesis, only the inevitable conclusion to the first chapter of the divorce of language from its natural referents. Through successive history, especially in times of political crisis, misnaming grew worse. Indeed, any increase in the volume of political oratory aimed at the masses was bound also to increase linguistic confusion; history showed that debasements of language and of civic responsibility went hand in hand.

Such dual debasement occurred, for example, in a period that South, from his days of translating at Westminster School, knew well: the decline of the Greek republics during the Pelopponesian War. This is how Thucydides describes the state of language as Athens and Sparta struggled:

in peace and prosperity, as well Cities as private men, are better minded, because they bee not plunged into necessity of doing any thing against their will, but War taking away the affluence of daily necessaries, is a most violent Master, and conformeth most mens passions to the present occasion. . . . The received values of names imposed for signification of things, was changed into arbitrary: For inconsiderate boldness, was counted true-hearted manlinesse; provident deliberation, a hansome Fears: modesty, the cloaks of cowardice; to be wide in every thing, to be lazie in every thing. A furious suddenness was reputed a point of valour. To re-advise for the better security, was held for a fair pretext of tergervisation. . . . In briefe, he that could outstrip another in the doing of an evill act, or that could perswade another thereto, that never meant it, was commended.[3]

The translation, that of Hobbes, provides a curiosity of its own. Hobbes appreciated the problem of linguistic debasement as keenly as anyone; but the solution he proposed in *Leviathan* (1650), to let the magistrate control the naming of good and evil, was interpreted by South and others as a major factor in promoting linguistic confusion after 1660.

The theory of the progressive debasement of language in political crises naturally led South and others to interpret the greatest political crisis of their lives, the regicide, in linguistic terms. The trial of Charles I allowed an orgy of naming good evil and evil good. In a sermon I discussed in the last chapter Thomas Sprat interprets the king's fall as caused by wilful redefinition of abstractions:

though He had manifestly the Right on His Side, yet His Enemies, by their Artifices, had got over most of the good, and plausible words, to be on theirs. Whilst the worst of their Actions were Sanctify'd, and made popular by the Specious Titles of *Liberty*, *Purity*, and *Reformation*: He Dy'd for the Laws, as a Malefactor; for the Church, the best Reformed Church, as an Enemy to the Cause of God.[4]

Sprat's interpretation of the prelude to the regicide offers a proleptic deconstruction of Dryden's fiction, three years later, of Charles II's conquest through words. In the world of history, the people tend not to believe words such as "liberty" and "reform" when a good man uses them; owing to fallen nature, especially its irrationality when reacting *en masse*, misnaming carries a subtly attractive conviction with it. At the end of his first sermon on the misuse of language, South too cannot refrain from discussing the regicide, as he often does in moral analysis. Before the king could be disposed of, his enemies knew that they had to "blacken" his name: "when any man is to be run down, and sacrificed to the lust of his enemies, as that royal martyr was, even his *good* (according to the apostle's phrase) *shall be evil spoken of*. He must first be undermined, then undone" (II, 137). South returns to a discussion of the regicide, under the same heading, many times in his other sermons on the misuse of language.

The generation that came to power after 1660 inherited a political language that, it was frequently told, the regicide had corrupted. South preached against such corruption, yet there is an air of despair about his sermons on words; for the duplicity of political speech was everywhere and the gullibility of audiences infinite. The power of evil seemed stronger, in this area, than the power of good. The conspiracy to subvert political language grew stronger with each crisis the nation endured.

[3] *Eight Books of the Peloponnesian War*, trans. Thomas Hobbes (London, 1629), p. 198 [188].
[4] Sprat, *A Sermon*, p. 21.

Moral: the misnaming of political realities had implications for any attempt to construct a theory of moral behavior. The national habit of misnaming might imply that calling things good or evil was only a sort of nominalism, resting not on inherent qualities in things, but on changing conventions. South and Stillingfleet both worried about moral nominalism and preached that good and evil were objective categories.

Stillingfleet's argument occurs in a sermon of 1669 on Isaiah 57:21, "there is no peace, saith my God, to the Wicked." Stillingfleet argues that the only way the wicked could have peace of mind would be if "wickedness is but a meer name of disgrace set upon some kind of actions, but that really there is no such thing as sin, or the differences of good and evil ... that those are names only imposed upon things by the more cunning sort of men to affright men from the doing some actions and to encourage them to do others."[5] For about 2,000 words in the first division after the exegesis of the text, Stillingfleet argues against the nominalist thesis. In a mixed proof, the division develops arguments mainly from experience, brings in, near the end, necessary reasoning, but never refers to Scripture.

Stillingfleet argues that good and evil are objective realities, independent of the opinion of the namer, because:

(a) the faculty of moral choice rests on the fact that choice between good and evil is possible
(b) no culture past or present has failed to differentiate between good and evil
(c) the experience of conscience tells us that we feel differently about doing good than doing evil
(d) everyone at least pays homage to the source of his existence
   (i) matricide and regicide are universally condemned
   (ii) worse than them is blasphemy
   (iii) how can these be condemned if objective good and evil do not exist?
(e) if there are people bad enough to follow the teachings of Hobbes's *Leviathan* that make things equally good and bad, "no Religion, no Law, no Kindness, no Promises, no Trust, no Contracts could ever oblige them not to do anything which they thought might be done with safety"
(f) the existence of God necessarily implies his own perfections, and the recognition of limited perfections in us necessarily implies an objective scale of good.[6]

There is perhaps little here to convince the thoroughly skeptical about the objectivity of good and evil. As in many of his proofs, Stillingfleet

[5] *FS*, p. 135.   [6] *FS*, pp. 135–41.

assumes an audience that is willing to be convinced of such objectivity, and looks to his text to give rational substance to this desire.

In the late 1680s, South gave four sermons on "the fatal imposture and force of words." His discussion of objective good and evil occurs near the beginning of his first sermon on the misuse of words, in the first division after the exegesis (II, 111–21). The placing, here as in Stillingfleet, is meaningful: the audience and preacher must agree that good and evil exist before their particular forms can be discussed. When South speaks of good or bad actions in this sermon, he makes clear that he means two hypothetically identical actions performed under the same circumstances; it is his thesis that one cannot be called good and the other bad. South argues in more general terms than Stillingfleet, depends more on analytical, necessary reasoning than on arguments from experience, and uses Scripture, though to no great extent. The objectivity of good and evil is a rational, a philosopher's issue; while Scripture speaks of good and evil actions, the precise problem of the universal applicability of the names, good and evil, is one that reason invents and must answer.

South defines good as that which is in accord with right reason or rational nature, a definition of long standing in the Aristotelian tradition. He briefly develops the positive side of the definition, then turns to two objections: that good depends on opinion or on positive law. The sources of the second objection, including Hobbes, are mentioned. South's arguments, unfortunately, are difficult to follow: to prove the absurdity of the two objections, he uses a kind of scholastic shorthand in which concepts familiar to his age, but not to ours, are moved quickly around. He analyzes two classic examples of imperatives to do good: obeying God and caring for one's neighbor. The first rests on a relationship of obedience, along with all other creatures, to God: "man naturally and necessarily stands" (119) in subordination, inside a hierarchy of being. To disobey is to deny one's essence. Duty towards one's neighbor is clear from Scripture; South touches briefly on Adam, Moses, the prophets, and Jesus, who said, "Whatsoever ye would that men should do unto you, do ye even unto them" (Matt. 7:12). A succeeding argument, of brief but equal length, develops "parity of right" as "the result of nature itself" (II, 120–21). The mixed proof appears in the form of arguments from Scripture and an examination of rational nature.

South and Stillingfleet frequently preach on questions of individual and social morality. The arguments about morality which I have summarized are usual in that, though they depend on a variety of sources, they lean, for their proofs, away from Scripture towards reason. This is mainly because, while it was perfectly obvious that Scripture inculcated morals, these preachers and their congregations enjoyed seeing how far reason alone could prescribe a moral life. They were unwilling to accept a morality founded only on authority; they wanted to base morality on an analysis of human nature and, in this, of course, they were in line with the entire Aristotelian tradition, key words and phrases of which come up frequently in South's first sermon on words. This process of analysis involves the mildest sort of rationalism. As I have said, South presumed that his audience was predisposed to assent. He and they were also conscious of the level of certainty that such arguments could reach, and that morals, not mathematics, were at issue.

The moral context of the misuse of language verges on the political. Hobbes raises his unruly head in the analyses of both South and Stilling-fleet; neither will allow the naming of good and evil to rest in the will of the Hobbesian magistrate. Stillingfleet uses regicide as an example of an objective evil, and South refers more than once in the sermon to the regicide of 1649. Moral and political contexts especially overlap in that both preachers assert that the link between language and things is broken because human beings have done something wrong; the break has not happened accidentally.

Philosophical or linguistic: a third context is scientific, in which value is subordinated to fact. Misuse of language in this context is not immoral, but merely something that happens, that can be observed as an interesting phenomenon of human activity, and that can be corrected by rational efforts. The first few chapters of book 3 of Locke's *Essay* provide a number of examples of dispassionately philosophical analysis of problems in linguistic communication. It was helpful to all, Locke writes, that language found general words to comprehend several particular things, but much confusion has resulted; both children and adults grow so accustomed to familiar words that they forget that words refer not to things but to ideas; and the meaning of even commonplace words and concepts, like "gold," depends on the experience of their users and hearers.[7] For Locke, problems of ambiguity in language are the natural result of its day-to-day use; we forget that words do not mean the same thing to us as to others. Frequency of use and inveterate sloth, not a conspiracy to mislead, have caused the present state of confusion.

In book 3 of Jonathan Swift's *Gulliver's Travels* (1726), Gulliver tells us about men who, distressed at the break between words and things, carry large sacks of objects on their backs; when they want to communicate, they take a thing out of the sacks and point to it, thus avoiding all ambiguity about their references, and indeed avoiding all words. Gulliver notes that this is a back-breaking process. The roots of this little satire lie deep in late seventeenth-century linguistic theory. Some thinkers, especially those associated with the Royal Society of London, stressed a revised connection

[7] *Essay Concerning Human Understanding*, pp. 402, 407–08; 406.

between words and things as a remedy for poor communication. In discussing style, as we have seen, Sprat suggests an ideal of conciseness, wherein the number of words should approximate the number of things spoken of. In the introductory matter to his essay on a universal language, John Wilkins says that all previous efforts to write such a language have failed because their authors associated their new sets of signs with existing languages, "without reference to the nature of things, and that common Notion of them, wherein Mankind does agree, must be chiefly respected, before any attempt of this nature could signifie any thing, as to the main end of it."[8] In the heyday of the early scientific revolution, Wilkins believed that the progressive degeneration of language could be cured by the right book that assigned new signs to things.

It is a disputed point how rigorously Wilkins and others held to their ideal of words as direct representations of things. It is generally agreed that Locke tends to speak of words as representing ideas, not things; he may have worked out his own theory as a critique of Wilkins's.[9] Histories of seventeenth-century linguistic thought have argued both a continuity and discontinuity between Wilkins and Locke in this area. South, on the other hand, is rarely a theorist about language; he is less concerned with what it is than with how it is misused for immoral or political reasons.

Whatever their agreement or disagreement on the primary referents of words, Wilkins and Locke share the view that it is the job of the philosopher of language to set matters straight and to offer remedies for linguistic abuse. Wilkins devises a series of marks, his "universal" language, that break words down into their notional constituents, and Locke devotes two chapters of the *Essay* to abuses of language and some means of correcting them. With the simple idealism that marks a number of publications of early members of the Royal Society, Wilkins writes that "the reducing of all things and notions, to such kind of Tables, as are here proposed (were it as compleatly done as it might be) would prove the shortest and plainest way for the attainment of real Knowledge, that hath yet been offered to the World." Considerably less sanguine about the possibilities of reform, Locke writes: "I am not so vain to think that any one can pretend to attempt the perfect *Reforming* the *Languages* of the world, no not so much as that of his own Country, without rendring himself ridiculous."[10]

Surveys of seventeenth-century thought on language often quote South's sermons to illustrate the theories of his contemporaries; isolated remarks of his, taken out of context, may seem to lean one way or the other

[8] *An Essay Towards A Real Character and A Philosophical Language* (London, 1668), sig. b2ʳ; see also p. 21.
[9] For opposing views, see Robert Adolph, *The Rise of Modern Prose Style*, pp. 199, 213–16, 239–40, and James Thompson, *Language in Wycherley's Plays: Seventeenth-Century Language Theory and Drama*, pp. 17–23.
[10] Wilkins, *An Essay*, sig.-blv; *Essay Concerning Human Understanding*, p. 509.

in the ongoing controversy about whether words are based on things or ideas. As I have said, South never regarded faulty communication as only a scientific problem. To quote him as if he did is, more often than not, to misrepresent him. South located human error, including errors in communication, in the deeper and darker recesses of human nature and society. On the one hand, this practice freed him from naïveté about the possibilities of reform; on the other, he is at times in need of a better scientific analysis of words. Even in his sermons on words, he can be observed using key terms of confusion as if they were value-free, when they are not.

Four sermons

South delivered his first sermon on "the fatal imposture and force of words" on 9 May 1686; the second, third and fourth are undated. In the third sermon he encourages Anglican clergymen "to serve the government, by testifying against any daring, domineering faction which would disturb it, though never so much in favour with it, no man certainly deserving the protection of the government, who does not in his place contribute to the support of it" (IV, 240). The faction that is at the same time daring, domineering, and in favor with the government seems to be Roman Catholicism; thus it appears that he gave the third sermon during James II's reign. The first sermon leads into the last three but could stand independently; the last three depend more on each other and may have been delivered after an interval of some time. The place where the sermons were delivered is not mentioned; their contents suggest a distinctly high church audience. The first sermon is theoretical in nature; the last three spell out the theory. The second details abuses of religious language, the third of political, and the fourth of language describing "the private interests of political persons." They vary in length from about 7,000 to over 9,000 words. The first was published for the first time in volume II (1694) of the *Sermons*, the last three together in volume VI (1717). The second and third sermons harshly attack religious and political figures and movements of the recent past. South left these for posthumous publication perhaps because, given the triumph of much that he disliked after 1688, he felt that they were of historical interest only. His pulpit campaign against the misrepresentation of church and monarchy had failed, and the new forms of both rested, he felt, on the very errors he had excoriated.

The text for all four sermons is the same: "Woe unto them that call evil good, and good evil" (Isa. 5:20). Here is an outline of the first sermon:

I *Exposition of the text*
    (1) nature of the woe denounced (II, 108–09)
    (2) cause of the woe: misnaming by the understanding (109–11)

II *Division and confirmation*
  (1) what is the nature of good and evil? (111–21)
     (a) that which is in accord (or not) with right reason
        (i)   opinion: good and evil are founded on opinion
        (ii) opinion: good and evil are founded in the will of the magistrate
        (iii) the absurdity of these two opinions
        (1) good and evil cannot keep changing
        (2) human law is not inherently moral
        (3) divine laws abrogate human laws
  (2) how good and evil operate on the human mind through words (121–22)
  (3) mischief follows from the misapplication of words (122–38)
     (a) most humans are enslaved by words
     (b) good and evil are accepted with implicit faith
        (i)   in particular instances, it is often difficult to distinguish good from evil
        (ii) most humans are slow and dull
     (c) two specific cases
        (i)   being deceived
        (ii) being misrepresented

Until II.3 the sermon is more unrelievedly theoretical than is South's wont. If the written form approximates the oral, the audience must have found the first half tough going. But suddenly, in three short paragraphs at the start of II.3, South compares the "generality of mankind" to "a drove of sheep or herd of oxen" and derides the "skillful manager of the rabble" who uses words such as *"popery and superstition, right of the subject, liberty of conscience, Lord Jesus Christ"* and who "may whistle them backwards and forwards, upwards and downwards, till he is weary"; he adds that few care about the meaning of a word, "only let it sound full and round, and chime right to the humor which is at present agog (just as a big, long, rattling name is said to command even adoration from a Spaniard)" (123). The sudden change in tone and topic, from a dry discussion of Aristotelian psychology to satire, common speech, and an ethnic joke, is, I think, carefully planned. South knows that his listeners have come to church expecting something livelier than Aristotelian philosophy. For the first two divisions of the confirmation, he holds off their expectations; then, in the third, he lets diatribe loose. The passage of sudden transition also exemplifies the "unseemly" South: his depiction of a rabble-rouser whistling the holy name mixes levity and the sacred in a manner that displeased many in his own and a later day. I do not doubt, however, that the congregation, so skillfully manipulated, loved it.

From the point of view of Wilkins's paradigm, the most remarkable thing about the sermon is its utter lack of an application. Neither in this or in the succeeding sermons does South offer remedies for the problems he discusses. He not only abandons the format he usually follows, but also rejects the obligation felt by secular philosophers in this area to set things right. He becomes a satirist in a nearly absolute and negative sense: he holds up the satiric mirror to human folly, but offers no positive models for improvement. Irène Simon has written of South's kinship with the "gloom" of the Tory satirists, Alexander Pope and Jonathan Swift.[11] The sermons on words, with their harsh view of mankind as sheep and oxen and their inability to find a program for change, arise from the depths of South's pessimism; his view of human nature is rarely positive, and these sermons give his sense of alienation full vent. Indeed in the first sermon, precisely at the point when we expect him to begin to offer some salutary applications to daily life, he gives only further instances of the "misapplication and confusion of those great governing names of *good* and *evil*" (133).

These sermons were written and delivered at the beginning of a dark period in South's life. His greatest hope – to be a bishop – was about to be frustrated. A Roman Catholic on the throne would lead to a reaction in 1688, in South's eyes, of an opposite extreme. The church as he wished it to be, the church of the old royalists, was not going to exist again in his lifetime. Perhaps these political developments help to account for the anger, which at times interferes with his logic, that informs the sermons on words. The theoretical nature of the first sermon puts a distance between the speaker and his emotions; in the last three South seems to lose control even over the satirical persona which is sometimes his specialty.

South selects fifteen words and phrases for discussion. I have set these out in tabular form to accentuate the process of thought, sometimes confusing, behind the analysis, and have reversed South's order of presentation. In the second and third columns appear the words and phrases whose misrepresenting power South attacks; in the first, I list the people, actions, and attitudes that the words allegedly misrepresent.

(a)	(b)	(c)
good or evil thing	*evil name for good*	*good name for evil*
II		
the church's opposition to popery	"popery"	

[11] Simon, "Robert South and the Augustans," 15–17.

attacks on the Protestant- ism of the church		"true Protestantism"
avarice and irreligion of the church's opponents		"reformation"
church's enforcement of law	"persecution"	
preaching against church privilege		"moderation"

III

royal enforcement of law	"arbitrary power"	
loyal counsellors	"evil counsellors"	
private interests		"public spirit"
the path to slavery		"rights of subjects"

IV

duels		"honor"
principle	"ill nature"	
lack of conviction		"good nature"
shallow penetration		"men of business"

Although the angry tone of the sermons carries them forward and to a certain extent unifies them, to put their ideas into schematic form isolates at least two variables that South does not call to our attention. The first concerns the logical relationship between (a) and (b) or (c). At the start this relationship is one of opposition. "Popery" and opposition to popery are spelled out in detail: South gives seven ways the Church of England opposes the Church of Rome. He makes this opposition so clear that even a Roman Catholic would have to assent to its reality, though pledged to the other side of the conflict. This full, initial discussion, a rhetorical ploy, encourages the reader to interpret subsequent relationships between things and words as oppositional, when in fact they are not. For example, "honor" is not opposed to duelling, except in the specific sense in which the former is defined; still, moral consensus holds duelling in disdain, and lets South's ploy pass. But some of his definitions are more contentious.

This brings us to the second variable, one of fact and value. Although an interpretation of language as a moral force seems reasonable, South allows his own moral, religious, and political feelings again and again to tamper with his definition of the thing named and the misnaming itself. One is at a loss to discover an objective norm. The speaker draws us into a hall of mirrors, none of which gives a true reflection of reality. Yet his contract with the reader seems to state that he is opposing illusion to reality, and misguided values to common sense and fact. For example, he ends the third sermon with the appeal to "let strict, naked, and undisguised truth take place in all things" (IV, 263). But at times South herein performs his own acts of clothing and disguising truth.

Let us take, for example, the opposition between "arbitrary power" and royal enforcement of the law. South first defines "arbitrary power" as "a prince's or governor's ruling his people according to his own absolute will and pleasure, either without law or against it" (IV, 243). Having set up an extreme definition (absolute, without or against law), South has no logical difficulty in making the claim that no power in England, at least after 1660, has been arbitrary. He then discusses the complementarity of king and Parliament in the English system, the benevolence of Charles I and Charles II, and how the alleged "arbitrary power" proves it is not so by allowing such a charge to be made against it in public. The argument nearly destroys itself when it asserts that, even if arbitrary power would exist, better it should be in the hands of a king than wielded by "a pack of spiteful, mean, merciless republicans" (247). At such a rhetorical moment, South lets his guard slip, and the objectivity of the entire enterprise of these sermons is called into doubt. The argument is also filled with a disproportionate number of rhetorical questions, and the bloody shirt of the regicide, forty years after the event, is raised to prove the dangers of dissent. Much of South's argument was, one suspects, beside the point for those who might have described governmental actions after 1660 as arbitrary. Surely they meant actions, less absolute than in South's definition, such as the expulsion of nonconforming clergy in 1662 and the abrogation of the Oxford parliament in 1681, praised by Dryden and made possible by a bribe from Louis XIV. South's definition carefully excludes such events.

The individual methods of argument of the last three sermons clash with their announced aims. On the one hand, South asserts that, once the specious naming of the opposition is cleared away, the truth is there for all to see; on the other, his sermons also indulge in specious naming. They will not or cannot enunciate the allegedly plain truth. This kind of counterstatement, where the particular units refute the general argument, differs from that of South's political sermon of 5 November 1675. There a counterstatement of images adds nuance and subtlety to what might have been simplistic propaganda; here the counterstatement does not enrich the main theme and, in a rather unpleasant way, seems to refute it. For the inability of the arguments to embody the thesis of the whole suggests a sort of hypocrisy. The author attacks others for what he himself does, or cannot avoid doing.

There are at least two ways to rationalize the conflict of statement and counterstatement. The first is to say that South was in full command of his matter and method and hoped that his audience would fail to notice the discrepancy between his announced intention and his performance. The sermons attack the "generality" of mankind as sheep and oxen, and if the reader accepts the arguments of the last three sermons, he is in the very category that is being satirized. Only by rejecting the arguments can he, paradoxically, reach the truth taught: that truth is hard to come by. An alternate explanation is less complex. South perhaps felt that his audience, already on his side and carried along by his angry presentation, would eagerly refuse to notice the inconsistency thereof. The frequent use of rhetorical questions that presume a community of shared beliefs may indicate that South knew that his audience would not be overly discriminating. Whether the reader is being trapped or taken for granted, however, the sermons betray what has to be called a cynicism about the intelligence of their audiences.

Did South, on the contrary, not realize that his arguments disproved his assumptions about the accessibility of truth? Was he ignorant of the full effect of his long presentations? Thus to interpret the sermons presupposes a lack of distance from method and text that is not characteristic of South. Likewise, it is one thing to be unaware of a discrepancy between aims and results in the short term, in the time of the sermons' composition and delivery; it is quite another to remain unaware years after the event, as the sermons are being prepared for publication. Still, biographical reasons are not wanting to explain why South might not have been in full control of his material in the last three sermons. During the reign of James II, two conflicting emotional drives tore at South. He supported the regime against its enemies; such support might secure him a bishopric and, to be fair to him, was highly consistent with his philosophy of kingship from 1660 on. Yet South was intelligent enough to hear the cracks in the foundations of that philosophy. James, he suspected, was too headstrong to last, and William of Orange waited in Holland for the call of South's enemies in England. James or William: in either case the church as South knew it was threatened. As South's sense of being threatened grew, he reacted, as humans will, by talking over the danger; his arguments grew inconsistent, and his voice rose to cover his anxiety. Perhaps on other topics he was able to simulate a rhetorical presence that effectively concealed his troubles; but, having chosen the truth of words as his topic, he alerts the reader to notice the very disjunctions that his divided self cannot avoid uttering.

The sermons depart from South's usual practice in another way. The depiction of truth as "strict, naked, and undisguised" is anomalous for South. He customarily depicts truth in images of depth and inaccessibility; he was never comfortable with the idea that truth was plain for all to see. The idea of accessible truth seems to appear, in the late seventeenth century, principally in the writings of those whom South opposed or of whose intentions he was suspicious; for example, in propaganda of the

Royal Society or, from a different point of view, in rationalist theology. For these different circles, truth would in theory always have been available to all, had not wrong scientific or philosophical theories hidden it from view. Sprat, for example, uses imagery of the nakedness of truth in his *History of the Royal Society*; the Socinian writers of the 1690s complain, against advocates of mystery, that truth is not hidden in a well, but is "like a City standing upon a Hill, which may be seen of all Men."[12] Scrape away the human confusion – either Aristotelian physics, false rhetoric, or scholastic categories – and truth will make itself known.

South habitually has a more pessimistic understanding of the relationship between subject and object wherein truth arises. For him, the object resists inquiry and does not want to let its secrets be known; the subject, radically altered by the fall, impatiently makes false starts and wrong guesses. "The mind of man," he writes in 1694, "is naturally licentious" (II, 390). Truth rarely appears, falsity often. In his last three sermons on words, South employs a model for truth from which he may have had a constitutional aversion. The inconsistencies of the sermons may partly arise from his inability to feel at home in his presuppositions.

Language and imagery

Showing more than South's customary bent for derisive language, these sermons glory in invective. South often attacked disestablished or non-established Protestants, and, in the second sermon, he openly admits that "church fanatics" present a greater danger to the Church of England than "church papists" (IV, 230). In this judgment South differs from the latitudinarian view expressed in, among other places, Gilbert Burnet's will. The second, third, and fourth sermons on words attack "church fanatics" again and again, and are inventive in their unkindness. I give a selection of epithets:

> half-witted Ahitophels
> speakers of creeping, whining, sanctified dialect
> quacks, mountebanks, and spiritual Proteuses
> a pack of designing hypocrites
> sanctified dunces
> stupid, schismatical
> half-witted corporation blockheads
> the brood and spawn of some republican cabal
> beggarly, broken, bankrupt malcontents ...

---

[12] Sprat, *The History of the Royal Society*, pp. 26, 28–29, 40, and 112–13; *An Impartial Account of the Word Mystery*, p. 13.

The course of interpretation I have been taking suggests that these attacks reflect back on the attacker: South may abuse what he most fears becoming, an outsider. But to isolate this kind of language perhaps gives it more psychological attention than it deserves. Those who came to hear South preach did not expect gentle language, and perhaps he was, in these epithets, more tending his curious reputation than revealing his soul.

Several patterns of imagery unify all four sermons. The first, involving animals and insects, illustrates the dull apprehensions of humanity and also, at times, the Hobbesian universe that allowed the violent change spoken of. Of arbitrary power wielded by a king or a republic, South writes: "it would be a much nobler death to be torn in pieces by a lion, than to be eaten up by lice" (IV, 247). False piety and fasting hide, he writes, their true intentions: "as it is observed in greyhounds, that the thinness of their jaws does not at all allay the ravening fury of their appetite" (IV, 274). The animal imagery reinforces the sense of the whole series that providence has abandoned a world where good and evil are so commonly misnamed. Humans act not in accord with a benevolent plan, but like animals, in pure self-interest; and strength and cunning seem irreversibly the victors.

Two other patterns also illustrate the insidious fatality of false words. South frequently compares words to poisoned food and drink and to fire and firearms. There is interesting variety in the latter: words are: magazines of arms, a fireship, burning churches, incendiaries, *boutefeus*, or torches used to light cannon, grenadoes, fiery darts, and so on. Again, taking these images cumulatively perhaps overly accentuates their grimness; in context, South's discovery of grounds of comparison between the Scottish covenant and a "great engine of battery" (IV, 232–33) surely brought with it a satisfaction at his own inventiveness. In these sermons South is not always so close to his project that he cannot be pleased with his own artistry.

The first sermon, on theory, is, as I have said, calmer than the last three. Perhaps by 9 May 1686, when the first was given, South had not greatly felt the press of change to his church and career; perhaps the other sermons were given when the future had become more ominous. The Aristotelian analysis of the first sermon keeps his anger at bay; partly to the same purpose, he brings classical history into his argument. In dismissing the possibility that good and evil rest on cultural opinion, he refers to two moral misnamings in classical history: thievery counted as a virtue in Sparta, and suicide commended similarly in Greece and Rome, as shown in the deaths of Cato and Atticus (II, 114). He illustrates the fondness of humanity for grand names by telling the story of Julius Caesar's calming of mutinous troops by giving them "the appellation of

Quirites," or knighthood (123–24). He quotes Seneca on flattery, and Cicero on the possibility that villains may be caught in their own schemes (126, 136).

These classical references tell us something about South's own reading. Some of these references are from Plutarch, a standard source for Graeco-Roman biography, but some, such as the anecdote about Caesar, are not; South's reading is wide. South does not hesitate to criticize Roman morality; especially Cato and Atticus, because of their republican sympathies, might have been easy targets for reproach. It is likely that South quoted Cicero and Seneca from memory. His quotation from Cicero's *Pro Milone*, which he names, is word-perfect. His quotation from Seneca's *Naturales Quaestiones*, which he does not name, is not. South writes, "Blanditiae, etiam cum excluduntur, placent" for Seneca's "habent hoc in se naturale blanditiae: etiam cum reiciuntur placent."[13] Throughout the humanist tradition, this kind of slight misquotation is not uncommon. South's error does not change the meaning, but does show his habit of quoting from the fund of material stored up in his memory from his days at Westminster School and Christ Church. It is not surprising that Cicero's *Pro Milone*, a much more popular text than Seneca's *Quaestiones*, is quoted correctly.

These references to classical literature are symbols of South's deeper commitment to traditional norms of thought and behavior. Although his sermons on the abuse of words end in a confusion of intentions, the beginning of the first sermon stands as a testament to the values and methods of composition that make him a great preacher. In his philosophical exegesis at the very start of the first sermon, South nearly overwhelms the problem he poses with his command of classical thought. He begins by reaffirming the Aristotelian and medieval doctrine that the human will is by nature capable of choosing only the good, and "shuns and flies from" the "odious deformity in vice" (109). Against this metaphysical analysis of human psychology, he places the evidence of experience: experience shows that, in spite of what human nature is, the "lives and practices of the generality of men ... are almost wholly took up in a passionate pursuit of what is evil, and in an equal neglect, if not an abhorrence, of what is good" (109). Metaphysical psychology also explains why this is so: although the will can only choose good, it depends on the understanding to present good to it. The intellect, fatally hurt by the fall, confuses good and evil. The intellect must choose between meanings that language places on things, and this is a difficult task. South gives a mini-parable of Attic brevity to illustrate his point: "One man gives another a cup of poison, a

---

[13] Both South and Seneca have roughly the same meaning: even when flattery is refused, it is pleasing. See Seneca, *Naturales Quaestiones*, II, text and trans. Thomas H. Corcoran (Cambridge, MA: Harvard University Press, 1972), p. 4.

thing as terrible as death; but at the same time he tells him that it is a cordial, and so he drinks it off, and dies" (110). The intellect is the only passage from the will's natural choice of the good to the disorder of experience, and the intellect, fatally open to conflicting opinion, habitually misnames good evil and evil good.

South never rests on the heights of metaphysics, as no successful preacher can. He invokes experience to complicate abstraction, then draws on biblical history to enrich both. He composes a Midrash of his own on the fall of Adam: God said that eating the fruit of the tree would bring death, and Satan misnames the primal act of choice as a bid for immortality and angelic perfection. "God commanded and told man what was good," South writes, "but the devil surnamed it evil, and thereby baffled the command, turned the world topsyturvy, and brought a new chaos upon the whole creation" (111). Biblical and colloquial, experiential and metaphysical language vie with one another to repeat the cosmic struggle on the level of style.

South's love of analogy is evident in these sermons; he tries to find the same pattern of activity repeated on metaphysical, moral, psychological, experiential, and political levels of reality. Each false act of speech repeats the act of temptation in the garden. The innocence told about in Scripture logically prefigures the natural, human drive towards the good, the true, and the beautiful. Granted a particular set of political beliefs, words of treason against Charles II or James II parallel and partake of the primal fault. Philosophy, experience, and Scripture are one in their teaching about the fatal imposture of words. The unity of reason and Scripture was the basis of all orthodox Anglican thought in the late seventeenth century, latitudinarian or high church. Only a few great preachers, like South, could image this unity in brief and dramatic segments of argument.

For South, the "new chaos" of the verbal universe arises from several sources. For Wilkins and Locke, whatever lip-service may be paid to Adamic language, this chaos is only a philosophical problem to be solved and, to a certain extent, remedied, by new verbal techniques based on clear analysis. The price of clarity is a divorce from the sort of analogical thinking that South loves. The new philosophy builds its new languages in painstaking fashion, in almost methodical doubt of what has gone on before. South, on the other hand, has little to offer in the great, gray area between theological and metaphysical analysis and the way the mass of people act. The leap to experience, as his last three sermons on words show, hurts him. Avoiding, perhaps scorning the new science of words, not really caring whether words refer to things or ideas, not paying close enough attention to his own point of view, he presents a flawed analysis of the disjunction between religious and political words and what they ideally represent. Only the linguistic analysis of the philosophers provides a safe path, if objectivity is at all possible, through the wasteland of propaganda. It is likely that South realized this in some limited way; but, confused by his own political and moral habits, perhaps deafened by his desire to amuse, he raised his voice in partisan invective to drown out his self-doubt.

5

South on the sacrament

The wedding feast

Among the several late seventeenth-century Anglican authors who extensively discussed the sacrament of the Lord's Supper was Jeremy Taylor
(1613–67), a theologian of the generation before South's; he was, after the
Restoration, raised to the Irish see of Down and Connor, a suitable reward
for his steady but undramatic royalism. In 1650 Taylor published his *Rules
for Holy Living*, one of several of his works that discuss the sacrament. As
C. W. Dugmore has made clear, Taylor's teaching on the sacrament is in
the high church or Laudian – it is difficult to formulate a single adjective
for this branch of the church at this time – tradition: that is, he firmly
insisted on the real, spiritual presence of Christ in the communication of
the elements of bread and wine, at the same time as he rejected the Roman
Catholic theory of transubstantiation, or that the bread and wine became
in substance the body and blood of Christ.[1]

In his discussion of 1650 Taylor stressed, as many other writers had and
would, the necessity of a solid preparation for receiving the sacrament. To
illustrate one of his main points, that preparation must be habitual as well
as immediate, he alludes to a text from Matthew's version of the parable of
the wedding feast (Matt. 22:1–14) which tells of a wedding guest who is
ousted from the feast because he is improperly attired. Taylor interprets
the text as applying to those who receive the sacrament without proper
preparation: "he that comes to this feast, must have on the wedding
garment, that is, he must have put on Jesus Christ, and he must have put
off the old man with his affections and lusts."[2] In his reading of Matthew
22, Taylor creates a symbolism useful for his immediate purposes: the text
about the wedding garment is brought up to illustrate a discussion about
the necessity of perduring reformation for a worthy reception of the
sacrament. The application is not hermetic or opaque. Without apology,

---

[1] C. W. Dugmore, *Eucharistic Doctrine in England from Hooker to Waterland* (London: SPCK, 1942),
pp. 90–102; see also Dugmore's sensible discussion of the difficulty of applying "Laudian" and
"high church" labels at this time, pp. 68–70.
[2] Taylor, *Whole Works* (London: Frederick Westley and A. H. Davits, 1835), I, 498.

the interpretation is accomplished, and the reader understands it quickly; the argument moves on.

Robert South had no great interest in preaching about the sacrament of the Lord's Supper; he did not make it one of his great themes, and in this he resembled his latitudinarian contemporaries, Stillingfleet and Tillotson, in whose writings the sacrament also does not greatly figure. South did include one sermon on the sacrament among the seventy-two he edited and published; on Palm Sunday, 8 April 1688, in Westminster Abbey, he preached on sacramental preparation, using for his text, "And he saith unto him, Friend, how camest thou in hither not having a wedding garment?" (Matt. 22:12), the same text employed by Taylor in his remarks in *Holy Living* on preparation. South's handling of the text, however, greatly differs from Taylor's, and this difference illustrates, in brief, the suspicion of metaphor and allegorical interpretation that had come to dominate the writing of prose, particularly exegetical prose, after 1660.[3]

South shows great nervousness about applying the text to the sacrament, and before discussing his method, it will be helpful to see the story of the improperly clad guest in its context. Matthew begins his account by telling us that Jesus "spake unto them in parables" (22:1). A king sends out invitations to his son's wedding, the invited guests refuse to come, mistreat the king's envoys, and receive their punishment; the king then sends his servants out "into the highways" to gather together "all as many as they found, both bad and good" (22:10).

And when the king came in to see the guests, he saw there a man which had not on a wedding garment: and he saith unto him, Friend, how comest thou in hither not having a wedding garment? And he was speechless. Then the king said to the servants, Bind him hand and foot, and take him away, and cast him into outer darkness; there shall be weeping and gnashing of teeth. For many are called, but few are chosen.   (22:11–14)

South begins his exegesis by noting that "the whole scheme of these words is figurative" (II, 80). That is, Jesus is not talking about a literal wedding feast, but through the literal story wants to communicate truths about his Father, himself, and their action in the world, "God's vouchsafing to the world the invaluable blessing of the gospel" (81), which meets with a varied response. Especially since Matthew has prefaced the account by saying that this is one of Jesus's "parables," this is fairly obvious exegesis; but South's exegetical inheritance insists that, if a text is not taken at its literal value, any alternate method of reading must be carefully

---

[3] Commentators relate a tradition that South preached a sermon in 1668, shortly after Taylor's death, that in part attacks his prose style. Although it is unlikely that South would preach a sermon against a Bishop of the Church of Ireland, Simon shows that in at least one paragraph of the sermon South quotes Taylor in distaste (Simon, I, 52–54).

explained. South then acknowledges that the primary, figurative meaning of the text, having to do with a call to participation in the kingdom of God, although once removed from literal meaning, is the "design of this parable," or the intention of the author. Accompanying this discussion is a warning that in reading the "analogy" of the parables, one cannot hope for exact, item-by-item correspondence of the "metaphorical part" and "the thing intended by it" (81).

South rarely labors so over the obvious. He is not yet, of course, where he wants to be, for he intends to move to a secondarily figurative meaning, that the invitation to the wedding feast implies not only the general call to belief, but a specific call to partaking of the sacrament. Taylor, who belongs to an exegetical generation not so constricted by the bonds of literalism, moves without effort, without even mentioning his tactic, to the second level of figuration; the history of Christian exegesis doubtless offers many instances of the same easy movement away from this very text. To get to this second level, South writes that there is "one principal privilege" of the gospel that the text "seems more particularly to aim at, or at least may more appositely and emphatically be applied to, than to any other whatsoever: and that is the blessed sacrament of the eucharist" (82).

At this point the strained apology for figurative interpretation begins to pay a dividend, for, still nervous, South gives three reasons that legitimate his interpretation, and these lay bare the heart of his theological method here and elsewhere. First, in a "genuine, proper, as well as common and received appellation," the word "supper" applies both to a wedding feast and to the eucharist; the idea of supper does not apply to the sacrament of baptism and, granting an analogical framework, the eucharist must be the sacrament that the text illuminates. Second, the eucharist can even be called a "*wedding supper*." Christ tells us elsewhere that he is wedded to the church in "nuptial endearments," and these "eminently and effectually" are present, if anywhere, in the reception of the sacrament of his body and blood. Third, history tells us that in some eastern countries the marriage covenant was sealed by the breaking of bread. South tells a story from Quintus Curtius Rufus, an obscure Latin historian of the first century after Christ, that at the wedding of Alexander the Great to the Persian princess Roxana, Alexander "divided a piece of bread with his sword, of which each of them took a part, and so thereby the nuptial rites were performed." Both marriage and the eucharist have the nature of a "covenant," and feasting symbolizes "full and perfect accord" (83).

South situates himself, by means of these reasons, in regard to various aspects of ancient and modern thought. The first testifies to his concern for the proper use of words and his desire to avoid the idiosyncrasy of linguistic usage that his contemporaries deplored: he assures us that it is commonly accepted that "supper" properly applies to both wedding and sacrament. The second shows his awareness, not often evident in his works, of a medieval exegesis that emphasized mystical readings of parts of the Old and New Testaments. The language of mystical marriage clashes with South's previously expressed concern for precise signification; he knows that the nature of the sacrament will not allow him to trim his argument only to what is fashionable in his own day. The third reason assumes the legitimacy of a search of ancient history for analogies to sacred Christian actions. This analogical reading of secular literature also conflicts with the otherwise ordered method South usually employs. Wilkins's model suggests that "Other *Parallel* or like *Scriptures*" may be introduced into the exegesis; to allude to classical literature does not stretch the point greatly. This context suggests, however, that South felt that classical literature itself was a kind of Scripture or inspired text in this case, that it was not by accident that the ancient wedding ceremony resembled a banquet, and that some kind of typological relationship between secular and sacred texts had been intended by a divine author. In his studied exegesis of the text, South shows himself as a man both in and out of his time, anxious to please his contemporaries and, in the same instant, faithful to earlier and less rationalistic methods of reading.

Text and sermon

There is an obvious question to be asked about South's choice of text; if he wanted to talk about sacramental preparation, and if he was nervous about reading Matthew 21:12 allegorically, why did he not choose a text that spoke in the literal sense about or gave an historical account of sacramental preparation? He could have used, for example, "For he that eateth and drinketh unworthily, eateth and drinketh damnation unto himself, not discerning the Lord's body" (I Cor. 11:29), or a number of other texts that would not have required extended apologies about figuration. The question is a good one, for it illuminates South's accomplishment in the sermon. Like all his works, it is written in the plain style: division, sentences, and paragraphs try to imitate the design of the things themselves – or at least the rational components that South's age liked to find in things. Yet more than in many of his sermons, self-regarding style here cuts across and moderates plain style. South equally accentuates how his subject is being grasped and communicated and what its dimensions are. The intellectual content of the sermon is, in fact, pedestrian; South eliminates from consideration, for example, most of the subtler questions about the sacrament that had agitated Anglicans for over a century. In the place of abstract inquiry, metaphor, image patterns, and aphorisms abound. The initial discussion about analogy and figurative interpretation forms part of this concentration of style over substance. In other words, there are, in this sermon, at least two main themes: sacramental preparation and something more subjectively subtle, that is, the very craft of interpretation and writing.

Here is an outline of the sermon:

I *Exposition of the text*
  (1) the whole scope and design of the parable of the wedding feast (II, 81–82)
  (2) how various circumstances suggest that preparation for the sacrament of the Lord's Supper is also meant by the text (82–84)

II *Division and confirmation*
  (1) a suitable preparation is necessary to receive the sacrament (84–95)
    (a) necessary
      (i) Old Testament and "heathen" practices
      (ii) what experience tells us
    (b) suitable
      (i)   the nearness of Easter
      (ii) habitual preparation
      (iii) actual preparation
  (2) the several parts of actual preparation (95–107)
    (a) self-examination
    (b) sorrow and remorse for sin
    (c) prayer
    (d) abstinence and fasting
    (e) almsgiving
    (f) charity
    (g) reading and meditation

The outlined contents present three anomalies. First, the exegesis is more detailed than is usual, owing, as I have shown, to South's self-consciousness in using a secondarily figurative meaning of the text to preach on. Second, there is, strictly speaking, no application. The second part of the division (II.2, a through g), however, listing seven ways to prepare for the sacrament, seems sufficiently applicatory for South to excuse himself, in this instance, from following the full Wilkins paradigm. Third, as he outlines his divisions, he announces that the second part will explain that "God is a strict observer of, and a severe animadverter upon, such as presume to partake of those mysteries, without such a preparation" (84). Although scattered sentences and paragraphs allude to this point, South never handles it separately, as he says he will; the seven practical steps of preparation take the place assigned to a discussion of God's strict observance of the unprepared.

I can think of no satisfactory explanation for this discrepancy between intention and execution, except that here one may glimpse something of the editorial process involved in publishing these sermons. Perhaps the preaching text had a final section on God's action, for which South substituted the seven stages of preparation; these were either originally composed for this publication, or taken from another sermon on the same theme. Like the cancelled section on God's action, the rest of that sermon is now lost. In an oral presentation, the discrepancy between outline and development would have been, I think, noticeable. This is not so in a printed version. Only repeated readings allow one to notice the problem; any reader who is not concentrating solely on the outline and its fulfillment will easily miss the omission.

South's particular grasp of the sacrament of the Lord's Supper is, obviously, preparation. At least two other divines, Taylor and Simon Patrick (1626–1707), a prominent latitudinarian and, after 1688, Bishop of Chichester and then of Ely, wrote extensively on this topic. Both Taylor and Patrick concentrate on the interior dispositions of sacramental preparation, especially an awareness of sin and the power of the theological virtues, faith, hope, and charity.[4] South's treatment stresses Christian action in the community, and thus departs from Taylor's and Patrick's treatment. Revised editions of *Ecclesiastes* recommend their writings as necessary readings for preachers who want to talk about the eucharist.[5] But it does not matter whether South knew their work, since Christian writers had gone over the themes they discuss again and again. Likewise, the originality of South's stress on action is improbable, for surely some other seventeenth-century texts read similarly. That action at the sacramental table and action in the world should be congruous is not a startling insight.

Those with a knowledge of and affection for the Christian church year may find South's choice of a subject on 8 April 1688 disappointing. Although Palm Sunday fell on this date, the sermon never mentions the triumphant narrative of Jesus' entry into Jerusalem, and it scarcely alludes to the church's imminent celebration of his passion, death, and resurrection. Instead, South interprets Palm Sunday through the prism of a rubric of the Prayer Book. After the order for communion is given, the Prayer Book sets out several rubrics concerning reception, among them one regarding frequency: "And note, that every parishioner shall communicate at the least three times in the year, of which Easter to be one."[6] To prepare the congregation of Westminster Abbey to make its Easter

---

[4] See Taylor, *Whole Works*, I, 497–99; III, 878–955; and Patrick, *Works*, ed. Alexander Taylor (Oxford: Oxford University Press, 1858), I, 180–232.

[5] *Ecclesiastes*, p. 181.

[6] *The Annotated Book of Common Prayer*, ed. John Henry Blunt (New York: E. P. Dutton, 1884), p. 399 and note.

"duty," South chose to preach, the week before, on dispositions and actions suitable for reception. He dislocates the meaning of Palm Sunday from its context in the Christian year to its relevance for the observance of church order.

Dugmore notes, without alluding to South, that the theme of intense preparation for receiving the sacrament was present especially in Laudian or high church writing. Latitudinarians such as Tillotson, he writes, felt that frequency of reception – the Prayer Book rubric was not meant to discourage more than thrice-yearly communion – might be hurt if preachers placed too great a stress on preparation. Dugmore's supporting evidence is suggestive, though not overwhelming on this point.[7] It is clear that Patrick stressed preparation in 1660, perhaps before the lines had begun to harden between high church and latitudinarian parties – if indeed there ever was a hardening along party lines on frequency of reception. Because prominent latitudinarians preached so infrequently on the sacrament, it is unlikely that evidence fully to corroborate Dugmore's thesis exists.

One way of defining the qualitative difference between South's treatment and others' is to evaluate his use of another frequently used image in sacramental preparation. One commonplace occurs in a number of sermons and treatises: that preparation for receiving Christ in the sacrament should approximate one's reaction to a visit from or to an earthly king. South uses the analogy thus:

> For who, that is to appear before his prince or patron, would not view and review himself over and over, with all imaginable care and solicitude, that there be nothing justly offensive in his habit, language, or behaviour? But especially, if he be vouchsafed the honour of his table, it would be infinitely more absurd and shameful to appear as foul and sordid there; and in the dress of the kitchen, receive the entertainments of the parlor.   (85)

South stresses the active preparation ("language, or behaviour") that characterizes his whole treatment. Though he does not slight interior dispositions, this passage and the sermon as a whole run the risk of playing down the role of divine help, or grace, in sacramental preparation. The sermon tends to make the gift of the sacrament God's thing, and its reception man's, and this kind of rationalism is not really orthodox. Given the human corruptibility South elsewhere preaches, and his stated opposition to Pelagianism (II, 254–57), it would follow that even preparation must be a graced activity. But this is one of the finer points that the sermon avoids discussing.

The second edition of *Certain Sermons and Homilies to Be Read in Churches* (1571), published to provide Anglican clergy with proper treatments of

---

[7] *Eucharistic Doctrine*, pp. 136, 159.

central Christian themes and doctrines, contains a sermon on sacramental preparation; this sermon also uses the commonplace of dining at a king's table. An Anglican classic, the book was republished even after 1660. The sermon on sacramental preparation reads, in part:

use the advice of the Wise Man, who willeth thee, when thou sittest at an earthly king's table, to take diligent heed what things are set before thee [Prov. 3: 21]. So now much more at the King of kings' table thou must carefully search and know what dainties are provided for the soul; whither thou art come, not to feed thy senses and belly to corruption, but the inward man to immortality and life.[8]

Not untypical of the homily's general approach, the passage stresses the necessity of faith in and knowledge of what the sacrament is. In its opposition of soul to sense, this version of the commonplace probably alludes to traditional Anglican opposition to transubstantiation: Anglicans argue the real but spiritual presence of Christ as the sacrament is received. This kind of careful discrimination too is generally absent from South's sermon.

In *Mensa Mystica* (1660), Patrick interprets the commonplace differently again; he stresses that even preparation for the king's visit is part of the king's gift.

As when a king comes into a city to stay there for some space, he doth not expect that the citizens (if they be poor) should provide all the furniture for him, which is a thing above their power; but he sends the grooms of his chamber before with such hangings and ornaments as may make the house they have prepared most befitting his majesty; so let us entreat the Lord, that after all our endeavours to set apart our hearts for him, to sweep the house as clean as we can, and for to receive such a glorious guest; he would be pleased to send his Holy Spirit, that may prepare the place for him, and adorn our souls with such traces, that his sacred Majesty may not disdain to come and make his abode with us.[9]

As early as 1660, Patrick has mastered the art of the ordered similitude. He restrains and concentrates his vehicle; both vehicle and that which it illustrates teach correct truths. Among these are that proper sacramental preparation may be impossible for believers (the "poor") and that kingly assistance, even before communion is received, may be necessary.

Patrick was not a Laudian ritualist; he seems confident that his audience will not mistake "hangings and ornaments" for church furnishings. The images refer entirely to interior preparations, or received "graces," habitually or immediately given to recipients of the sacrament. To the extent that it gives God more to do, and acknowledges human poverty, Patrick's treatment is more orthodox, or at least more sensitive to Scripture than South's. These passages from the *Homilies* and Patrick suggest,

---

[8] *Certain Sermons and Homilies Appointed to Be Read in Churches* (London, 1683), p. 282.
[9] *Works*, I, 214.

by way of contrast, a want of thought or emotion in South's use of the commonplace of the kingly visit. Knowingly or not, here and elsewhere in the sermon, he drew back from drawing on certain riches that his own Anglican tradition made available to him on the subject of sacramental preparation.

Anglican tradition

By narrowing his purchase on the sacrament to preparation, South avoids discussing more than a theory of grace and action. That part of the Anglican tradition on the sacrament left in pales in importance to what is left out. In the 150 years before South gave his sermon, four principal themes dominated Anglican discussion of the eucharist.

(1) *The nature of the sacrament*: Anglicans taught that Christ was truly received with and through the elements of bread and wine, but not in them. That is, they apparently universally rejected the Roman Catholic doctrine of transubstantiation as a correct formulation of how the body and blood of Christ were communicated to the believer. Fully approved by the Council of Trent at its thirteenth session in 1551, this doctrine explained that the bread and wine were changed in substance into the body and blood of Christ. Anglicans considered this doctrine a scholastic folly and violation of the rules of sense evidence. These rules were important to Anglican apologetics, particularly since divines used witnesses to miracles as part of the proof for the authenticity of Scripture; a violation of sense evidence in one area, they felt, might lead to a probative chaos that would affect other areas of doctrine.

South wrote from time to time against transubstantiation. Because he felt that Protestant sects presented a greater danger to the Church of England than Roman Catholics did, and because he thus exposed himself to the charge of romanizing, he may have experienced a sense of relief in finding in transubstantiation a Roman doctrine he could unreservedly assail. The sermon on sacramental preparation, however, almost completely ignores the controversy over substantial change in the elements. Only in several references to "spiritual eating" and "spiritual food" (88, 91), does one find, perhaps allusions to specifically Anglican doctrine in this area.

(2) *The institution of the sign*: Roman Catholic theology had traditionally taught that the words of institution ("On the night before he died, Jesus took bread ... ") provided the occasion for the instantaneous consecration of the bread and wine. In the seventeenth century, Anglican theologians often reflected on what actions were necessary so that the elements of bread and wine might achieve sacramental reality. The institution narrative, prayers and actions accompanying it, and a special prayer of invo-

cation to the Holy Spirit were discussed in this regard. As Richard F. Buxton analyzes the matter, some combination of these actions and words was generally thought to be efficacious; Buxton stresses the continuity of more precise definition with what went before as the controversy, if it was that, unfolded.[10] The discussion became involved with revisions suggested in the Prayer Book, and surely South knew about these; nothing in the sermon on preparation, however, shows this knowledge. He carefully excludes theological reflection about the institution of the sign from his consideration.

(3) *The eucharist as sacrifice*: before and after South lived, Anglican divines were anxious to insist both that the sacrament was central to Christian life and that it in no way replaced or diminished the unique sacrifice of Christ on the hill of Calvary. One sacrifice, once offered: this was a cardinal tenet not only of Anglican but of European Protestant faith. The word "sacrifice" might be used in a number of senses to refer to the sacrament, but not so as to suggest that it was a "propitiatory" sacrifice for sin; the sacrifice of Calvary was propitiation enough for all time.

In South's later years and soon after his death, nonjurors and high church theologians began to call the sacrament, usually in guarded ways, a propitiatory sacrifice; they also began to write about the presence of Christ not only through but in the elements. As J. H. Overton writes:

The nonjurors assigned the very highest importance to the Holy Eucharist as the central act of Christian ownership. Not only so; they insisted strongly on its sacrificial character. Everything that could elevate the Holy Sacrament and bring out prominently its sacrificial aspect would be likely to find acceptance with them.[11]

Although South sympathized with the plight of the nonjurors, he showed no interest at all in adopting their revisionist frame of mind and terminology. There is, I think, no sign anywhere that South held a high church sacramental theology, and certainly not in his treatment of sacramental preparation. The nature and institution of the sacrament of the Lord's Supper, and the changed understanding of these occurring in South's later years, were topics that do not appear to have interested him.

(4) *Frequency of reception*: "at the Restoration," writes J. Wickham Legg, "with a population unaccustomed to approach the Holy Table, even at Easter, it was exceedingly uphill work to carry out the Church's intention

[10] Buxton, *Eucharist and Institution Narrative: A Study in the Roman and Anglican Traditions of the Consecration of the Eucharist from the Eighth to the Twentieth Centuries*, Alcuin Club Collections, no. 58 (Great Wakering: Mayhew-McCrimmon, 1976), pp. 110–32, 153–76.
[11] Overton, *The Nonjurors: Their Lives, Principles and Writings* (London: Smith, Elder, 1902), p. 291; see also the survey of some of these writers in C. F. Secretan, *Memoirs of the Life and Times of the Pious Robert Nelson* (London, 1860), pp. 172–79.

of a celebration [of the sacrament] on every day for which a collect, epistle, and gospel were provided."[12] Legg assembles the evidence on frequency of reception after 1660, as well as the repeated exhortations of the clergy towards this end. Party politics in the church did not seem to weaken the general opinion that more frequent reception was desirable.

Of this there is nothing in South's sermon. Because of the close relationship between preparation and reception, the omission is bothersome. This is not only a matter of South's not conforming to contemporary church practice; to deal with preparation and not frequency also seems intellectually sloppy. As Dugmore notes that Tillotson worried, the two activities had to be related if sound practice were to develop: an overemphasis on preparation may easily have cut down frequency of reception. Taylor, for one, handles the topics concurrently: in his *Worthy Communicant* (1660), his method of presentation shows the reader how frequency and preparation go hand in hand.[13] South does not develop this side of things at all. It is reasonable to suppose that he was either against or indifferent to frequent reception of the sacrament.

In reading South and other seventeenth-century divines, one must be careful not to read back into that time categories of controversy that developed later in English church history. One aspect of the sermon on preparation, its discussion of conversion, seems, nevertheless, decidedly evangelical. South sums up habitual preparation for the sacrament in the idea of conversion; he expresses doubt whether conversion refers to the sacrament of baptism, to later (presuming infant baptism) changes of heart, or both. South uses the phrases "new birth" and "new man" to refer not to baptism, which is their classical, Pauline reference, but to

that mighty spiritual change which we call conversion ... [of] a man, whose nature is renewed, whose heart is changed, and the stream of whose appetites is so turned, that he does with as high and quick a relish taste the ways of duty, holiness, and strict living, as others, or as he himself before this, grasped at the most enamouring proposals of sin. (90)

The eucharist is intended to preserve "that spiritual life, which we do or should receive in baptism, or at least by a thorough conversion after it" (91). Later developments in Anglicanism lead one to press South's thought to see if he means that conversion is the larger category that encompasses baptism. Is he in an anti-sacramental, or an evangelical position? The development of his ideas, however, gives way before such questioning. He does not seem to be concerned, here and elsewhere in the sermon, with fine distinctions about sacramental life.

---

[12] Legg, *English Church Life from the Restoration to the Tractarian Movement, Considered in Some of Its Neglected or Forgotten Features* (London: Longmans, Green, 1914), p. 21.

[13] Dugmore, *Eucharistic Doctrine*, pp. 136, 159; Taylor, *Whole Works*, III, 938.

Explanation for South's avoidance of major and minor points of controversy about the sacraments can be sought in several directions. Nothing
about this sermon contradicts the tone and content of his whole body of
work: politically high church, he was not so in regard to the sacramental
life of the church. For South, the sacraments involved a personal relationship with God with which the theological technician had better not
tamper, except perhaps to list, as this sermon does, ways in which to
prepare for the sacramental encounter.

South's sense of ordered rhetoric also prompts him to avoid complication. Having chosen the Wilkins model – second nature to him by 1688 –
he stays to the stated topic, preparation. The model did not encourage
forays into allied topics, in this case, the nature of the sacrament or
frequency of reception; its strength lay in the full exploration of one, not
parallel themes. It encouraged thoroughness, not subtlety or paradox, and
made the pleasures of second thought or afterthought forbidden.

The occasion of this sermon offers the fullest explanation of its non-
controversial nature. It is possible that many in the congregation at
Westminster Abbey on Palm Sunday 1688 would only be receiving the
sacrament once that year, on the following Sunday. For some the yearly
communion would be a pious duty undertaken for personal reasons; for
others it would have more worldly benefits. Office-holders, for example,
may have felt obliged to prove that they were members of the national, not
the disestablished or Roman churches. Throughout the seventeenth and
eighteenth centuries, reception of the eucharist in Anglican churches was
not without its technical, legal repercussions. Perhaps South felt that,
given the wide variety of personal dispositions in a congregation, the
preparation for the annual communion was no time to bring up differences in doctrine that might make it more difficult for the weak and
alienated to accomplish their duty.

South shared the latitudinarian belief that the saving truths of Scripture
were few and plain. The preacher had better stress that the salvation of his
congregation rested on its adherence to a few, important, truths than to
belabor it with theological theories. This kind of common-sense thinking is
present throughout seventeenth-century Anglicanism, from the work of
William Chillingworth in the 1630s to that of Locke at the end of the
century. Applying the spirit of this intellectual canon to another level,
South's sermon on the sacrament avoids getting into technical discussion;
he makes the sacrament simply a matter of God's revelation – not very
carefully explained – to individual believers who must work hard to be
ready for it. The image of a preacher who waters down doctrine to make it
acceptable is surely a strange one for South; he is rarely this accommodating. The sacrament, however, was a special case, a central act of
religion that even he may have felt should be kept apart from politics.

The argument of this sermon offers a number of excellent examples of the mixed proofs favored by seventeenth-century Anglican divines. Let us take as an illustration South's discussion of the necessity of preparation. This takes up about 1,500 words, in preamble to the most distinctive part of the sermon, the seven ways of preparation. It is doubtful that South really sets out to prove the necessity of preparation for the sacrament, a point with which no congregation, almost by the fact of their attendance, would argue. Rather he wants to show the congruence of scriptural, heathen, and experiential evidence in supporting the proposition; this assembly of sources, not the proposition itself, makes the argument interesting. South begins by discussing how preparations for death and for meeting a prince or patron offer useful models for sacramental preparation (84–85). He writes of Jewish priests who carefully prepare to enter the sanctuary or to celebrate the sabbath (85–86); he also discusses sacrifices made by "heathens" and preparation thereto (87). He begins to end the argument in a return to experience, which shows that "business" makes "the recollections and disciplines of the spirit" difficult (87–88). His last example returns again to the "very commendable" Jewish practice of washing before meals, and how Christians might find symbolic relevance in this as they approach "God's table" (88).

South punctuates his movement from one sort of evidence to another with highly self-conscious signposts. He draws the reader's attention to his methodology in various ways. Some signposts concern social behavior:

The very rules of worldly civility might instruct men how to order their addresses God.   (85)

our washing is to be like our eating, both of them spiritual; that we are to carry it from the hand to the heart, to improve a ceremonial nicety into a substantial duty, and the modes of civility into the realities of religion.   (88)

Or reason and revelation:

the necessity of men's preparing themselves for the sacred offices of religion was a lesson which the mere light and dictates of common reason, without the help of revelation, taught all the knowing and intelligent part of the world.   (86)

Or the forceful lessons of experience:

he that shall thoroughly consider what the heart of man is, what sin and the world is, and what it is to approve one's self to an all-searching eye, in so sublime a duty as the sacrament, must acknowledge that a man may as well go about it without a soul, as without preparation.   (87)

The sermon playfully and repeatedly calls attention to its own methodology. South here celebrates the unanimity of its sources of evidence.

The sermon also simultaneously presses forward two arguments. The

first is the argument at hand, concerning the necessity of preparation for
the sacrament. The intellectual content of this first argument is slim, the
exception to the rule in South's sermons. The second argument uses
methodology as an emblem of an entire theological project. The different
types of evidence – from reason, Scripture, experience, history and so on –
always argue, by the very fact of their coexistence, that the truths of
Christianity are not narrowly based on partisan evidence. Usually the
form of a sermon makes this point without a great deal of comment; the
sermon on sacramental preparation is different only in that it calls so much
attention to its probative resources. This *concordia discors* of truths, a
wholeness amidst difference, argues that the truth of Christianity, resting
on reason and faith, revelation, history, and experience, should be irresistible to an intelligent person. Each argument is an emblem of the over-
powering and uniform witness of different sources of truth.

Imagery

The image patterns of the sermon, arising naturally from text and subject-
matter, concern clothing, dirt and cleansing, and eating. The imagery is
abundant and occasionally humorous. At one point it reflects back on
itself in a startling way. In talking of fasting, his fourth "actual" preparation, South explores the paradox that deprivation of food is a kind of
nourishment: "fasting is the diet of angels, the food and reflection of souls,
and the richest and highest aliment of grace. And he who fasts for the sake
of religion, *hungers and thirsts after righteousness*, without a metaphor" (102).
The brief apology "without a metaphor," presumes that the audience has
grown conscious of the metaphorical nature of the immediately preceding
and, perhaps, of the sermon as a whole. The oral delivery of this passage
would have made its tone clearer than the printed page can. Did South
draw attention to the artificiality of his discourse in other oral ways that
now escape us? Why does he break his thought in this way? He is probably
not, thirty years into his preaching career, nervous about his preaching
style. He has written a contract with the audience which the later reader
has difficulty reconstructing: an invitation to enjoy, with the preacher, his
artifice in building a sermon.

The most highly developed image pattern, growing out of the text,
concerns clothing. South deftly turns this imagery this way and that,
talking about, for example, tailoring and pockets, and it always refers in
some way to preparation. No one can get the necessary garment "for
nothing" (81), and it must always fit the occasion (88). Preparations for
next week's communion should be as careful as one's choice of "Easter
dress" (89). Self-examination is the only tailor that makes the garment of
suitable preparation (96). Preparation involves actions such as clothing

the naked and feeding the hungry; "God and man will find it a very unfit garment for such a purpose, which has not in it a purse or pocket for the poor" (103). Failing to carry out one's Christian duties after receiving the eucharist will "fatally unravel all again" the good done in preparation (107). South's wittiest development of the imagery addresses the self-examination of those who refuse to face up to their sins. He calls such failures "short reckonings" and continues: "What pitiful fig-leaves, what senseless and ridiculous shifts are these, not able to silence, and much less to satisfy, an accusing conscience!" (97). In other places South explores the relation of the sins of his own time with Adam's; here he only touches on the theme, backing away quickly from it, and unable to resist the pun in "shifts."

South uses the image patterns of this sermon tamely: the imagery of clothing makes no counterstatement to complicate the argument. One looks in vain, for example, for a reference to frequency of reception, the theme always awaited, yet never appearing in the sermon. One is tempted to find, in South's emphasis on clothing, or the outside of things, an imagistic confirmation of the self-consciousness about form evident in the sermon. Is South preparing, in overt comment and in imagery, form from content, and what does this mean? The reality of the work calls us back from such interesting speculation: as preparation must be suitable to the sacrament – South attacks "humoursome, singular, and phantastic" preparations (107) – so the imagery always suits the argument. The edge of self-consciousness is always there in a way different, I think, from other sermons; but the discipline and order of plain style metaphor do not desert South at this point. The sermon worries about and celebrates its author's bent for analogy, but the argument presses forward.

South and Busby

Besides the approaching Easter communion, besides South's desire to keep the central matter of Christianity free from excessive complication, another factor may have deeply influenced South in his decision to reduce his treatment of the sacrament to the theme of preparation. Sacramental preparation involved, for any former Westminster pupil, special memories of Busby. Philip Henry's recollections, narrated by his son, tell of Busby's special care in preparing his boys for receiving the sacrament:

It was the ancient Custom of *Westminster-School*, that all the King's Scholars who stood *Candidates* for an election to the University, were to receive the Lord's Supper the *Easter* before, which he did with the rest in St. *Margaret's-Church*, at Easter, 1647, and he would often speak of the great Pains which Dr. *Busby* took with his scholars, that were to approach to the solemn Ordinance, for several weeks before at stated times; with what Skill and Seriousness of Application, and manifest Concern for their Souls, he opened to them the Nature of the Ordinance, and of the Work they had to do in it; and instructed them what was to be done in preparation for it; and this he made a Business of, appointing them their Religious Exercises instead of their School Exercises.[14]

For once, the classical texts were set aside at Westminster School; only preparation for the sacrament was important enough to achieve this radical change in daily order.

South stood for election to Christ Church in 1651; if Henry's account describes, as it purports to do, perennial practice, South received the sacrament for the first time on Easter of the year. Thirty-seven Easters later, in 1688, South followed Busby's example, displacing the obvious themes of Palm Sunday in order to prepare his listeners "to approach to the solemn Ordinance." The poignancy of this act of homage to his master's practice increases when one considers that Busby himself, a very faithful canon of Westminster Abbey and, in 1688, 82 years old, very likely sat in his stall listening to his favored pupil preach on a favored theme. Both Busby and South fully accepted the truth of the sermon's theme; the self-conscious wit of the presentation has added meaning when understood as part of a warm rivalry of teaching between student and master.

[14] Matthew Henry, *An Account of the Life and Death of Mr. Philip Henry*, pp. 10–11.

6

South and mystery

Latitudinarians and mystery

In his study of eighteenth-century sermons, James Downey punctuates his treatment of six eighteenth-century preachers with acknowledgment of their forefathers and teachers, the Anglican divines of the late seventeenth century. Downey repeats what has been the accepted wisdom concerning the doctrinal content of latitudinarian theology, especially that of Archbishop Tillotson; this wisdom holds that Tillotson and others avoided and perhaps enervated the mysterious content of religion in the interests of constructing a rational and easily practiced Christianity. Downey writes:

Anglicans of the seventeenth and early eighteenth centuries, abhorring what seemed to them the degeneracy of Rome and the intolerance of Geneva, sought a more responsible basis of faith. Reason appeared to be the only alternative. ... As in all his preaching, Tillotson was solicitous to show how reasonable and beneficial Christianity can be. Mystery and sacrifice are not so much condemned as set aside as redundant. In their desire to make Christianity intellectually respectable, Latitudinarians robbed it of two of its most precious possessions, mystery and passion. ... [Sterne] is untroubled by the mystery and paradox which surround Christianity. He accepts the authority and teaching of the Church because it is the Church and because it has never occurred to him seriously to question it. The same is true of the Bible. At many points his interpretation of religion betrays the influence of Archbishop Tillotson, from whom he had borrowed so freely in his sermons.[1]

Mystery, passion, sacrifice, and paradox – it is not unfair to say that many available treatments agree with Downey that these are absent from Anglican theology of the period.

The absence or presence of mystery in any theologian's work is no small matter. A tolerance, explication, or cultivation of mystery comes near to the heart of the ticklish matter of distinguishing theological rationalism from rational theology and natural from scriptural religion. If the Judaeo-Christian tradition of beliefs can be rendered non-mysterious and

[1] Downey, *The Eighteenth Century Pulpit: A Study of the Sermons of Butler, Berkeley, Secker, Sterne, Whitfield, and Wesley* (Oxford: Clarendon Press, 1969), pp. 14, 20, 129.

expressed in one kind of epistemological medium popular in the seventeenth century, clear and distinct concepts, why must the mind ever go beyond itself to formulate truths about God? If religion becomes, as it may for many, a code of morality only, cannot the superstructure of the Bible, church, and an interpreting ministry be abandoned? Most of all, would not a religion of reason command widespread assent, and therefore end the violent religious controversies that have marred human history? Downey makes a fundamental critique of late seventeenth-century Anglicanism. If that critique is correct, then the Whiggish interpretation of Anglican theology at that time is also true: that, conscious of their tendencies or not, theologians paved the way for an enlightened era when humankind finally realized the irrelevance of everything except reason in approaching God.[2]

On the face of things, to characterize Anglican theology at this time as devoid of mystery and sacrifice is strange. Indeed, the published works of Burnet, Stillingfleet, Tillotson, and other latitudinarians – and those of other theologians like South – include explicit defenses of mystery and of the real sacrifice of Jesus to atone for human sins. Tillotson published six sermons in the 1690s that argue the presence of mystery in scriptural revelation; in the same period Burnet instructed the clergy of Salisbury and Stillingfleet the faithful of the City of London on the same theme. It is not obvious that South should be included in Downey's generalizations, and South, as I will show, approached mystery in his own way; yet he was one with the latitudinarians in the broad orthodoxy of his writings on mystery, and it would be dishonest to distinguish his work from theirs by making him out to be a unique defender of mystery. Like Stillingfleet, South also wrote long prose tracts in this area. He entered an involved controversy with William Sherlock, Dean of St. Paul's, about what concepts might be used to rationalize the Trinity without embracing tritheism. Sustained latitudinarian and high church acts of preaching and writing seem to deny the accepted wisdom.

In her chapter on "Anglican Rationalism," Irène Simon has helped to restore balance to the intellectual history of the late seventeenth century by her discussion of South's and Tillotson's sermons of the 1690s that defend mystery.[3] Nevertheless, Downey's account and the tradition that lies behind it should not be carelessly dismissed, and there are two good reasons why they will continue to appeal. First, the study of Anglican theology after 1660 still suffers from neglect. Stillingfleet and Tillotson have no biographies other than those written by their immediate disciples; studies of their patterns of thought as integrated wholes are also wanting.

---

[2] For this approach, see Leslie Stephen, *History of English Thought in the Eighteenth Century*, 3rd edn. (London: Smith and Elder, 1902), I, 76; and Mark Pattison, *Essays*, II, 48.

[3] Simon, I, 116–30.

Both a theologian and an historian – as well as, in his later years, an interpreter of church law – Stillingfleet presents special problems to anyone trying to understand his many works as parts of an integrated whole, if indeed such an integration exists.[4] Little work has been done from a developmental point of view; common sense must suppose that over a thirty-year period the thoughts of these divines changed, but no one has yet undertaken to show us how. We do not know, for example, whether Tillotson's energetic defense of the Trinity in the 1690s was a new or old task for him, a departure from his moralistic sermons or a development of doctrine latent in his morality.

There is, besides, the problem of quantity and quality. That only 6 out of over 250 of Tillotson's sermons set out explicitly to defend mystery may reinforce the view that this project did not greatly interest him. Yet interpretation cannot rest on mere counting. It is necessary to devise other norms by which to judge how much weight an individual sermon or set of sermons should have in an overall assessment. It is clear to me, however, that far too much emphasis has been placed on a few sermons of Tillotson that equate religion with happiness, to the detriment of many other sermons that place harsher demands on the morals and minds of his congregations. In the next section, I will analyze the Trinitarian writings of Stillingfleet, Tillotson, and Burnet only to provide a context in which to understand South's work; I leave the construction of a qualitative and developmental model of understanding latitudinarian theology to other scholars.

In contrast to the latitudinarians, South attended to a defense of mystery and of the doctrines it involved throughout his career. Between the 1660s and 1695, besides his two lengthy prose tracts at the end of that period, South preached five sermons – out of seventy-two, a far greater percentage than Tillotson – which argued with opponents of mystery.[5] From at least the Christmas of 1665, he showed a thorough knowledge of Socinian thought; Socinian writings seem to have been part of his reading at Christ Church in the years before and after the Restoration. By the time a major outpouring of Socinian writings began in the 1690s, he was thoroughly familiar with the continental backgrounds of the movement. More importantly, in a 1694 sermon, which I will examine in detail, he gives evidence that his defense of mystery is not an afterthought in his theology. The sermon recapitulates, in argument and imagery, some of the

[4] For a study of one integrating theme in Stillingfleet, see Robert T. Carroll, *The Common-Sense Philosophy of Religion of Bishop Edward Stillingfleet, 1635–1699* (The Hague: Martinus Nijhoff, 1975).
[5] South argues with Socinian writings in at least the following five of his sermons: on John 1:11 (Christmas 1665), on Colossians 2:2 (between 1663 and 1670), on 1 Corinthians 2:7 (29 April 1694), on John 7:17 (undated), and on Acts 24:15 (undated).

dominant themes of his preaching career. In both quantity and quality, South was a mystery-theologian.

The Socinian pamphlets to which the divines respond in the 1690s formidably argue their case against mystery and traditional formulations of the doctrines of the Trinity, the Incarnation, and the sacrifice of Jesus.[6] Though the Anglican divines try to pin the stigma of novelty on the pamphlets, a number of new and old streams of seventeenth-century thought flow into them. The pamphlets rely on a deeply Protestant sense of the inviolability of the relationship between the individual and the scriptural text, though their vision of this relationship, rationalistic in conception, lacks the affective sense of much English Protestant noncon-formism. They repeatedly reject the idea that an individual believer needs to turn to the Councils of the Church or to learned commentaries to understand the meaning of the key doctrines of Christianity. They agree with the maxim of the divines, who learned it from William Chilling-worth, a Caroline theologian, that the saving doctrines in Scripture are plain and few. The pamphlets transfer to theology the Cartesian quest for certainty, interpreting clear and distinct ideas as the only guarantor of it. They import and freely quote from the writings of continental Socinians. They make the first use in English scriptural theology of the textual criticism of Richard Simon, the French sometime Oratorian; they distin-guish good from bad manuscripts and editions in a way that English divines, somewhat complacent in this area, find hard to keep up with. Although different pamphleteers enunciate different anti-Trinitarian traditions – Arian, Socinian, Unitarian – they agree that the preexistence of the divine Logos who becomes the man-God in Jesus is not a scriptural doctrine.

The Socinian pamphlets also give as pure an expression as one can find at this time in England of one central theme of Enlightenment thought: that a republic of reason had replaced a monarchy of title. In the third set of pamphlets, Stephen Nye, a frequent contributor, writes:

the *Common-wealth of Learning* owns none of these Titles, Dean, Bishop, Arch-bishop and such like; it has no regard for 'em. That *Serene Republick* estimates all Men, by *only* their Performances, in what they undertake to maintain, or to oppose: *Here*, it serves but only to make a Man ridiculous, to character or write himself, by any of the (specious) Titles or Advantages of this World; by his *Fortune* not by his *Merits*. If I have really removed, or helped to remove, the *Darkness*; that the Men of Mystery would bring into Religion ... it will avail my Opposers nothing, nor blemish me at all, that they are great *Pensioners of the World*, and I am *free of those Biasses*.[7]

---

[6] For discussions of the authorship and contents of the pamphlets, see Robert Wallace, *Anti-Trinitarian Biography* (London, 1850), I, 218–342; and Herbert McLachlan, *The Story of a Nonconformist Library* (Manchester: Manchester University Press, 1923), pp. 53–87.

[7] *Considerations on the Explications of the Doctrine of the Trinity* (London, 1694), p. 44.

Such an attack on authority caused a particular anxiety in the adherents of an established religion. Moreover, the introduction of politics and titles into theological arguments alarmed those who pretended that the work of titled clerics with university degrees was an apolitical enterprise. Tillotson especially avoided discussing the political aspect of a theology defended by an establishment. Indeed only South, long used to defending the political basis of Anglican doctrine, dared fully to attack such an argument.

For Anglican divines of the late seventeenth century, "mystery" in a general sense refers to truths which the human mind cannot comprehend; that is, it can assent to their existence but not understand the manner of their existing. The union of body and soul in human activity and the foreknowledge of God are examples frequently given of mysteries in this general sense. A scriptural mystery is a revealed truth about which the mind must make the same distinction concerning existence and manner of existence. The mysteries *par excellence* of Christianity, and in fact those debated in the 1690s, are the existence and manner of existing of God as three-in-one and of Jesus as God and man. A third doctrine, the sacrifice of Jesus for sin, depended on the resolution of the first two: if Jesus was God, how and why the Father willed him to suffer and die remained a mystery; if he was not, various theories of the exemplarity of and rewards for his human suffering were worked out.

Anglican divines differed even on the level of a description of what mystery is. Gilbert Burnet's description has a tentative air about it: "some theory, or point of Doctrine that we believe; because we are persuaded that it is revealed to us in Scripture, tho' we cannot distinctly apprehend how it can be; and that in the common view which is offered concerning it, it seems to contradict our common Notions."[8] South gives four marks of mystery in a characteristically firmer fashion: (1) mystery is a truth, not an absurdity or something internally contradictory; (2) its existence was revealed by God in Scripture; (3) human reason could not have discovered its existence; and (4) it continues to be incomprehensible by "bare human reason."[9] Even in defending it, Anglican response to mystery was not uniform: it ranged from reluctant acceptance of something that went against the modern temper to enthusiasm that that temper was confounded. Mystery remained a permanent condition of the acceptance of a few theological truths, at least in this life; the afterlife of bliss would clarify mystery, though in an intuitive rather than a ratiocinative mode of knowledge. The Socinians, on the other hand, readily accepted the idea of mystery, but in the matters at issue only as relative to time and place; their most common expression of this relativity was that the plan of God in regard to the human race was once a mystery, but, with the unfolding of

[8] *Four Discourses Delivered to the Clergy of the Diocese of Sarum* (London, 1694), p. 26.
[9] *Animadversions*, pp. 3–6.

the drama of Jesus in suffering, humiliation, and redemption, God's plan
became clear and distinct.

Stillingfleet, Tillotson, and Burnet

The first divine into the lists was Edward Stillingfleet, who, in a sermon on
7 April 1691, challenged the argument of *An Impartial Account of the Word
Mystery As It Is Taken in Holy Scripture,* a pamphlet published earlier in the
year in the first Socinian collection, *The Faith of One God.* In a rare crossing
of latitudinarian and high church lines, South later praised the sermon for
baffling and overthrowing the pamphlet's argument.[10] By an unknown
author, *An Impartial Account* begins by defining three meanings of mystery
in Scripture and shows how Jesus demystified them; it then analyzes six
scriptural texts, showing how they are not Trinitarian in meaning. In one
instance the author employs the critical method, new in controversial
literature such as this, of comparing different textual readings; he concludes this section by saying that when Scripture terms a doctrine a
mystery, the doctrine is "called so only with respect to some Circumstances of Time, Place, and Person."[11] About halfway through, the
pamphlet abandons a strict order of presentation; the second half slyly
praises Sherlock for rendering the Trinity so intelligible (and, therefore,
not a mystery), insists that Protestants who accept the Trinity lay themselves open to accepting other philosophical interpretations of Scripture
such as transubstantiation, and derides the elderly Oxford professor, John
Wallis, for trying to explain the Trinity by means of analogies from
geometry. "Must all our disputes," asks the writer, "depend only upon
meer Metaphysicks ... Confusion of Words, and incomprehensible
Notions, whereby the Divine Light, which ought to enlighten the most
simple Men, is altogether darkened?"[12]

Arguments over the human analogies used to illuminate divine mysteries run through the Socinian pamphlets, Anglican responses stimulated by
them, and, indeed, much commentary on the Trinity since the early
centuries of the church. A Protestant theologian developed such analogies,
either in a metaphysical or homelier mode, with diffidence, for such
analogies were associated with the medieval theology of the schools that
some early reformers rejected. In the present, philosophizing upon Scripture implied that some intellectual system was equal in value to Scripture;
it also implied the existence of universities where the system was taught, a
more or less official body of interpreters, and perhaps some kind of
tradition outside of Scripture that might be taken as necessary to interpret
it properly. Such a tradition interfered with a strict application of the *sola*

[10] *Animadversions,* p. 6.   [11] *An Impartial Account,* p. 12.   [12] *Ibid.,* p. 22.

Scriptura, the theory that Scripture alone sufficed to tell believers what they needed to believe to be saved. In practice, Anglicans of the late seventeenth century held to this theory and continued to attack Rome for its emphasis on extra-scriptural tradition; in various ways, they also relied on the tradition that has interpreted Scripture as Trinitarian since the first centuries of the church. Some Anglicans found themselves in the awkward position of attacking Socinians for flaunting a church tradition which their own Protestant commitment predisposed them to disregard.

Quoting at least two of the pamphlets in *The Faith of One God*, Stillingfleet's sermon of 1691 refuses to become bogged down in arguments about individual texts. As his point of entry into the debate, Stillingfleet picks not the Trinity or Incarnation, but the allied doctrine of the sacrifice made by Jesus for sinners. Since, in Socinian theory, Jesus was not God during his earthly life, the idea that God sacrificed his own Son is grossly irrelevant; Socinians propose instead the theory that God exalted Jesus as his son as a reward for a life of obedience and humility that needs no ascription of divinity to make it exemplary. To counter this theory, Stillingfleet picks as his text, "This is a faithful saying and worthy of all acceptation, that Christ Jesus came into the World to save Sinners, of whom I am the chief" (I Tim. 1:15). About 9,000 words long, the sermon was preached at St. Lawrence Jewry, a City church and the home pulpit of Tillotson. Choosing this pulpit for this sermon, Stillingfleet makes his enterprise one of solidarity with Tillotson, and hints that the sermon is only the first chapter of the establishment's reply to the Socinian pamphlets.

There is no exegesis at the start and no application at the end; the body of the sermon itself serves as both, for Stillingfleet sets out to write an extended instruction for present and future use about how one reads a passage whose meaning is disputed. He divides his topic into two questions: given two, conflicting senses of a passage, which is "most agreeable to the Revealed Word of God," and "which doth offer fairest for the Benefit and Advantage of Mankind?"[13] Even an outline shows the sermon's great historical value, for it gives a full example of how Anglicans of the time thought Scripture should be read:

I *Agreeableness to the revealed word of God*
   (1) which of two senses in dispute do we choose? (454–56)
      (a) the plain and easy, not forced and intricate sense
      (b) that which most fits the whole scope of the New Testament
      (c) that which generally has been received by the Christian church

[13] *FS*, pp. 453ff.

   (d) that which best agrees with the character of Jesus and his
       disciples
       (i) Jesus demands that he be accepted as God
       (ii) John and Paul testify to his divinity
 (2) *an objection*: to insist on belief in mysteries abuses the credulity of
     mankind (456–57)
 (3) *answer* (457–63)
   (a) God may justly demand our belief in what we do not com-
       prehend
       (i)   his own eternity
       (ii) his own spiritual nature
       (iii) his own foreknowledge
   (b) there are worse absurdities in the suggested replacements for
       traditional doctrines
       (i)   Jesus more eminent, without divinity, than John the
             Baptist
       (ii) an abstraction, wisdom, is made flesh, rather than a
             person, God
       (iii) a man is rapt up into heaven rather than sent down
       (iv) man becomes God, not God man
       (v)   suffering of an innocent rather than a predestined savior
       (vi) a mere man raised to godliness rather than divine con-
             descension
   (c) clear revelation, not incomprehensibility as such is the norm
       for necessary articles of faith
II *Agreeableness to the benefit and advantage of mankind*
   (1) the sense tending most to esteem and love of Jesus (464)
   (2) to hatred of sin (464–65)
   (3) to strengthening one's hope for salvation (465–66)

It is to be noted that nowhere does this scheme say anything about bad
manuscripts and editions. It assumes the integrity of the text. At this point
in the controversy, specialized textual criticism is foreign ground for
Stillingfleet; only later does he employ the new criticism to effect.[14] He
refuses to address *An Impartial Account* in its text by text analysis, and
instead offers a list of literary, historical, and moral norms for an acceptable reading. Reason on its own must not confront each text in a discrete
fashion; the believer must read Scripture within a long tradition of
interpretation and piety. Though such interpretation presupposes a knowledge of the whole Scripture that might be available to any believer, it also
demands the kind of learning which only the historically trained specialist
has at his command.

---

[14] See his *Vindication of the Holy Trinity* (1696), in *Works*, III (London, 1710), 479–82.

Stillingfleet uses a number of conventional arguments, as well as some peculiar to himself. At somewhat greater length than other anti-Socinian writers of the time, he develops the absurdities of the Socinians' replacements for traditional doctrines, and accuses them of creating the very difficulties that their drastic break with tradition attempts to avoid. A trifle nervous about his allegiance to extra-scriptural tradition, he insists that it is apostolic and does not arise from "modern *Inventions*, or *criticisms*, or Pretences to *Revelation*" (454); he wants to make clear that he is not defending the formulations of the schools or private inspiration. He also stresses the continuity of the Trinity, the Incarnation, and the sacrifice of Jesus with other mysteries. This, it seems to me, is a point worth noticing. Almost all Anglican arguments put the scriptural mysteries in continuum with other truths, also incomprehensible, about God; in I.3.a.i–iii, Stillingfleet argues that God's eternity, spiritual nature, and foreknowledge are mysteries and, once we accept them, there is no reason to reject others. Although he alludes to "*Mysteries* in Arts, *Mysteries* in Nature" and to a "Spire of Grass" as a "*Mystery*" (457), Stillingfleet does not develop the relationship of divine to natural mysteries, as others, notably Tillotson, do. The sermon discusses the spirituality of God in so decided a way that it would be jarring to stress the continuity of knowing him and physical nature.

It would appear that although Stillingfleet, unlike the Socinians, finds mystery indubitably in Scripture, he does not rejoice over his discovery. He portrays himself – and this may well be a mask devised for a critical audience – as a reluctant defender of mystery. Christianity would be more acceptable in modern times, he notes, if it contained only clear and distinct ideas. But Protestant Christianity is founded on Scripture, and "our business is to consider, whether any such things be contained in that *Revelation* which we all own; and if they be, we are bound to believe them, although we are not able to comprehend them" (453). Tillotson and others affect similar reluctance, though South, as we shall see, does not. This feigned or real reluctance to accept mystery may differentiate latitudinarian from high church theology in this matter.

Lastly, as the outline shows, Stillingfleet develops at some length, at the end of the sermon, the benefits of mystery to the believer. The presence of mystery, as opposed to the Socinian alternative, raises love for Jesus Christ, hatred for sin, and strengthens hope of salvation and reward. The traditional interpretation of the sacrifice of Jesus "is indeed an Argument great enough to raise our Admiration, to excite our Devotion, to inflame our Affection"; the Socinian alternative, in contrast, seems "flat and low" (464). The last paragraph of the sermon speaks of strong consolation, hopes of forgiveness, the depths of despair without Jesus, lively faith, comfort, and inward satisfaction. Throughout the centuries Christian preachers have asked congregations to let the consoling revelation of Jesus arouse these emotions in them. Such encouragement to strong feelings is not everywhere in Stillingfleet; he is not Wesley, and a characterization of his sermons as rational essays is not without merit. Nevertheless, he is not devoid of passion; he does not depart from standard Christian practice in this respect. The 1691 sermon frustrates a simplistic application of the model of the passionless latitudinarian; the reality is more complex.

Tillotson preached four sermons defending and explaining the Christian mysteries in the Christmas seasons of 1679 and 1680 at his parish church, St. Lawrence Jewry; as the Socinian controversy of the 1690s heated up, and perhaps because his own orthodoxy had been called into question, he revised and enlarged the sermons, publishing them in 1693 as *Sermons Concerning the Divinity and Incarnation of Our Blessed Saviour*. In the same year he delivered and published two more sermons on the sacrifice and satisfaction of Jesus and on the unity of God. The six sermons provide a coherent view of Anglican rules for scriptural interpretation in the face of Socinian simplification. As I have noted, the sermons also provide the reading necessary to correct the view that Tillotson lacked interest in doctrinal mystery or, indeed, doctrine itself. Tillotson intended the sermons, which range from 6,000 to 10,000 words in length, to be a manual of Anglican Trinitarian and Incarnational thought. Especially at the start of the revised sermons of 1679–80, he suppresses local references; he later alludes to previous sermons of the series as if they were chapters of an ongoing book.

The four sermons of 1679–80 show the power the Wilkins model had over Tillotson's mind. No single sermon follows the model exactly, but the four sermons taken as a whole, even though they were delivered in two segments over a year apart, faithfully follow Wilkins's standard pattern of explication, exposition, and application. The beginning of the third sermon makes clear that the first two are to be regarded as explications of the one text used for all four: "The Word was made flesh, and dwelt amongst us; and we beheld his glory, the glory as of the only begotten of the Father, full of grace and truth" (John 1:14). Stretched out over two sermons, the long explication joins parts of Wilkins's model that we rarely see together: Tillotson explores the doctrinal aspects of the Word and his Incarnation and also ancient and current contextual aspects, such as those heresies that John addressed and their current manifestation in Socinian writings. At the start of the third sermon, Tillotson divides the text into three points, two of which this sermon and the third the last sermon develops. The last twenty pages of the last sermon serve as an application, "a practical Inference or two," for the whole set.[15]

[15] *Sermons Concerning the Divinity and Incarnation of Our Blessed Saviour* (London, 1693), p. 215.

The structures of the two other sermons published in 1693 bear a closer resemblance to the Wilkins model, and have observable explications, expositions, and applications. The explications of both are somewhat longer than is usual. Unlike Stillingfleet, Tillotson decided to address obsessive Socinian care about textual analysis. The expositions or confirmations of these sermons tend to be feisty, for Tillotson knows that he is in battle. Inside these expositions, the divisions are shorter; Tillotson does not develop a few major points, as is his wont, but tries to defend traditional doctrine in a number of ways the Socinian pamphlets suggest. In the sermon on the unity of God, after the explication, Tillotson admits that the doctrine of the Trinity may cause problems for the doctrine of the unity of God. Here is what the outline of his attempt to solve these looks like:

II *Division and confirmation*
   (1) there is a difference between the speculations of the schoolmen and the simplicity of scriptural teaching
   (2) how the Trinity as three-in-one is a mystery and the desirability of implicit faith
   (3) "person" is not used in Scripture to describe the three-in-one, but it is difficult to find a better term
   (4) even pre-Christian literature tends to see three distinctions in God
   (5) Scripture clearly teaches both Trinity and unity
   (6) Scripture does not teach a plurality of gods
   (7) reason can assent to the incomprehensible so long as there is a good reason for this assent.[16]

The development of the last point goes on for some pages; here Tillotson addresses the charge in *An Impartial Account* that acceptance of the Trinity leads to acceptance of absurdities such as transubstantiation. In this section, Tillotson gives clear evidence of knowing the distinction between a scriptural doctrine and philosophical theories which try to explain it. He notes, for example, that the idea of substantial change, a theory, is not in Scripture, and that the Trinity, a doctrine, is.[17]

In all six sermons, Tillotson's grand strategy is the same. He situates Anglican acceptance of mystery between two rationalisms: the simplifying rationalism of the Socinians, that, in order to conform Scripture to reason, rejects doctrines which cannot be expressed in clear and distinct ideas, then returns to the text to strain mysterious meanings through a rationalist sieve; and the encumbering rationalism of the medieval schools and

---

[16] *A Sermon Concerning the Unity of the Divine Nature and the Blessed Trinity*, (London, 1693), pp. 25–26; hereafter referred to in the notes as *Unity*.
[17] *Unity*, p. 50.

Catholic tradition, that invents complicated terminology to replace scriptural simplicity. One rationalism pretends to know too little, and the other too much. In his analysis, a deft recreation of the Anglican *via media*, he invokes "the general *Tradition* of the *Christian* Church ... which next to *Scripture* is the best and surest confirmation of the great *Point*." He thus admits that he leans on something outside Scripture, a general tradition of very old and sure standing. His emotional sympathies seem to tend towards the Socinian position; he expresses his admiration for their way of argument, and pleads his own limitations as a theologian when he refuses to construct theories, other than the plain words of Scripture themselves, to enclose mystery. Like Stillingfleet, he wears the mask of reluctant acceptance: "I look upon *Mysteries* and *Miracles* in Religion," he writes, "to be of the same nature, and that a great Reverence is due to both when they are certain, and necessary in the Nature and Reason of the thing: But neither of them are easily to be admitted without necessity, and very good evidence."[18] Mysteries are so improbable that only Scripture acceptably testifies to their existence.

Both Stillingfleet and Tillotson find mystery in something they call the "plain" sense of Scripture; those who deny the presence of mystery in revelation, they say, can do so only by twisting the plain sense. Tillotson writes:

There is no end of Wit and Fancy, which can turn any thing any way, and can make whatever they please to be the meaning of any Book, though never so contrary to the plain design of it, and to that sense which at the first hearing or reading of it is obvious to any man of common sense.[19]

This principle of interpretation rests on a deeper theological truth held by both Anglicans and Socinians: if everyone has to believe certain things to be entitled to receive the benefits of redemption, then God has to make Scripture's enunciation of those things obvious to and assimilable by a wide range of hearers and readers. The fairness of God therefore dictates that something like a plain sense of Scripture should exist.

The plain sense, however, is a term whose meaning grows more elusive the more one tries to figure it out. Who is this man of "common sense" who finds the saving truths of Scripture plainly there? Stillingfleet and Tillotson note that anti-Trinitarian interpretation has existed since the days when the gospel of John was composed. That common sense led interpreters to heterodoxy is surely a reasonable possibility. Socinians maintain that, historically, the plain sense was really that held by titled believers who belonged to an establishment powerful enough to have its own way. The winners of theological controversies, for a number of reasons, get to own the plain sense, and those who lose do not.

---

[18] *Sermons*, pp. 115, 71, 149–50, 183; *Unity*, p. 29.   [19] *Sermons*, pp. 76–77.

Many Protestants of Tillotson's time solved the problem of the plain sense by saying that it was a gift of the Holy Spirit; God is in Scripture, authenticating its plain meanings, and sealing them into the minds and hearts of believers. The rational orientation of much late seventeenth-century Anglican theology did not encourage its practitioners to adopt this kind of spiritual interpretation. This view had an historical connection with the sects of the Interregnum and with nonconformist thought in general, which did not cease to thrive at the Restoration; Anglicans also felt that spiritual interpretation was individualistic and tended to make chaos out of the ordered theology they desired. For Anglicans, of course, the plain sense of Scripture does not provide a sole point of argument. As Stillingfleet suggests, common-sense plain readings form only one item in a long list of norms for correct interpretation. The full implementation of these norms, however weak one link in the chain might be, was held to authenticate the mysteriousness of Scripture.

Tillotson gives an example, noted by others, of Socinian avoidance of plain meaning. Socinus and some of his followers held that the prologue to the gospel of John does not affirm the preexistence of the Logos and its incarnation in Jesus. John's phrase, "In the beginning was the Word" (John 1:1), refers to the time when the gospel began to be spread, not to time immemorial. The rest of the prologue was then construed accordingly. Tillotson spends almost 3,500 words refuting this reading, arguing that the general tradition of the church, the guardian of the plain sense, never held this. He buries the Socinian interpretation in a barrage of derisive adjectives: violent, unreasonable, pitiful, wretched, precarious, arbitrary, strained, forced, biassed, incredible, rash, rude, inconsistent, new, and odd.[20] His annoyance shows that it is indeed difficult to write about the plain sense with objectivity; the plain sense is only obvious until someone, also pleading common sense, comes up with something plainer. Tillotson's barrage of adjectives hides his insecurity about his premises.

Lastly, Tillotson's six sermons stress the continuity of the incomprehensibility of scriptural mysteries and that of natural mysteries. In his sermon on the unity of God, he lists physical and spiritual mysteries which prepare us for accepting mysteries in Scripture: how material things are one, how seeds contain the form of a mature organism, and how the soul works through the body. Even before one gets to the unity of the Trinity and of man and God in Jesus, the infinity, foreknowledge, and self-causation of God resist efforts at comprehension. Tillotson also develops the idea that human actions and customs provide analogies helpful towards understanding how God mysteriously reveals himself in Scripture. Pagan mys-

[20] *Sermons*, pp. 57–83. Stillingfleet partly answered Socinian interpretation of John 1 by parodying it; see "A Discourse Concerning the Sufferings of Christ" (1696), *Works*, III (London, 1710), 242–43.

teries, however corrupt, prepare for the mysteries in Scripture; pagan and
Jewish sacrifices hint at the sacrifice of the Son by the Father, and
primitive monotheism at the Judaeo-Christian idea of the one God.[21]
These discussions, the last two of which are extended, in no way try to
deny mystery. Tillotson tries only to take away some of the utter strangeness of scriptural revelation. He ventures into biology and a sort of
anthropology in a spirit of faith; the book of nature also reveals God and,
not surprisingly, confirms Scripture. He does not see the dark side of his
arguments, as Stillingfleet, a deeper thinker who avoids most of these
analogies, surely did: if a thriving experimental philosophy began to solve
physical and psychological mysteries, perhaps an equally thriving rationalism might be encouraged to solve the divine.

One more latitudinarian entry into the Socinian controversy of the
1690s merits notice. It is that of Gilbert Burnet, Bishop of Salisbury in the
early 1690s, who occasionally exercised his right to assemble and instruct
the clergy of his diocese in sound practice and doctrine. In 1694 he
published four of these talks to his fellow ministers, the second of which,
"Concerning the Divinity and Death of Christ," answers the Socinian
writings. In his introduction, Burnet likens the Socinians to "libertines,"
who also denied mystery, but like Tillotson he praises the "Justice and
Charity" of the former.[22] Although he was a prominent latitudinarian and
although he complains that in trying to explain mystery "Ancients and
Moderns have perhaps gone beyond due bounds" (31), Burnet attempts
some theoretical analogizing of his own. He discusses historical notions of
"Lord" and philosophical relations within human faculties in order partly
to illuminate the Trinity and Incarnation (35–42). As long as they
affirmed abiding mystery, latitudinarians apparently felt free to add to the
store of analogies built up over the centuries towards such illumination.
The nature of Burnet's audience – presumably more theologically sophisticated than a lay audience – also allowed him to speculate upon scriptural
doctrine.

In other respects, Burnet's talk follows well-worn latitudinarian paths.
He aligns limited knowledge of the natural world with that of the divine
(27–29), admitting the argument of the continuity of the acts of understanding God and his creation. Like Tillotson, he notes that expiatory
sacrifice was widespread before the time of Jesus, and that God used this
practice to prepare the world for his own remarkable activity; "for there
was not any one sort of things, which the whole world knew better than all
that belong'd to Sacrifices" (43). He complains that the Socinians twist
the plain sense with new significations (46–47). The closeness of Burnet's

---

[21] *Unity*, pp. 38–43; *Sermons*, pp. 188–89; *A Sermon Concerning the Sacrifice and Satisfaction of Christ*
(London, 1693), pp. 9–14; *Unity*, pp. 8–15.
[22] *Four Discourses*, p. 11. Further page references will be given in parentheses in the text.

arguments to Stillingfleet's and Tillotson's leads one to suspect that they met to coordinate their responses to the Socinian pamphlets. Their world was not large; besides meeting in the House of Lords, they shared a commitment to William III for which, high churchmen pointed out, they had been rewarded with the sees of Canterbury, Salisbury, and Worcester. Their defensiveness about these rewards, given soon after the oaths, brought them closer together. Meetings called to set political agenda may well have turned to theological discussion; such latitudinarian summit sessions provide the simplest explanation for the common elements in these bishops' anti-Socinian writings. Burnet and Stillingfleet, before and after such meetings, may have mined Tillotson's sermons of 1679–80, made available to them in manuscript; each added his own arguments according to his theological temper and his audience.

South's contribution

Robert South's contribution to the Socinian debate has two parts: a sermon of 29 April 1694 answering the pamphlets and, before and after this, two long tracts of tortuous controversy with William Sherlock, Dean of St. Paul's, over the proper methods to be used in answering the Socinians. The controversy begins with Sherlock's *Vindication of the Doctrine of the Holy and Ever Blessed Trinity* (1690), written in answer to the earliest Socinian tracts. In his preface Sherlock states, somewhat strangely, that he learned a great deal as he wrote the book, and that the ending is clearer than the beginning.[23] The lack of revision implied here provides South with much to find fault. The title-page gives Sherlock's name, and the book does not seem to exploit any literary distance between the Vindicator and the author himself. South answers the *Vindication* with his 382-page *Animadversions Upon Dr. Sherlock's Book Entituled A Vindication of the Holy and Ever Blessed Trinity* (1693), the title-page of which announces the author as "A Divine of the Church of England," with South's name nowhere given. From the start, the Animadverter assumes the role of a defender of doctrinal purity, outraged that Sherlock's sloppy work has been taken as representative of the Church of England's position. The distancing of author from Animadverter allows South to lift the argument above personal grievance; the personal argument of South and Sherlock over the 1689 oaths was common knowledge. Sherlock picks up the distancing mode in his reply to *Animadversions*: *A Defense of Dr. Sherlock's Notion of A Trinity in Unity* (1693); its title-page gives no author's name, only a subtitle, "In a Letter to a Friend." The fiction is maintained throughout

---

23 *Vindication*, sig. A2v. For further discussion of the Sherlock–South argument, see W. H. T. Dodds, "Robert South and William Sherlock: Some Unpublished Letters," *Modern Language Review* (1944), 215–24.

that a "friend of the Dean" writes this defense for an interested third party. South responds to *A Defense* with his 312-page *Tritheism Charged Upon Dr. Sherlock's New Notion of the Trinity* (1695), again under the authorship of "A Divine of the Church of England." By this time the controversy had grown so bitter as to evoke responses from others on both sides; William III personally ordered it to cease.

Involving over a thousand pages of detailed argument, the controversy makes for extremely difficult reading, even after its broad outlines, which I will give, are understood. Only Sherlock's *Vindication* offers positive arguments; South's two responses are uniformly negative, and Sherlock's *Defense* is a sad attempt to keep himself from drowning in the Animadverter's superior arguments. South gave himself four years to write his first response and a year to write his second; Sherlock seems to have rushed both the *Vindication* and *Defense* into print. Although South's sermons in the 1690s and before are not without invective, it is probably his attacks on Sherlock which gave him the reputation, especially for nineteenth-century commentators, for language unbecoming to an Anglican clergyman. The speaker of *Tritheism Charged* pretends that in the matter of harsh language he is more sinned against than sinning; the invective of *Animadversions*, the earlier work, renders this pretense patently false.

In his *Vindication*, Sherlock constructs a model of mutual self-consciousness to help explain the mystery of three-and-one in the Trinity; South attacks the orthodoxy of Sherlock's model, claiming it creates three separate gods. Further arguments about the nature of person ensue. When Sherlock tries to clear up the ambiguities of his theory, South accuses him of maintaining contradictory positions. The following quotation from *Tritheism Charged* shows the special bitterness of this controversy:

But why do I dispute against such sottish Paradoxes, which all the Schools in *Christendome* would hiss, or rather spit at the Author of them for? But this poor ambitious *Animalculum Gloriae* has been always affecting to signalize his little Self by the Character of holding what the whole World besides denies, and of denying what it holds.[24]

In trying to interpret the matter and manner of South's attack on Sherlock, it is necessary to contemplate two options. Did South bitterly assault Sherlock because of the contents of the *Vindication* and *Defense*? That is, did he truly feel that the arguments in them were not only bad but caused the church itself to be ridiculed? Socinian pamphlet-writers did, in fact, use Sherlock's theorizing to show that a Dean of the church defended mystery by substituting a mishmash of abstractions for it; Sherlock's theories showed that the establishment did not know what it was talking about. Or

---

[24] *Tritheism Charged*, p. 203. "Animalculum" seems to be a variation of the medieval Latin, "animalicum," or "lowly animal."

was South's opposition essentially personal? Had he been lying in wait, since Sherlock had attacked his reputation about keeping secrets about the oaths, for the Dean to make a false move in print? My own view is that both options are tenable, although only the second explains the special bitterness of South's replies. South's Animadverter and Charger seek publicly to ridicule not only Sherlock's theories, but Sherlock himself.

Because of their length, and because in them South composes for a reading audience only, the two attacks on Sherlock offer a somewhat different version from the sermons of South the writer. They show first of all South's passion for accuracy and attention to detail. He abhors Sherlock's sloppiness of thought and composition. Sherlock, he insists, puts forward new ideas with insufficient care about their implications; in the matter of consciousness in God, the *Vindication* gives no thought to the possibility of tritheism present in the theory. South says that ambition caused Sherlock to shoot higher than his natural ability allowed; even his own preface corroborates the charge that his method of composition is sloppy.

Animadversions also attacks Sherlock's use of words: South repeatedly ridicules his faulty definitions, usage, and knowledge of English, Latin, and Greek spelling and grammar. South enlisted the help of Michael Mattaire, a younger Busby favorite, to trace Sherlock's errors in Latin and Greek; some of these errors are substantial, although many others, involving wrong accents and breathing marks in Greek, are not. Yet South shows a precision about usage that, except for these writings, we would not know about. In the midst of the Trinitarian controversy, for example, it is useful to receive the following precise distinction between the meaning of the verbs "understand" and "comprehend": Sherlock "promiscuously joyns together words, as if they were of the same Import and Extent of Signification, when really they are very different. For to *understand* a thing, is to know it in any respect, or degree, in which it is knowable; and to *comprehend* a thing, is to know it in every respect in which it is knowable." In many similar ways he corrects Sherlock's usage.

South depicts his adversary as a writer who thinks his ideas so grand that he can be careless about details. The ideas being wrong, only the carelessness remains; or rather, the ideas can only exist in the details, and if these are incorrect, no argument stands. South's small essay on small errors is worth quoting:

And now, if either he, or any one else for him, shall pretend to slight and despise this charge, and tell me that Faults and Mistakes here alledged by me, are *small Things*; so, say I, is the point of a Dagger too; but for all that, it may stab a Man to the Heart; and I think, it matters not how small the thing is, which wounds a Man's Credit, if it chance to bleed to Death of the Wound. But there are some

Things in the World, the *Knowledge* of which seems but small, but the *Ignorance* of them is not so. And certainly of all Men living, such as will be Writers, are concerned to treat tenderly, and to take every step with the utmost Caution, where they do not find a *Grammatical* Bottom firm under them. For my own part, I dare account nothing small, or despicable, which may either do a Man a great mischief, or is necessary to prevent one.[25]

Death at knifepoint, or death by drowning: South's exact metaphors deflate Sherlock's exposition as well as any list of Greek errors can. In four sermons, which we have seen, South satirizes the misuse of words in politics, religion, and personal affairs; each misuse causes chaos in its own sphere. The controversy with Sherlock gives evidence of South's purer interest in words and their meanings. Here precise signification becomes a value in itself, the controversialist's firm ground, and the writer's line of life.

Second, South's reproof of Sherlock's ambition emerges not only from personal animosity but from long-held belief. To satisfy his egotism, South charges, Sherlock treats theological tradition as inconsequential, then, under attack, tries to rewrite tradition to fit his theories. He pretends that the Fathers of the Church support his own rationalization of mystery. South had solid knowledge in this area. Especially in the work of Bishop Fell, knowledge of the Fathers had become part of the tradition of Christ Church, and *Animadversions* and *Tritheism Charged* return again and again to patristic texts to show that they do not say what Sherlock alleges them to say. South repeatedly calls Sherlock "this *Eureka* man" and a "theological Quack," a specialist in the quick invention and remedy to solve any difficulty.

A theologian's ignorance of or misinformation about Christian tradition was a special sin for South. In politics and theology, tradition held back the tide of revolution. Like the latitudinarians, South attacked the "school-men" when it suited him; unlike them, he made tradition a cornerstone of his theological methodology. Convinced he lived in a time of swift political and doctrinal decline, he felt that tradition was God's gift to the Church of England to survive the flood of change. South did not espouse tradition for convenience's sake, only to answer Sherlock, as a latitudinarian perhaps did to answer, for the moment, Socinian pamphlets. Sherlock offended South's lifelong allegiance to the wisdom of the pre-reformation past.

Lastly, South's use of an authorial persona in *Animadversions* and *Tritheism Charged* invites analysis, especially in regard to how this persona might qualify the invective of both books. Even though the careful structure and imagery of his sermons invite it, South has never been

---

[25] *Animadversions*, pp. 7, 354.

subjected to very stringent literary analysis. Critical opinion about these books has not advanced much beyond what G. M. Webster tells us of contemporary reaction: "The general opinion was that though Sherlock had entered too lightly upon a subject beyond his powers, South's mingling of abuse of his opponent with the exposition of the Divine Mystery was most offensive to good taste."[26] Critics of his own day seem to have made nothing of the distance South tried to maintain between himself and the abusive Animadverter and Charger by assigning the authorship of these works to a "Divine of the Church of England."

In his preface, the Animadverter writes of his shock at the silence of the church in not condemning Sherlock for his heterodoxy. These sentiments echo those of South in other contexts. They are, however, mildly anachronistic in the 1690s, when many, including South, ruefully admitted to the enervation of the church as a defender of doctrine. In his dedication of volume III (1698) of the *Sermons* to Narcissus Marsh, South praised the vigor of the Church of Ireland, in contrast to the torpor of his own church, in prosecuting heresy. The naïveté of the Animadverter suggests more than a nominal difference between himself and South. Moreover, several times in *Tritheism Charged* South invents a speaker different not only from himself but also from the speaker of the previous *Animadversions*. For example, the Charger writes wittily about Sherlock: "the Animadverter ever yet took him for as easy a Combatant as heart could wish, and bids me acquaint him further, that he shall be readier to engage in a Controversial Duel with him, than with any Man alive, provided that he does not bring his *Meaning* for his *Second*."[27]

South's closing years overlapped the era of the wittiest inventions of multiple narrators that English literature can show. John Arbuthnot, Alexander Pope, and Jonathan Swift, friends and literary co-conspirators, often engage in extended exercises that distance narrators from authors. Perhaps only one of emotional tone, South's distance from the Animadverter and Charger is minimal compared to the pattern of much Scriblerian writing, where narrators sometimes affirm authorial positions by stating the opposite to them. This technique was thriving at least by the time of John Dryden's *MacFlecknoe* (1682), whose narrators praise the dullness the poem satirizes; the technique of the distanced, ironic narrator reached its apogee in Swift's *Tale of A Tub* (1704), *Gulliver's Travels* (1726), and *A Modest Proposal* (1729). Is it possible that South, in the 1690s, creates the same type of ironic narrators? If such is the case, can we properly consider that the vituperation of these characters may be construed not to be South's own, but that of characters South uses in order to express hostility, and at the same time to distance himself from it? These characters are

---

[26] Webster, p. 229.   [27] *Tritheism Charged*, p. 392.

rigid, conservative, backward-looking, and angry; they are also unrealistic about what the present establishment can do about penalizing Sherlock's heterodoxy.

In the dedicatory epistle to *Tritheism Charged*, the Charger asks the two universities to censure "such *Propositions as have of late so much impugned our* Faith, *and disparaged our* Church; *as that of* Oxford *had passed before upon such* Doctrines, *as undermined and struck at our* Civil Government."[28] Oxford was in fact condemning local writings supporting Sherlock, an action stopped by William III's veto of further argument. The Charger refers the reader back in time, perhaps to the resistance of Oxford to James II's changes, and more likely to the university's condemnation of opposition to passive obedience in 1683.[29] The Charger's *laudatio temporis acti* reveals him to be what South elsewhere calls "a good old Church of England man," for whom fidelity to tradition was all in all. South had affection for this type, which he contrasted with the revolutionaries of the Interregnum and the time-serving politicians of Charles II's reign. The character resembles South in some ways and not in others: South had enough realism to pursue a bishopric under James and take the oaths to William. Through his narrators, South is able to take a somewhat simpler and more outraged view of Sherlock's writing and ecclesiastical politics than an informed estimate of the political scene of the 1690s would have allowed.

To divide South from his narrators runs the risk of committing the crime of which South accuses Sherlock: interpretational novelty unknown to centuries of commentators. Truly, one must move tentatively in such matters. Yet their abstruse nature has kept commentators away from these late works of South. Neglect of South's literary intentions and artistry may be owing to an understandable avoidance of the weighty Trinitarian material. Also, the device of an ironic narrator is particularly susceptible to misinterpretation; the device intends to make interpreting readers unsure of what evidence to take for the fiction's true statement, and occasionally doubtful that one exists. Unlike South, Swift had the pleasure of writing for a closed interpreting community, the Scriblerians, who greeted irony as an old friend when they met it. In later years, particularly in the nineteenth century, Swift's writings, like South's, encountered the dullness of critics who could not find, within or through the grossness, the soul of wit.

South's 1694 sermon

South concludes his sermon of 1694 with another attack on Sherlock and his ilk, who in principle or practice attempt to explain away the Christian

---

[28] *Tritheism Charged*, sig. A3r.
[29] See William Jane, *The Judgment and Decree of the University of Oxford* (Oxford, 1683), which condemned twenty-seven propositions and authors that were opposed to passive obedience.

mysteries. Somewhat more clearly than in the tracts, in the sermon South explains why he considers this attempt dangerous: "such innovators break down those sacred mounds which antiquity had placed about these articles, and then heretics and blasphemers rush in upon them, trample them under foot, and quite throw them out of our creed" (III, 408). Although the language overdramatizes the problem, the history of the Socinian delight in Sherlock's work makes the pattern South describes fair game for "heretics." The process of explanation and debasing becomes especially troublesome when the church refuses to step in and denounce false theories; the sermon, unlike the Animadverter's and Charger's writings, has given up hope that the church will ever again perform its role as a guardian of doctrine.

An outline of South's 9,000-word sermon looks like this:

I *Exposition of the text*
   (1) Aristotle's definition of wisdom compatible with St. Paul's; God's wisdom always meets opposition (379–80)
   (2) the power of God's wisdom conquers opposition (380–81)
II *Division and confirmation*
   (1) God's revelations are necessarily mysterious (381–88)
      (a) as unequal to finite, limited human minds
      (b) as spiritual and abstract
      (c) as irreducible to the common methods for observing nature
         (i)   Christ's satisfaction for sin
         (ii) regeneration
         (iii) bodily resurrection
   (2) the ends of religion are mysterious (388–401)
      (a) the *agenda* are simple, the *credenda* obscure
      (b) mysteriousness fits the *credenda*
         (i)   distance preserves respect and awe, as even the religion of the gentiles shows
         (ii) religion should humble pride in reason
         (iii) mysteriousness prompts us to inquire more deeply, and we need university theologians to help us
         (iv) mysteriousness prompts thoughts of a hereafter, where all will be explained to us
III *Application*
   (1) it is reasonable to depend on the wisdom of the whole church (402–04)
   (2) it is a sophistry to say that whatever is incomprehensible by reason cannot exist (404–05)
   (3) it is a vain presumption to pretend to clear up all mysteries (406–07).

South's exegesis of his text, "But we speak of the wisdom of God in a mystery" (I Cor. 2:7), is brief. He takes one idea, wisdom, and discusses its Aristotelian and Pauline dimensions, and its power; thus he avoids arguments which he senses depend more on one's presuppositions than on the meaning of the words. He takes the philosophical road and discusses the presence of mystery in revelation not simply as a textual fact but as the necessary result of the meeting of the finite human mind and God's self-revelation.

South uses few of the latitudinarian arguments for mystery in the sermon. Towards the end he discusses how humans do not understand several things about themselves, such as their psychological unity, and about God, such as his foreknowledge; why, he asks, should the Trinity and the sacrifice of Jesus be any different (406–07)? Near the beginning of the sermon he notes how spirituality and abstraction puzzle the mind; keeping to this theme, he never lowers his argument to stress, as Tillotson does, the continuity of physical and divine mysteries. In this, his approach resembles Stillingfleet's.

Reading this sermon in the context of latitudinarian work in its area accentuates its great stress on the discontinuity between understandings of human and divine realities. For example, South places his treatment of the sacrifice of Jesus under the heading of matters which resist "the common methods and observations of nature." The offering of the Son by the Father "was such a transaction, as we can find nothing like or analogous to in all the dealings of men, and cannot but be owned as wholly beside, if not also directly contrary to all human methods" (386). When the Socinians try to apply what they have observed in created beings to what they want to know about God, it is inevitable that they come to reject mystery; one cannot transfer models of learning from one sphere to another. Thus South takes a view opposite to that of Stillingfleet and Tillotson, who preface discussion of the satisfaction of Jesus with historical surveys of sacrifices before him which make his own more intelligible. He stresses the discontinuity of scriptural mysteries with all other human learning; this means that the human race never has or will be ready to accept them. The Father's sacrifice of his Son to make reparation for human sin stands apart as a revelation which will always surprise the believer and confound those who try to reduce it to human analogies.

Mystery for South is not something to be accepted with reluctance; it is an inevitable and even desirable scriptural fact. He gives two considerations that explain its inevitability: the immensity of the divine essence and existence – like others, South sees the mystery of God as a problem of infinity – and the feebleness of human intelligence. "Heaven, I confess," he writes, "enters into us, as we must into that, by a very narrow passage" (382). The human mind can never understand God, and certainly not his mysterious operations. As in many other sermons, South takes a pessimistic view of the human mind and heart, which will, on their own, err. The mind is "naturally licentious, and there is nothing which it is more averse from than duty: nothing which it abhors more than restraint" (390). Webster notes that South became a Calvinist in his early years at Oxford.[30] The epistles of St. Paul and the writings of Augustine also provided ample opportunity for South to fathom how sin affected even the higher human faculties.

South writes: "all knowledge is a kind of conquest over the thing we know" (391). Mystery is not only inevitable but desirable because it disciplines humans where they most need to be disciplined: in their unbounded desires to know, possess, and conquer. South does not let his discussion of this theme remain only on the psychological and moral level; he places it also in the context of biblical history. The futile yet irresistible confrontation with mystery remedies the fall of Adam: "man would be like God in knowledge, and so he fell; and now if he will be like him in happiness too, God will effect it in such a way, as shall convince him to face that he knows nothing" (395). Returning to the theme set in the exegesis, that Paul's wisdom confounded the philosophers of his time, South says that the gospel was "set up, as it were, in triumph" over secular philosophy. He puts new life into this traditional idea by placing it in the context of the human assault on sacred truth, first seen as Adam advanced on the Tree of Knowledge, and now as Socinians attempt to understand mystery.

Any serious thinker who writes in volume reveals central themes and methodologies around which subordinate ideas and arguments cluster, and in the light of which they come into focus. For Stillingfleet and Tillotson, the relationship of Scripture and reason is one such point of departure. They accept that the God who speaks through both cannot work at cross-purposes; yet mystery challenges the reconciliation of revelation and reason that their many writings had preached and practiced. In the 1690s they firmly defend mystery, but it is clear that they do so or pretend to do so with some uneasiness and reluctance. South, on the other hand, welcomes mystery; having been prompted by the Socinian pamphlets to discuss it at length, he discovers that it has become central to his thinking and helps organize themes that have long preoccupied him. For him, mystery is not just another problem to be solved; it uniquely illuminates his previous teaching about morals, psychology, and sacred history. One of his earliest sermons, for example, had been on Adam and the fall; thirty years later his earlier preoccupation finds its fulfillment in his thought on mystery. Mystery welds disparate themes into a system: it enables him to see the weakness and pride of the human intellect and the history of human sin in new relation to one another.

Mystery frees South from rationalism, and he knows the price:

man naturally is scarce so fond of the offspring of his body, as of that of his soul. His notions are his darlings; so that neither children nor self are half so dear to him as the only-begotten of his mind. And therefore, in the dispensations of religion, God will have his only-begotten, this best-beloved, this Isaac of our souls (above all other offerings that a man can bring him), to be sacrificed, and given up to him.

(396)

God, Abraham, the Anglican theologian of the late seventeenth century: to accomplish the great work, each has to sacrifice his first-born. South refuses to compare Jewish and Christian sacrifices until he has discovered an action analogical to sacrifice in the modern world; mystery abases reason in 1694, but only in the way that God and Abraham have abased themselves before.

South also discovers, in this sermon, that mystery illuminates the bases of his political thought. Alone among those responding to the Socinian pamphlets, he is willing to face their political argument. For a rationalist, there is something contradictory about using philosophy to justify mystery; mystery can only be construed to rest on other grounds, such as the self-interest of its advocates or political gain. Mystery can serve, for example, to keep an elite in power by canonizing that elite's claims to leadership. South addresses this argument and, in a way, agrees with it; mystery demands and justifies an interpreting elite. The church, like the cosmos, is hierarchical. This is the divine order of things, and South twice argues in 1694 that the origins of a permanent teaching order in the church are divine: "God has appointed a standing order of church interpreters to declare and dispense these mysteries," and "the schools are and must be the standing nurseries of the church" (403, 397). South's defense of a "standing order" of preachers was, without a doubt, self-serving; in the divine order of things, he implies, something like Christ Church must exist. South was, on the other hand, consistent. His dependence on the idea of hierarchy is evident from his earliest days of writing; his work on mystery revived its importance to him.

South reinforces the argument of his 1694 sermon with sustained patterns of imagery, a strategy suited to an analogical point of view. Once again the imagery mitigates the harsh, forward progress of the Wilkins model, helping to make its linear progress turn in on itself as the reader begins to recognize repeated imagistic signposts. Two related clusters of images emerge. The first involves light, the sun, darkness, and blindness; the second spatial images of depth that, being dark, relate to the first. Light is a traditional symbol for knowledge, and the sermon suggests that a kind of half-light, or alternating light and darkness, fittingly symbolizes finite understanding of mystery. This imagery recapitulates the standard Anglican theory concerning faith, which rests on moral not mathematical certainty; humans remain free to make an act of faith or not, the evidence for it being good but not necessarily compelling.

Half-light or alternating light and darkness appeal, moreover, to a perversity in human nature that is attracted more by strangeness than excellence: "it is not the worth or excellency, but the strangeness of a thing which draws the eyes and admiration of men after it; for can anything in nature be imagined more glorious and beautiful than the sun shining in his full might, and yet how many spectators and wonderers does the same sun find under an eclipse?" (392). For God to have revealed all clearly would have led to disenchantment; mystery, the sun in eclipse, more cleverly plays on human fascination with strangeness.

The sermon uses the image of full light twice, and a temporal distinction defines its value. The Socinians are "blessed new lights" who want "a clear account" and "an open explicit scheme" of divine things; they cannot stand living in half-light, and would destroy it, although they would have "to outlive not only Methuselah, but even the world itself" (407). On the other hand, all mystery will be cleared up "in the broad light of an everlasting day." Part of the experience of heaven will be the disentanglement of the dark knots of mystery that finite intelligence theretofore experienced. Yet even everlasting day will not provide the clear and distinct ideas demanded by Socinians; "knowledge shall be then intuitive, and above discourse; not proceeding by a long circuit of ante-cedents and consequents, as now in this vale of imperfection it is forced to do" (400–01). The image of full light is positive in the context of time eternal; to want full light in finite time foolishly runs against the nature of human knowledge.

One of South's artistic habits, as I have said, is to maintain an image pattern in a variety of ways, some of his own invention, some suggested by other sources, including classical history and Scripture. Two scriptural allusions, from the gospels of St. Luke and St. John, carry out the pattern of limited and full light. Using a Lucan idea, South writes of the Socinians that "this is their hour, and the power of darkness." The original words, ascribed to Jesus himself, occur after his arrest and just before he is led to the house of the high priest: "When I was daily with you in the temple, ye stretched forth no hands against me: but this is your hour and the power of darkness" (Luke 22:58). The typology is a bold one for South: the Socinians are those arresting Jesus. Jesus either remains himself, alive in spirit in the church, or is the church and its divines, who, like Jesus, do not strike back at their persecutors. The image may express a new aspect of what South felt about the passivity of the church under attack; that he casts this inaction in a typology of redemptive suffering suggests his gradual coming to terms with it. The reference is brief, however, and perhaps one should not make too much of it in terms of South's development at 60 years of age. At the very least the striking allusion dramatically maintains the pattern of light evident in the sermon.

The second allusion concerns, at least in part, the man born blind, whose cure the ninth chapter of St. John's gospel narrates. Because late seventeenth-century philosophy is not without reference to blind men cured for the purposes of epistemological experiment, it is not certain that South alludes only to Scripture. His blind man first appears in a discussion of spirituality: one may as well expect a man born blind to know color and geography as to "apprehend what a spirit, an angel, or an immaterial being is" (384–85). In another context, blindness results from the fall: all humans are subsequently born blind, and faith, their only purchase on the supernatural, "is properly a seeing with another's eyes" (395). If South intends a biblical allusion, the Socinians become a kind of false messiah or miracle-worker, promising a quick reversal of the effects of sin; South uses similarly derisive imagery later in the sermon. If South intends a philosophical allusion, one need look no farther than Locke's *Essay Concerning Human Understanding*, published a few years before the sermon, for a parallel. Locke sets up a complicated problem for a man born blind, suddenly given sight, to solve: having known the difference between a cube and a sphere by touch, will he know it by sight? Locke says no, and draws the conclusion that our knowledge is conditioned by experience and previous learning more than we commonly think.[31] To blend scriptural and philosophical allusions is suggestive of meaning: even if Socinian miracle-workers could give the blind man sight, the realities of God would remain a mystery to him. Blindness before mystery is less a physical and individual than a moral and historical condition; it is only mitigated by moral regeneration and the reversal, allowed to God alone, of Adam's sin.

In the verbal world of the sermon, truth, discoverable only in half-light, dwells in the earth's depths. South's sense of the inaccessibility of truth again stimulates his powers of metaphor.

Truth, we are told, dwells low, and in a bottom; and the most valued things of the creation are concealed and hidden by the great Creator of them from the common view of the world. Gold and diamonds, with the most precious stones and metals, lie couched and covered in the bowels of the earth; the very condition of their

[31] *Essay Concerning Human Understanding*, pp. 145–46. Hobbes writes similarly of a man born not blind, but deaf and dumb, who has to figure out the Pythagorean theorem; as one might suspect, in a Hobbesian world the man is not cured before the problem is posed (*Leviathan*, p. 20). For a full treatment of this philosophical topos, see Michael J. Morgan, *Molyneux's Question: Vision, Touch and the Philosophy of Perception* (Cambridge: Cambridge University Press, 1977).

being giving them their burial too. So that violence must be done to nature, before
she will produce and bring them forth.   (389–99)

South turns the likeness around and probes it for meaning after meaning.
Truth resembles precious stones because both are hard to get at, because
the "common view" does not appreciate them, because the hiddenness of
both is of their essence, and because "violence must be done to nature"
before they can be possessed. On the human level, violated nature includes
both supposed truths that must give way to truth itself and the psyche of
the seeker. The seeker must become uncertain and wary of his intellectual
nature, and entertain the darkness of ignorance, before he encounters
knowledge. Many passages in the sermon speak of mystery in terms of
depth; South weaves Scripture into this pattern also, quoting, near the
end, St. Paul: "O the depth and unsearchableness of the things of God"
(Rom. 11:33). With a final sneer at the Socinians, South concludes: these
were St. Paul's "thoughts of these dreadful and mysterious depths; and the
same, no doubt, will be the thoughts and judgment of all others concerning them, who have any thing of depth themselves" (409).

Lastly, two images of depth also illustrate what Mitchell calls South's
"unseemly" language.[32] The "articles of our faith," South writes, "are
those depths in which the elephant may swim; and the rules of our practice
those shallows in which the lamb may wade" (390). The contrast of
animals is proverbial, although their application to theological matters is
surely South's alone. Though many in his own time and later found the
practice indecorous, South was never loath to mix the sacred and the
humorous together in this way. If the combination has to be defended
here, it might be pointed out that elephants are proverbially dumb, and
the elephant wading into deep water reinforces, in a comic tone, a major
theme of the sermon: that human intelligence is out of its depths when it
tries to understand the mysteries of God. The image is also structurally
justified, since it helps fill out the pattern of depth that South has so
carefully built up.

In his application South again mixes the sacred and the comic; he is
closing his castigation of those who pretend to "clear up" mysteries,
meaning Socinians and also Sherlock, whom the next paragraph will
attack:

The attempts of which sort of men I can liken to nothing so properly as to those
pretences to infallible cures, which we daily see posted up in every corner of the
streets; and I think it is great pity, but that both these sort of pretences were *posted
up together*. For I know no universal, infallible remedy, which certainly cures, or
rather carries off all diseases, and puts an end to all disputes, but death: which yet,
for all that, is a remedy not much in request. Quacks and mountebanks are

[32] Mitchell, *English Pulpit Oratory*, pp. 315, 316.

doubtless a very dangerous sort of men in physic, but much more so in divinity: they are both of them very large in pretence and promise, but short in performance, and generally fatal in their practice.

(406; also III, 20, for parallel imagery)

South goes on to say that the "depths" and "bottom" of divinity and philosophy resist the knowing of those with solid learning, and all the more of intellectual mountebanks.

South's sermons are filled with images of physical as a surrogate for moral disease, imagery found also in other imaginative literature of his time. In this witty variation, South seems, uncharacteristically, to lose control: why the posting of cures and pamphlets is simultaneous is not clear. But the introduction of death by either is apt: it sums up and mirrors much of the sermon. The "remedy not much in request" will terminate the useless endeavors of the Socinians and Sherlock; perhaps South also shows weariness towards the end of his own involvement in these arguments. Death will provide the transition to the intuitive knowledge that will displace ratiocination. Perhaps, however, the anti-mystery quacks will not reach this stage; their rationalistic medicine is "much more" dangerous than that of physic. That is, it can endanger not only mortal but also immortal life. Self-denying assent to mystery reverses the fall and restores life; the quick remedy to lack of knowledge, repeating the sin of Adam, invokes death.

Conclusion

Study of South's 1694 sermon on mystery and allied texts again exemplifies his curious relationship to the latitudinarian divines of his day. In the controversy over mystery, Burnet, South, Stillingfleet, Tillotson were on the same side against rationalistic trends in religious thought. Each summoned up a lifetime of skill in controversy and learning to argue for the traditional mysteries of the Trinity and the real nature of the sacrifice of Jesus. Although the political differences between South and the latitudinarians widened in the 1690s, essential sameness remained in their fundamental positions on the Christian mysteries. This essential sameness represents the mainstream of Anglican thought in the late seventeenth century, and provides the hermeneutical key with which the entire theological projects of these various divines ought to be opened.

Study of the individual arguments of these divines in the matter of mystery also reveals critical differences. As in his defense of kingship, at least until 1685, South again takes the high road in his defense of mystery. He rushes to embrace, as the latitudinarians do not, pre-rational and supra-rational intellectual commitments. Skilled at rational arguments from reason and Scripture, he is also at home in that which resists reduction to clear and distinct ideas. The latitudinarians warily entered this area; although they defended mystery, they did so, by their own admission, reluctantly.

South's openness to mystery and hostility to rationalism supply the core content of the term, "high church," as it is correctly applied to him. His predilection for the pre-rational allowed him to write a sacramental theology of kingship; the same bias towards mystery motivated him in the 1690s controversy with the Socinians. This controversy enabled him to come home, as it were, theologically; after his experience of kingship frustrated his high theology of it, he rediscovered an area that richly rewarded his desire to see history and nature in analogous terms. It is curious that South did not seem to entertain a high church theology of the sacrament of the Lord's Supper itself. This central mystery did not become a governing center of analogy for him. High church movement in this area occurred at the end of South's active life of writing. He had spent his imaginative energy, perhaps, in the controversies over kingship and the Trinity, and had none left for a new battlefield.

A study of South's 1694 sermon on mystery also reinforces what I take to be the major innovation of his homiletic manner: his ability to construct patterns of imagery from Scripture, experience, history, and elsewhere. At times these patterns are decoratively rhetorical, at times counter to the central argument, and at times revelant of what South saw as unifying analogies of creation. With high artistry they always unify the constructs in which they appear. Such patterns may be seen in a number of the longer poems of the late seventeenth century. Outside of South, there is sparse evidence for their existence in the prose essays of the period – especially, for example, in the essays of Dryden. South's analogizing adds gravity and humor, variety and consistency to his works. Reading late seventeenth-century sermons is not a task for the easily bored or distracted; but South's image-making, like a fire in a cold house, mellows the discipline of scholarship.

Appendix 1

A list of South's sermons that can be dated

There follows, in chronological order, those of South's sermons (approximately one-half) that can be dated. I only include sermons published in the six volumes for whose editing South was responsible (1692, 1694, 1698, 1715, 1717, 1717). After the date, I list the place of delivery, when we know it, the scriptural text, the date of publication, and occasional notes.

Besides the usual abbreviations for months and books of Scripture, the following are used:

CC	Christ Church
CC (BU)	Christ Church, Before the University
SMO	St. Mary's, Oxford
SMO (BU)	St. Mary's, Oxford, Before the University
WA	Westminster Abbey

Date	Place	Text	Date publ.	Notes
24 July 1659	SMO	1 Kgs. 13:33	1670, 1692	"Interest Deposed" at Oxford Assizes
29 July 1660	SMO (BU)	Matt. 13:32	1715	"Scribe Instructed" at Clarendon visitation
10 Dec. 1661	SMO (BU)	Matt. 7:26	1698	On obedience and salvation
9 Nov. 1662	St. Paul's	Gen. 1:27	1679, 1692	Dedicated to Lord Mayor and Aldermen of the City of London; on man as God's image
30 Jan. 1663	Whitehall	Judg. 19:30	1717	Brief dedication to Charles I; on conscience and rebellion
5 Nov. 1663	WA	Rom. 13:5	1717	On conscience
1664	CC (BU)	John 15:15	1694	On the love of Christ for his disciples

153

1665	CC	Prov. 3:17	1679, 1692	Before the Court; on the pleasure of religion
25 Dec. 1665	SMO (BU)	John 1:11	1698	On Jesus as Messiah
25 Nov. 1666	Lambeth	Tit. 2:15	1679, 1692	At episcopal consecration of John Dolben; dedicated to Dolben
Easter 1667	–	Acts 2:24	1698	On the resurrection
1677	WA	Prov. 10:9	1694	On reason and religion
Good Friday, 1668	CC (BU)	Isa. 53:8	1698	On the Messiah's suffering for sin
30 Apr. 1668	CC	Luke 21:15	1717	On the ascension
29 May 1670	WA	Matt. 5:44	1698	Anniversary of Restoration; on loving one's enemies
29 May 1672	WA	Rom. 11:33	1698	Anniversary of Restoration ; on the methods of Providence passing human understanding
Michaelmas Term, 1672	CC (BU)	1 Cor. 8:12	1698	On conscience
17 Oct. 1675	CC (BU)	Judg. 8:34	1692	On ingratitude
5 Nov. 1675	WA	Ps. 144:10	1698	On the care of Providence for kings; see 3
30 Apr. 1676	WA	1 Cor. 3:19	1692	On worldly wisdom and "politicians"
10 Nov. 1678	CC	1 Sam. 25:32	1694	On the prevention of sin
22 Feb. 1685	WA	Prov. 16:33	1692	On Providence and contingencies; includes description of Cromwell in a "greasy hat"
(1685)	(WA)	Prov. 22:6	1717	On educating children; written for a Westminster School reunion, and never delivered because of intervening death of Charles II
3 May 1685	CC (BU)	2 Cor. 8:12	1692	On intentions and actions; brief attack on Monmouth rebellion and Rye House Plot

9 May 1686	–	Isa. 5:20	1694	On misuse of words; see 4
8 Apr. 1688	WA	Matt. 22:12	1694	On preparation for the sacrament; see 5
14 Oct. 1688	CC (BU)	Prov. 12:22	1692	On lying
5 Nov. 1688	WA	Isa. 5:4	1717	On the ingratitude of England for divine mercies; see 3
2 Nov. 1690	CC (BU)	Rom. 1:20	1694	On natural religion and sin
1 Nov. 1691	CC (BU)	1 John 3:21	1694	On conscience, a positive view; see 3
1692, perhaps Pentecost	WA	1 Cor. 12:4	1698	On the gifts of the Holy Spirit
30 Oct. 1692	CC (BU)	1 John 3:21	1694	On conscience, a positive view; see 3
29 Oct. 1693	CC (BU)	Luke 11:25	1698	On conscience as a light
29 Apr. 1694	WA	1 Cor. 2:7	1698	On mystery; see 6
5 Dec. 1697	WA	Job 22:2	1698	On merit; attack of Pelagian and Roman interpretation
11 Sept. 1698	CC (BU)	Heb. 11:24	1715	On reward and duty as motives for action
15 Oct. 1699	CC (BU)	Matt. 6:21	1715	On the commitment of one's heart

Appendix 2

Wilkins's paradigm for explication

In his *Ecclesiastes* (6th edn., 1679), John Wilkins gives three separate paradigms for the explication, development, and application of a sermon. Because I have often referred in detail, in earlier chapters, to an individual divine's use of part of Wilkins's norms for explication, a facsimile of the full paradigm follows (photo: British Library).

1 *EXPLICATION* is either of the

Text ; by

Unfolding difficulties in the sense, for which we are to consider,

The *Phrase is self*, according to the Original, and various Readings.

authentick Translations.

The *Circumstances* of the Text and Context, in respect of

Persons concerned in it,

Who.

To whom or of whom.

Occasion of it

Time

wherein it was written

Place

Scope or End of it.

The *Analogy of Faith.*

Other *Parallel* or like *Scriptures.*

Dividing of the Text in order to the better distinguishing of the chief parts of which it consists.

Doctrines deduced from it, by

Clearing their inference, if there be occasion for it,

Stating the true *sense* and meaning of the Subject to be insisted upon. The method of which will be various, according to the different natures of the Subject, whether *Doctrinal,*

Doctrinal, namely some Proposition concerning the *Truth* of any thing that we are to know, or believe, which is to be explicated by

Distinguishing the chief terms of it, according to their various Acceptions, substituting a *more usual* word, for one that is *less usual* ; one that is *proper*, for one that is *figurative.*

Shewing in several Conclusions, in what sense, and with what limitations each word is to be understood.

Practical, concerning some *virtue* or *duty* to be done, or *sin* to be avoided. In the unfolding of which, the matters to be enquired after, are the

Quid nominis, as to the

Various *aequivocal senses*, wherein the word is used,

Synonimous Terms, or such other words as are commonly used to express the same thing.

Quid res, as to the

Causes and *Properties.*

Kinds and *Parts.*

Opposites and *Affinities.*

Appendix 3

Some laws and required oaths, during South's lifetime, that tested religious and denominational allegiances

Note on sources: at least for records before 1688, the indispensable guide is *The Stuart Constitution: Documents and Commentary*, ed. J. P. Kenyon (Cambridge: Cambridge University Press, 1966), which includes most of the Acts of Parliament and royal declarations with which religious Englishmen and women had to contend in South's lifetime. Sometimes Kenyon gives documents in abbreviated form, and he stops at 1688. For full texts and supplementary reading, the reader may consult *Acts and Ordinances of the Interregnum*, ed. C. H. Firth and R. S. Raitt (London: HMSO, 1911), and *The Statutes of the Realm* (London, 1810–28), V (1625–85), and VI (1685–94).

At various times in their reigns (1662, 1672, 1687, and 1688), Charles II and James II attempted both to extend their constitutional powers of dispensation and to release Roman Catholics from the penal laws that had accrued since the reign of Elizabeth I. Each attempt brought each monarch into direct opposition with the legislature; the 1688 confrontation, wherein seven bishops opposed James and got away with it, initiated the final stage of James's reign. South's reactions to these royal tactics are not recorded. It is unlikely that South was displeased with at least Charles's attempts to extend his prerogatives, and South was never as anti-Catholic as some of his contemporaries, especially Tillotson, seem to have been. Five principal laws or set of laws in South's lifetime required oaths that affected religious allegiance: the Solemn League and Covenant of September 1643; the Engagement of January 1650; the Act of Uniformity of early 1662; the Test Acts of spring 1673 and fall 1678; and the substitution of new for old oaths at the accession of William and Mary in late 1688 and the first half of 1689.

The Solemn League and Covenant: dominated by Presbyterians, the House of Commons wrote and took a lengthy oath in September 1643 to preserve the reformed religion of the Church of Scotland; to extirpate popery and prelacy; to preserve the rights of Parliament and the king; to fight rebellion; to promote peace; and to defend all who joined the Solemn

158

League. A further Act of Parliament (5 February 1644) directed that the oaths be taken by, among others, all ministers, all men above the age of eighteen, and all church congregations. Wood tells us that commissioners visited Oxford to investigate noncompliance.

Although the act specifically preserves the monarchy, the provisions of the oath, because they oppose episcopacy, were extremely offensive to many Anglicans. Richard Busby, we are told, stayed home the day the commissioners came to administer the oath to the masters of Westminster School. Since South was 10 years old during this time, he did not have to take the oath; he later praised those who did not.

The Engagement oath: almost a year after the execution of the king, Parliament legislated that all men over the age of 18 had to swear a simple oath "to be true and faithful to the Commonwealth of England, as it is now established, without a King or House of Lords" (2 January 1650). The instructions for taking the oath stipulate that anyone "that now hath, or hereafter shall have" any remunerative public office must take the oath. Rather nastily, the Act also prescribes that anyone who had a case pending in court had to take the oath before the case could proceed.

The Engagement oath was, in a sense, less offensive to many upholders of Anglican polity than the Solemn League and Covenant. The 1650 Act does not mention the episcopacy, although perhaps abolition was taken for granted. The major stumbling-block to taking the oath was, of course, an implicit assent to the legitimacy of the regicide, or at least to that government which sanctioned it.

South was still short of 18 in 1650, but the Act provides for the "hereafter"; in order to keep his Studentship, it is likely that South had to take the Engagement oath at some point. If South took the oath, Wood's complaint about his ease amidst the sufferings of others has merit. South's subsequent, strident advocacy of high royalism does not sit comfortably with his compliance, if this occurred, in the 1650s. To be fair to him and many others, however, the world is quite a different place in one's thirties from what it is at the age of 18, and personal ambition is not the only factor involved in such changes of perspectives.

The Act of Uniformity: perhaps without the wholehearted support of Charles II, the royalist Parliament of 1662 legislated that all ministers in holy orders, professors and tutors in the universities, and schoolmasters had to swear consent to everything contained in the Prayer Book, opposition to taking arms against the king, and repudiation of the Solemn League and Covenant.

Whatever his infidelities before 1662, South would have welcomed the Act of 1662. the Act was, in a sense, the major text South preached on for the rest of his life. In leaving funds to Christ Church for use by ministers in its attached livings, South's will of 1716 stipulates that they must confirm, in their public worship, the letter of the Act of Uniformity, passed over fifty years before.

The test Acts of 1673 and 1678: essentially anti-Catholic measures passed over Charles's opposition, these Acts required an oath of supremacy (borrowed from the 1606 version) and a denial of belief in transubstantiation. The 1678 Act, during the Popish Plot, included a renunciation of jesuitical equivocation. The 1673 oaths were aimed at royal appointees; the 1678 oaths only involved members of the two House of Parliament.

Except for the implicit message the Acts give of limiting the king's power, South would have had no objection to their contents. Though he spoke against transubstantiation, this was not a major theme. He tended to regard Protestant nonconformists as more of a threat to church and state than Roman Catholics.

The 1689 oaths: the Act of 1688 containing the oaths abrogates some previous formulas of sovereignty and details at length those who must take new oaths: prelates, nobility, judges, and all those who were required to take previous oaths of supremacy. Various penalties for noncompliance are listed, as they are in all the laws discussed here; noncomplying clergymen were to be deprived of their livings, as had been the case in 1662. The Act explicitly abrogates the promise not to take up arms against the king from the Act of Uniformity. The new oaths promise allegiance to William and Mary and repudiation of the papal authority in England. The first half of the oath, a simple promise of allegiance, bears a resemblance to the engagement oath; the critical difference in 1689 was that the head of the previous government was still living, about 200 miles away.

South took the oaths on 31 July 1689, the last day when it was possible to do so without penalty; I suspect that the courts were busy that day with similarly reluctant compliers. South sympathized with those who in conscience would not take the oaths, the nonjurors, and remembered them in this will. His will also required some recipients of monies to conform to the Prayer Book worship decreed by the Act of Uniformity. The 1688 Act had not abrogated this part of the 1662 law and oath, but South's insistent allusion to 1662 makes his position clear. His compliance in 1688 was real, confined to the letter of the law, and ornery.

Bibliography

Works by Robert South

Animadversions Upon Dr. Sherlock's Book, Entituled A Vindication of the Holy and Ever Blessed Trinity. London, 1693

Bodl. Ms. Engl. hist. d.1. 29781 (RS and Archbishop Sancroft; account of argument with Sherlock)

Bodl. Ms. Rawl. D. 110 (early works)

Bodl. Ms. Rawl. D. 1151 (early works and Oxford orations)

Bodl. Ms. Tanner. XXX. 91, 109 (RS and Archbishop Sancroft)

Bodl. Ms. Tanner. XXXIX. 81 (dispensation for Wales parish)

"Dr. South's Notebook," Muniments Room, Westminster Abbey

Posthumous Works of the Late Reverend Robert South. London, 1717

Sermons Preached Upon Several Occasions. 7 vols. Oxford, 1823

Sermons Preached Upon Several Occasions. Oxford, 1679

Tritheism Charged Upon Dr. Sherlock's New Notion of the Trinity. London, 1695

Twelve Sermons Preached Upon Several Occasions. London, 1692

Twelve Sermons Preached Upon Several Occasions. 2nd vol. London, 1694

Twelve Sermons Preached Upon Several Subjects and Occasions. 3rd vol. London, 1698

Twelve Sermons Preached at Several Times and Upon Several Occasions. 4th vol. London, 1715

Twelve Sermons and Discourses on Several Subjects and Occasions. 5th vol. London, 1717

Twelve Sermons and Discourses on Several Subjects and Occasions. 6th vol. London, 1717

Works of other seventeenth-century preachers, theologians, and philosophers

An Impartial Account of the Word Mystery As It is Taken In the Holy Scripture. London, 1691

Barrow, Isaac. *Works,* ed. John Tillotson. 4 vols. London, 1683–87

Burnet, Gilbert. *Bishop Burnet's History of His Own Time.* 2nd edn. enlarged. 6 vols. Oxford: Oxford University Press, 1833

A Discourse of the Pastoral Care. London, 1692

An Exposition of the Thirty-Nine Articles of the Church of England. London, 1699

Four Discourses Delivered to the Clergy of the Diocese of Sarum. London, 1694

Eachard, John. *The Grounds and Occasions of the Contempt of the Clergy and Religion.* London, 1670

Eikon Basilike: The Portraiture of His Sacred Majesty in His Solitudes and Sufferings, ed. Philip A. Knachel. Ithaca: Cornell University Press, 1966

Fell, John. *The Character of the Last Daies*. Oxford, 1675

   The Life of Richard Allestree. London, 1848

   The Life of the Most Learned, Reverend and Pious Dr. H. Hammond. London, 1661

   A Sermon Preached before the House of Peers on December 22, 1680. Oxford, 1680

Hickes, George. *Christian Priesthood and the Dignity of the Episcopal Order*. 3rd edn. 2 vols. London, 1727

   A Sermon Preached Before the Lord Mayor . . . on the 30th January, 1682. London, 1683

Hobbes, Thomas. *Leviathan*, ed. Michael Oakeshott. Oxford: Basil Blackwell, 1947

Jane, William. *The Judgment and Decree of the University of Oxford*. Oxford, 1683

   A Sermon Preached on the Day of the Public Fast, April the 11th, 1679. London, 1679

Jordanus, Hyacinth. *Theorica Medicinae Sancti Thomae Doctoris Angelici*. Naples, 1643

Kennett, White. *Parochial Antiquities . . . in the Counties of Oxford and Bucks*. Oxford, 1695

Locke, John. *The Correspondence*, ed. E. S. DeBeer. 8 vols. Oxford: Clarendon Press, 1976–89

   An Essay Concerning Human Understanding, ed. Peter H. Nidditch. Oxford: Clarendon Press, 1975

   A Paraphrase and Notes on the Epistles of St. Paul to the Galatians, 1 and 2 Corinthians, Romans, and Ephesians, ed. Arthur W. Wainwright. 2 Vols. Oxford: Clarendon Press, 1987

   Some Thoughts Concerning Education, ed. John W. and Jean S. Yolton. Oxford: Clarendon Press, 1989

   Two Treatises of Government, ed. Peter Laslett. Cambridge: Cambridge University Press, 1988

Nelson, Robert. *A Companion for the Festivals and Fasts of the Church of England*. London, 1704

Nye, Stephen. *Considerations on the Explications of the Doctrine of the Trinity*. London, 1694

Parker, Samuel. *A Discourse of Ecclesiastical Politie*. London, 1670

Patrick, Simon. *Works*, ed. Alexander Taylor. 9 vols. Oxford: Oxford University Press, 1858

Pocock, Edward. *Theological Works*, introd. Leonard Twells. 2 vols. London, 1740

Proclamation for a General Fast, A. London, 1678

   London, 1679

   London, 1680

Sherlock, William. *A Defence of Dr. Sherlock's Notion of A Trinity in Unity*. London, 1694

   A Vindication of the Doctrine of the Holy and Ever Blessed Trinity, and the Incarnation of the Son of God. London, 1690.

Sprat, Thomas. *The History of the Royal Society of London*, ed. Jackson, I. Cope and Harold Whitmore Jones. St. Louis: Washington University Press, 1958

   A Sermon Preached before the Honorable House of Commons . . . January 30th, 1678. London, 1678

   Sermons Preached on Several Occasions. London, 1697

Stillingfleet, Edward. *Fifty Sermons Preached Upon Several Occasions*. London, 1707
Works. 6 vols., London, 1707–10
Taylor, Jeremy. *Whole Works*. 3 vols. London: Frederick Westley and A. H. Davis, 1835
Tillotson, John. *A Sermon Concerning the Sacrifice and Satisfaction of Christ*. London, 1693
A Sermon Concerning the Unity of the Divine Nature and the Blessed Trinity. London, 1693
A Sermon Preached November 5, 1678. London, 1678
Sermons. 14 vols. London, 1695–1704
Sermons Concerning the Divinity and Incarnation of Our Blessed Saviour. London, 1693
Toland, John. *Christianity Not Mysterious*. London, 1696
Wilkins, John. *Ecclesiastes, or A Discourse Concerning the Gift of Preaching*. 6th edn. London, 1679
An Essay Towards A Real Character, and A Philosophical Language. London, 1668
Sermons Preached on Several Occasions Before the King at Whitehall. London, 1677

Other sources

Aarsleff, Hans, ed. *From Locke to Saussure: Essays on the Study of Language and Intellecual History*. Minneapolis: University of Minnesota Press, 1982
Abbey, Charles, J. *The English Church and Its Bishops, 1700–1800*. 2 vols. London: Longmans, Green, 1887
Abbey, Charles J. and John H. Overton. *The English Church in the Eighteenth Century*. 2 vols. London: Longmans, Green, 1878
Adolph, Robert. *The Rise of Modern Prose Style*. Cambridge, MA: MIT Press, 1968
Alkon, Paul K. "Robert South, William Law, and Samuel Johnson," *SEL*, 6 (1966), 499–528.
Annotated Book of Common Prayer, The ed. John Henry Blunt. New York: E. P. Dutton, 1884
Atkins, G. Douglas. *The Faith of John Dryden: Change and Continuity*. Lexington, KY: The University Press of Kentucky, 1980
Barber, John. *The Character of the Reverend and Learned Dr. Robert South*. London, 1716
Barker, G. F. Russell. *Memoir of Richard Busby, D.D. (1606–1695), With Some Account of Westminster School in the Seventeenth Century*. London: Lawrence and Bullen, 1895
Bennett, Joan. "An Aspect of the Evolution of Seventeenth-Century Prose Style," *Review of English Studies*, 17 (1941), 281–97
Birch, Thomas. *The Life of the Most Reverend John Tillotson*. London, 1752
Bosher, Robert S. *The Making of the Restoration Settlement: The Influence of the Laudians, 1649–1662*. New York: Oxford University Press, 1951
Boswell, James. *Life of Johnson*, ed. George Birkbeck Hill, rev. L. F. Powell. 6 vols. Oxford: Clarendon Press, 1934–64
Brink, C. O. *Horace on Poetry: Prolegomena to the Literary Epistles*. Cambridge: Cambridge University Press, 1963
Buxton, Richard F. *Eucharist and Institution Narrative: A Study in the Roman and Anglican Traditions of the Consecration of the Eucharist from the Eighth to the Twentieth Centuries*. Great Wakering: Mayhew-McCrimmon, 1976

Cantalupo, Charles. "Hobbes's Use of Metaphor," *Restoration*, 12 (1988), 20–31

Carleton, J. D. *Westminster*. London: Blackie and Son, 1938

Carroll, Robert T. *The Common-Sense Philosophy of Religion of Bishop Edward Stillingfleet, 1635–1699*. The Hague: Martinus Nijhoff, 1975

Certain Sermons or Homilies Appointed to Be Read in Churches in the Time of Queen Elizabeth ... Oxford, 1683

Christ Church, Oxford. Disbursement Books, 1681–85, 1696–1700; Chapter Books, 1648–88, 1688–1712

Clark, George. *The Later Stuarts, 1660–1714*. 2nd edn. Oxford: Clarendon Press, 1955

Clark, J. C. D. *Revolution and Rebellion: State and Society in England in the Seventeenth and Eighteenth Centuries*. Cambridge: Cambridge University Press, 1986

Cohen, Murray. *Sensible Words: Linguistic Practice in England, 1640–1785*. Baltimore: The Johns Hopkins University Press, 1977

Cressy, David. *Bonfires and Bells: National Memory and the Protestant Calendar in Elizabethan and Stuart England*. Berkeley and Los Angeles: University of California Press, 1989

Dodds, W. M. T. "Robert South and William Sherlock: Some Unpublished Letters," *Modern Language Review*, 39 (1944), 215–24

Dowdell, Victor Lyle. *Aristotle and Anglican Religious Thought*. Ithaca: Cornell University Press, 1942

Downey, James. *The Eighteenth-Century Pulpit: A Study of the Sermons of Butler, Berkeley, Secker, Sterne, Whitfield and Wesley*. Oxford: Clarendon Press, 1969

Dryden, John. *Of Dramatic Poesy and Other Critical Essays*. 2 vols. Ed. George Watson. London: Dent, 1962

   Poems and Fables, ed. James Kinsley. London: Oxford University Press, 1962

   Works, II, ed. H. T. Swedenberg and Vinton A. Dearing. Berkeley and Los Angeles: University of California Press, 1972

Dugmore, C. W. *Eucharistic Doctrine in England from Hooker to Waterland*. London: SPCK, 1942

Evelyn, John. *Diary*, ed. E. S. DeBeer. London: Oxford University Press, 1959

Every, George. *The High-Church Party, 1688–1718*. London: SPCK, 1956

Filmer, Robert. *Patriarcha and Other Political Works*, ed. Peter Laslett. Oxford: Basil Blackwell, 1949

Firth, C. H. and R. S. Raitt, eds. *Acts and Ordinances of the Interregnum* (1642–1660). 3 vols. London: HMSO, 1911

Form of Common Prayer for God's Blessing Upon His Majesty and His Dominions, A. London, 1679

Forshall, Frederick. *Westminster School: Past and Present*. London: Wyman and Sons, 1884

Freiling, Keith. *A History of the Tory Party, 1640–1714*. Oxford: Clarendon Press, 1924

Gascoigne, John. *Cambridge in the Age of the Enlightenment*. Cambridge: Cambridge University Press, 1989

Green, I. M. *The Re-establishment of the Church of England, 1660–1663*. Oxford: Oxford University Press, 1978

Hargreaves-Mawdesley, W. N. *Oxford in the Age of John Locke.* Norman: University of Oklahoma Press, 1973

Harrison, John, and Peter Laslett. *The Library of John Locke*, 2nd edn. Oxford: Clarendon Press, 1971

Harth, Phillip. *Contexts of Dryden's Thought.* Chicago: University of Chicago Press, 1968

Hearne, Thomas. *Remarks and Collections*, 11 vols. Ed. C. E. Doble. Oxford: Oxford Historical Society, 1885–1921

Hiscock, W. G. *Henry Aldrich of Christ Church.* Oxford: Holywell Press, 1960

Henry, Matthew. *An Account of the Life and Death of Mr. Philip Henry.* 3rd edn. London, 1712

Holmes, Geoffrey. *The Trial of Dr. Sacheverell.* London: Eyre and Methuen, 1973

Hume, Robert D. *Dryden's Criticism.* Ithaca and London: Cornell University Press, 1970

Hutton, Ronald. *The Restoration: A Political and Religious History of England and Wales, 1658–1667.* Oxford: Clarendon Press, 1985

Jacob, Margaret C. *The Newtonians and the English Revolution.* Ithaca: Cornell University Press, 1976

Jewel, John. *An Apology for the Church of England*, ed. John E. Booty. Ithaca: Cornell University Press, 1963

Kempe, John Edward, ed. *The Classic Preachers of the English Church.* 2 vols. London: John Murray, 1877–78

Kenyon, J. P. *The Popish Plot.* 1972; Harmondsworth: Penguin Books, 1974
  Revolutionary Principles: The Politics of Party, 1689–1720. Cambridge: Cambridge University Press, 1977
  ed. *The Stuart Constitution: Documents and Commentary.* Cambridge: Cambridge University Press 1966

Knachel, Philip, ed. *Eikon Basilike: The Portraiture of His Sacred Majesty in His Solitudes and Sufferings.* Ithaca: Cornell University Press, 1966

Knowlson, James. *Universal Language Schemes in England and France, 1600–1800.* Toronto: University of Toronto Press, 1975

Lanham, Richard A. *The Motives of Eloquence: Literary Rhetoric in the Renaissance.* New Haven and London: Yale University Press, 1976

Legg. J. Wickham. *English Church Life from the Restoration to the Tractarian Movement, in Some of Its Neglected or Forgotten Features.* London: Longmans, Green, 1914

Lives and Last Wills and Testaments of the Following Eminent Persons, The. London, 1728

McAdoo, H. R. *The Spirit of Anglicanism: A Survey of Anglican Theological Method in the Seventeenth Century.* London: Adam and Charles Black, 1965

McLachlan, Herbert. *The Story of A Nonconformist Library.* Manchester: Manchester University Press, 1923

Mallett, Charles Edward. *A History of the University of Oxford*, II: *The Sixteenth and Seventeenth Centuries.* London: Methuen, 1924

Marvell, Andrew. *Poems and Letters.* 2 vols. 3rd edn. Ed. H. M. Margoliouth, rev. Pierre Legouis. Oxford: Clarendon Press, 1971

Memoirs of the Life and Writing of Mr. Kettlewell. London, 1718

Mitchell, W. Fraser. *English Pulpit Oratory from Andrewes to Tillotson.* London: SPCK, 1932

Morgan, Michael J. *Molyneux's Question: Vision, Touch, and the Philosophy of Perception*. Cambridge: Cambridge University Press, 1977

Nepos, Cornelius. *De Latinis Historicis*. New York: G. P. Putnam, 1929

Novarr, David. *The Making of Walton's Lives*. Ithaca: Cornell University Press, 1958

O Hehir, Brendan. *Expans'd Hieroglyphics: A Critical Edition of Sir John Denham's Cooper's Hill*. Berkeley and Los Angeles: University of California Press, 1969

    Harmony from Discords: A Life of Sir John Denham. Berkeley and Los Angeles: University of California Press, 1968

Overton, John H. *Life in the English Church (1660–1714)*. London: Longmans, Green, 1885

    The Nonjurors: Their Lives, Principles, and Writings. London: Smith, Elder, 1902

Pattison, Mark. *Essays*. 2 vols. Oxford: Clarendon Press, 1889

Pechter, Edward. *Dryden's Classical Theory of Literature*. Cambridge: Cambridge University Press, 1975

Pope, Walter. *The Life of the Right Reverend Father in God, Seth, Lord Bishop of Salisbury*. London, 1697

Prowse, Abigail. *Life of Bishop George Hooper*. Lambeth Palace Ms. 3016

Reedy, Gerard. *The Bible and Reason: Anglicans and Scripture in Late Seventeenth-Century England*. Philadelphia: University of Pennsylvania Press, 1985

    "Stillingfleet's *Fifty Sermons*," *Papers of the Bibliographical Society of America*, 73 (1979), 254–57

Richardson, Caroline. *English Preachers and Preaching, 1640–1670. A Secular Study*. London: SPCK, 1928

Rymer, Thomas. *A General Draught and Prospect of Government in Europe*. London, 1681

Salvian. *A Treatise of God's Government and of the Justice of His Present Dispensations in This World*, trans. R. T. Intro. Thomas Wagstaffe. London, 1700

Secretan, C. F. *Memoirs of the Life and Times of the Pious Robert Nelson*. London: John Murray, 1806

Seneca. *Naturales Quaestiones*. 2 vols. Cambridge, Mass.: Harvard University Press, 1972

Sergeaunt, John. *Annals of Westminster School*. London: Methuen, 1898

Shapiro, Barbara J. *John Wilkins, 1614–1672. An Intellectual Biography*. Berkeley and Los Angeles: University of California Press, 1969

Simon, Irène. "Robert South and the Augustans," *Essays and Studies*, n.s. 28 (1975), 15–28

    Three Restoration Divines: Barrow, South, Tillotson. 2 vols. Paris: Société d'Edition "Les Belles Lettres," 1967, 1976

Simon, Walter G. *The Restoration Episcopate*. New York: Bookman Associates, 1965

Slaughter, M. M. *Universal Languages and Scientific Taxonomy in the Seventeenth Century*. Cambridge: Cambridge University Press, 1982

Spiker, Sina. "Figures of Speech in the Sermons of Robert South," *Review of English Studies*, 16 (1940), 444–55

Statues of the Realm, The. 11 vols. in 12. London: [The Record Commission], 1810–28

Stephen, Leslie. *History of English Thought in the Eighteenth Century*. 2 vols. 3rd edn. London: Smith and Elder, 1902

Sutherland, James R. "Restoration Prose," in *Restoration and Augustan Prose*. Los Angeles: William Andrews Clark Memorial Library, 1956

Sutherland, L. S. and L. G. Mitchell, eds. *The History of the University of Oxford*, V: *The Eighteenth Century*. Oxford: Clarendon Press, 1985

Swift, Jonathan. *The Correspondence*. 5 vols. Ed. Harold Williams. Oxford: Clarendon Press, 1963–65

Sykes, Norman. *From Sheldon to Secker: Aspects of English Church History, 1660–1768*. Cambridge: Cambridge University Press, 1959

Tanner, Lawrence E. *Westminster School, A History*. London: Country Life, 1934

Tatler, The, ed. Donald F. Bond. 3 vols. Oxford: Clarendon Press, 1987

Thompson, Henry L. *Christ Church*. London: F. E. Robinson, 1900

Thompson, James. *Language in Wycherley's Plays. Seventeenth-Century Language Theory and Drama*. University, AL: University of Alabama Press, 1984

Thucydides. *Eight Books of the Peloponnesian War*, trans. Thomas Hobbes. London, 1629

Vickers, Brian. "The Royal Society and English Prose Style: A Reassessment," *Rhetoric and the Pursuit of Truth. Language and Change in the Seventeenth and Eighteenth Centuries*. Los Angeles: William Andrews Clark Memorial Library, 1985

Wallace, Robert. *Anti-Trinitarian Biography*. 3 vols. London, 1850

Ward, Charles. *The Life of John Dryden*. Chapel Hill. University of North Carolina Press, 1961

Warton, Thomas. *The Life and Literary Remains of Ralph Bathurst, M.D*. London, 1761

Webster, G. M. "The Life and Opinions of Robert South, D.D." B.D. thesis, Exeter College, Oxford, 1957

Wilkinson, John. *The Supper and the Eucharist: A Layman's Guide to Anglican Revision*. New York: St. Martin's Press, 1965

Williamson, George. *The Senecan Amble: A Study in Prose Form from Bacon to Collier*. Chicago: University of Chicago Press, 1951

Wilson, F. P. *Seventeenth-Century Prose*. Berkeley and Los Angeles: University of California Press, 1960

Wood, Anthony. *Athenae Oxonienses, An Exact History of All the Writers and Bishops Who Have Had Their Education in the University of Oxford*. 4 vols. Ed. Philip Bliss. London, 1820

Life and Times. 5 vols. Ed. Andrew Clark. Oxford: The Historical Society, 1891–1900

Wykes, David. *A Preface to Dryden*. London: Longman, 1977

Index

Adam and Adamic language 88–89, 90, 105

Adolph, Robert 47

Alexander the Great 76, 109

Alkon, Paul 27

Allestree, Richard 12, 13, 14–15

Ammianus Marcellinus 67–68

Andrewes, Launcelot 47

Anglican tradition of the Lord's Supper 115–17

Anne, Queen 30

Arbuthnot, John 141

Aristotle 88; and Dryden, John, 33, 34–35; and RS, 21, 93, 97, 102, 103, 104, 144

Atkins, Edward 41

Atkins, G. Douglas 29

Atticus, Titus Pomponius 103

Bacon, Francis 4n

Barrow, Isaac 15n

Bennett, Joan 50

Birch, Thomas 48

body politic, used in sermons 61, 66–68, 70, 76, 85

Boyle, Robert 4n

Brett, Arthur 14–15

Bromley, William 42–43

Boulton, Ralph 14

Burke, Edmund 28

Burnet, Gilbert 18; on mystery, 127, 136–37, 150–51; on RS oath taking, 10; on sermon delivery, 46; will, 7, 8, 9, 10, 79, 102

Bury, Arthur 40

Busby, Richard 42, 54; communion preparation and RS, 121–22; corporal punishment, 20n, 24n; influence on students, 19, 22–23, 28; no oath in 1645, 9, 22–23, 22n, 159; will, 10

Buxton, Richard 14

Caesar, Augustus 71, 76

Caesar, Julius 51, 72, 103–04

Cato, Marcus Porcius 103

Certain Sermons and Homilies 113–14

Charles I 100; Thomas Sprat on, 71, 72, 91

Charles II 9, 55, 80, 159; death, 24, 154; and Dryden, John, 89–90, 91; and RS, 57, 60, 63, 65, 100, 105, 142

Chaucer, Geoffrey 29

Chillingworth, William 118, 126

Christ Church 23, 46; high church royalism, 19, 42, 68; and RS, 7–8, 13–15, 17–23, 38, 39, 41, 87, 104, 122, 125, 146, 153–55, 160; Studentships, 19–20; teaching at, 21–22

Cicero, Marcus Tullius 47, 51, 104

Clarendon, Edward Hyde, Earl of 14, 41, 81

Common Prayer, Book of 112

Craddock, Thomas 14

Cromwell, Oliver 4, 12, 22, 41

Curll, Edmund 7, 11

Denham, John 64n

Descartes, René 105, 124, 126, 133, 147, 151

Dolben, John 13, 41

Donne, John 12, 47

Downey, James 122–23

Dryden, John 1, 19, 23; *Absalom and Achitophel*, 28, 87, 89–90, 91; *Annus Mirabilis*, 28, 41; and classical authorities, 33–35; on education of clergy, 28–31; *Essay of Dramatic Poesy*, 34; essays, 151; "Heads of An Answer to Rymer," 34; *MacFlecknoe*, 141; metaphorical language, 31; mixed proofs, 32–35; mixing genres, 31–32; *Religio Laici*, 29; and RS, 27–35; translations, 30

Dugmore, C. W. 107, 113, 117

Eachard, John 49, 50, 52

education, RS and John Locke compared on, 24–27

education of clergy 18, 28–31, 44–45, 59, 127, 128, 146

Evelyn, John 71n

faith, Anglican theory of 147

Fell, John 49, 58, 140; biographer, 12; and Christ Church royalism, 19; clandestine liturgy, 13; political theology, 65–68; and pulpit levity, 15, 32; and RS, 14–15, 17

168

www.ingramcontent.com/pod-product-compliance
Ingram Content Group UK Ltd.
Pitfield, Milton Keynes, MK11 3LW, UK
UKHW010047140625
459647UK00012BB/1659